Bridges to Literacy

To My Father, Selden C. Dickinson,
Esse Quam Videri

and My Mother, Dorothy M. Dickinson,
Reader of My Bedtime Stories

Bridges to Literacy

Children, Families, and Schools

Edited by

David K. Dickinson

BLACKWELL
Oxford UK & Cambridge USA

Copyright © Basil Blackwell Ltd 1994

First published 1994

Blackwell Publishers
238 Main Street
Cambridge, Massachusetts 02142
USA

108 Cowley Road
Oxford OX4 1JF
UK

Library of Congress Cataloging-in-Publication Data
Bridges to literacy : children, families, and schools / edited by
   David K. Dickinson.
       p.   cm.
   Includes bibliographical references (p.   ) and index.
   1. Reading—Parent participation.   2. Family literacy programs.
3. Children—Books and reading.   I. Dickinson, David K.
LB1050.B74   1994   93–27158
649'.68—dc20   CIP

ISBN 1–55786–372–5 (hardback)
       1–55786–373–3 (paperback)

British Library Cataloguing in Publication Data

A CIP catalogue record for this book is available from the British Library.

Typeset in 10 on 12 pt Palatino
by Graphicraft Typesetters Ltd., Hong Kong
Printed in the United States of America.

This book is printed on acid-free paper

struction that goes on there. Home as a context for literacy development has been a frequent theme in emergent literacy research, but the writers of this volume increase our understanding of the complexity of "studying" it. There is no such thing as "the home" in the abstract, just as there is no such thing as "the family." Homes include the idiosyncratic characteristics and cultures of all the family members in addition to the broader trends, practices, and mores of so-called mainstream culture. All of the layers influencing the home contain ideas about the nature of children and how they learn, as well as the nature of parents and teachers and how they foster the child's literacy.

From this book we gain respect for the diversity of family backgrounds and values about literacy. In the past, many of our school programs did not attempt to reach families, except through programs that attempted to dictate what parents "ought to do." Though this book respects families and describes early childhood schooling programs reaching out to them, it also reveals tension about family practices that do not seem to provide adequate bridges to the literacy practices of the schools and eventual workplaces. This tension between imposing a "mainstream model" and neglecting the literacy needs of children and families does not go unnoticed in this book.

Though we must always keep in mind that our ideas about "children's needs" are some people's perceptions at some point in time – that is, they are relative – this book seems to provide a true bridge by focusing on family practices that complement school practices and on adjusting school practices to family practices. I was struck with the importance the designers of the programs attributed to various forms of bedtime reading or book sharing. In comparison with my own collection of bedtime reading, *Bridges* seems to need more ties to writing. In spite of the place writing seems to have in the program descriptions, this book like many others still has little to say about the actual role of writing at school and at home. Perhaps we will have a second edition soon in which the writing bridges will be more explicit.

The second theme that *Bridges* provided for me was the importance of talk – talk for its own sake, as well as talk for literacy's sake. In my bedside reading collection, family members' talk was crucial, the absence of it no less than the presence. Talk seems to be a glue that binds human beings together – face to face and across time and distance. The writers of this book provide us with new appreciation of talk within the family as a bridge to literacy. The talk in storybook reading is an obvious tie, but the contributors to this book have a wider vision of written language. They lead us to understand how certain kinds of talk, such as mealtime conversation, conversation in cars, conversation about events provide content and structure to children as they become literate.

Early childhood specialists often react to literacy programs with apprehension. They are afraid that "teaching reading" or "teaching writing" will take something precious away from young children. They are afraid that programs for children from low-income families, minority families, or families with other factors associated with low school achievement will focus on academic subjects and neglect children's human needs – needs to talk, to play, to engage with other children and adults. The programs and research in this book assert that talk in family and play situations can be the kind of talk that supports and becomes part of children's literacy development.

In the first two themes, families and talk, I felt a pull of conservatism: The old tried and true method was still at work. In the third theme, faint but perceptible nevertheless, I sense a bridge to the future. The writers in this book clearly have broader ideas of literacy, including modern technology, than one would have found even a decade ago, as shown in their interpretations of the family and of the role of talk. The definitions of reading (and writing) that the writers use reflect an understanding that reading and writing are more than decoding and encoding, even for the beginner. They no longer treat reading and writing as tied solely to marks on a page. They treat the evanescent speech exchanges of parent and child sharing a storybook as part of reading; they investigate the invisible perturbations of air created through mealtime talk as being part of reading development. These concepts of reading may seem conservative – storybook reading is good; talking with your child is good – but they are also radical. They suggest truly new conceptions of literacy.

Back in my own bedtime-reading stack, I see the electronic media that our young children take as part of their world, whether or not they themselves own or use them. Our writers certainly have attested to the presence of television in children's lives, but not yet has enough been said and done about the images of literacy on the television. Our picture of the diversity of families and their literacy often fails to address the diversity of models that young children experience vicariously through the television. My students and I have surveyed young children in an urban, minority school setting and found that almost every child had some familiarity with computers in their extended families prior to their experience in school – not just video games (although we cannot ignore the importance of all kinds of "edutainment") but actual computers – and was able to expound on educational and work purposes within their families for these computers. In another study, we found low-income, African-American kindergarteners to use sophisticated teaching and politeness routines with computers on their first exposure to them in the classroom, routines that were beyond those used by their teachers in teaching them. There is much to learn about literacy from television, computers, faxes, and even telephones; I expect to read about these, too, in the second edition of *Bridges*. But for now, the current *Bridges to Literacy* has provided a down-to-earth look at effective, specific programs to provide bridges between home and school and a look to the future for literacy, children, their parents, and teachers.

ELIZABETH SULZBY

Acknowledgments

My work on this book as been supported, in part, by grant #90-CD-0827 from the Administration for Children, Youth, and Families, awarded by Project Head Start. My early interest in and initial contact with those working on family literacy programs was fostered by a small grant from the W.T. Grant Foundation. I thank both for their financial assistance. I also thank my wife, Mary Fischer, for her emotional support as this book has added one more element of complexity to our lives. Finally, I thank Catherine Snow for her intellectual and professional support and Allyssa McCabe for her encouragement and advice as I began work on this book.

Introduction: Directions in Literacy Theory and Intervention Programs

David K. Dickinson

As we move toward the close of the 20th century there is an increasing need to develop and institutionalize new approaches to raising the literacy levels of large numbers of people. In the United States growing numbers of families and children are living in persistent poverty. Around the world demographic changes are resulting in a rise in the number of ethnic minorities and immigrants with languages and cultures different from that of the dominant group. And often families in these minority groups have not had traditions of literacy. All of these realities increase the chances that many children will have trouble becoming fully literate. At the same time, in technologically advanced countries, economic forces are impelling new standards. No longer is minimal technical literacy sufficient for many jobs; instead, workers need to be able to read and write challenging texts.

As the importance of literacy as a societal issue has loomed larger, the body of relevant research and theory has expanded. New approaches to vexing problems are characterized by their range and sophistication. They have emerged from such diverse fields as developmental and cognitive psychology, sociology, linguistics, and anthropology. More applied approaches have been taken by varied types of practitioners including early childhood educators, parent educators, adult literacy instructors, librarians, and family literacy workers. To varying degrees these groups are aware of each other, but communication among them has not been optimal (Dickinson, 1988).

This book was born of a desire to build bridges of understanding and respect between those of us interested in fostering the literacy development of disadvantaged populations, and to broaden our awareness of the diverse ways bridges to literacy are being provided for children and their families. Every chapter except the first one, which reports the results of an important longitudinal observational study, is contributed by researchers who discuss a sustained program of intervention. Because understanding of the applied methods comes from a sense of practical specifics, authors include information about the details of interventions that should be very helpful to practitioners. But techniques alone will serve us poorly in the long run; therefore each approach is situated within its theoretical framework.

In this introduction I first chart the recent history of theoretical and applied work that has brought us to where we are today. Next, I outline some key questions that need to be confronted, and offer an overview of what is to come. Throughout I attempt to enhance clarity by minimizing references to studies other than those dealt with in this book; instead, I refer to chapters in which many background studies are cited and relevant new research is reported.

Advances in Literacy Theory

Starting in the 1970s there was a resurgence in reading theory, leading to recognition that reading is a constructive act in which children draw upon their oral language skills (e.g., vocabulary, syntactic skills) and a vast array of background knowledge about the physical world, about people, and about texts and written language. As understanding of the complexity of the reading process deepened, attention turned to the genesis of the skills employed. This shift of attention led to the discovery of emergent literacy, the cluster of behaviors involving uses of print and oral language that appear during the preschool years. These behaviors make clear the fact that, prior to formal literacy instruction, children are constructing literacy-related knowledge (for much more about the early roots of literacy see the foreword and chapters 1–8 and 11; see also Mason & Allen, 1986; Sulzby & Teale, 1991).

Early childhood has long been believed to be an important formative period, with Project Head Start and other initiatives of the 1960s being an early expression of how this belief was transformed into social policy. Emergent literacy research validated the importance of early childhood for literacy, and added an important new element. Previously the pathway from early childhood experiences to later literacy was thought to begin with general, rather diffuse competencies such as "intelligence", "language", or "emotional adjustment," which flowered into literacy once children received formal reading instruction. Emergent literacy work opened the possibility that, in addition to the likely importance of such generic abilities, preschool children also construct knowledge and acquire skills that are more directly linked to later literacy. Thus, preschool children reared in literacy-rich environments could now be seen as constructing vital literacy-related concepts and displaying them in playful "pretend" readings of books and "scribble writing" (e.g., Harste, Woodward & Burke, 1984). Examination of the oral language of such children also revealed varied subtle ways that oral language patterns reflected the impact of the literate culture they were joining (for more on oral language see especially chapters 1, 4, and 5).

It now became possible to see the enduring disparities between social classes in literacy development as reflecting differential access to literacy-specific experiences during the preschool years (chapter 5), a position supported by findings that measures of home literacy environments are more predictive of later literacy than are measures of social economic status (chapter 6). Such findings naturally led to a search for ingredients of home and school environments that translate into emergent literacy (chapter 1).

Homes in literate cultures include a host of characteristics with potentially important impact on children's emergent literacy: Parents model literacy uses, reading and writing materials are widely available, topics of conversation may range widely, etc. Not surprisingly, book reading quickly emerged from the welter of possible features, bolstered by years of correlational research pointing to its importance and new anthropological research (Heath, 1982, 1983; Heath and Branscombe, 1986) and longitudinal developmental work reinforcing its central importance (Wells, 1985a, 1985b).

Book reading had long been known to correlate with later literacy, but new theoretical insights led to closer inspection of the interactions that occur while books are read. By the early 1980s reading was coming to be seen as an active process of meaning construction (Dickinson, 1987), and literacy as an intensely social activity, with skills acquired and practiced in the context of social interactions and used to serve social ends (chapters 1, 5, and 11). The attention to interaction during book reading led to recognition of the potential cognitive and linguistic richness of talk during book reading and to realization that, just as happens with language learning, effective mothers change the demands they place on children as children mature (Goldfield & Snow, 1984; Snow, 1983; chapters 1, 5, and 11).

Thus, by the later part of the 1980s the theoretical groundwork was laid for intervention programs in which book reading, accompanied by high levels of cognitively challenging interaction, play a central role. Book reading also became an attractive candidate for home intervention programs for practical reasons: 1) It is a discrete activity that can be duplicated nearly anywhere; 2) it is often a regular feature in family and classroom routines; 3) it is broadly valued within literate cultures; and 4) once established as a routine, it is nurtured by the emotional closeness that arises as books are enjoyed together.

Changing Responses of Program Developers

Concern for the welfare of families and children has been a long-standing tradition in the United States, but there has been an enormous increase in the number of institutionalized programs since the 1960s (Weiss & Jacobs, 1988) when many intervention programs began, some including home components and some focusing only on the child. In the 1970s and increasingly in the 1980s the ranks of these first-generation intervention programs were augmented by programs supporting families (Weiss & Hite, 1986; Zigler & Weiss, 1985). In general, programs in the 1970s tended to have an affective focus striving to help parents better serve their child's emotional and social needs and to teach them more effective child-rearing practice.

In the late 1980s I attempted to identify as many programs as possible in the United States that support the language and literacy development of children. To this end I combed through descriptions of 500 programs in the files of the Harvard Family Research Project, the vast majority of which served children from birth to five years of age. I sought programs involving children from the age of three to adolescence that were not focused specifically on children who were not physically handicapped. In addition, I pursued networks of personal contacts, did a computer search of articles back to 1974, scanned professional publications for program descriptions, and used newsletters and presentations at professional conferences to request information. These intensive efforts, however, led to identification of only 43 programs.

Surveys returned by these 43 programs led to my selection of 29 that most closely met my criteria. I conducted telephone interviews with 14 of these and analyzed the remainder from their survey responses. Programs distinguished themselves by the age of the children they served (only preschool vs. inclusion of elementary), the nature of the population they served (high or mixed vs. only low socioeconomic status [SES]), and whether primarily preschool-based or not. One prototypical non-preschool program serving a mixed clientele is New Parents as Teachers, which offers parenting advice and support as well as screening for early developmental problems to all new parents in Missouri. An example of a non-preschool type program for low-income populations is Avancé, which serves Hispanic adults and children in San Antonio and provides both parenting and adult literacy courses. Here parents have the opportunity to spend time practicing what they have learned with their children who are enrolled in the child-care classes provided by the program.

I found the importance of language and literacy to be unevenly distributed across programs. In general they were more central for programs affiliated with preschools, for programs serving lower-income and minority groups, and for programs serving elementary school-aged children. I also found that the range of literacy activities included in most programs to be limited. Enhanced use of books by parents was given nearly the same relative priority rating by preschool-based programs (3.9 on a 5 point scale) and non-preschool programs (3.8), but encouraging children to write had a much lower priority for non-preschool programs (2.5, a rating indicating relatively minor importance) than for preschool ones. Interestingly, stimulation of oral language achieved the highest rating in preschool-based programs (4.7), though ranked substantially lower in non-preschool programs (3.4). Limited concern for fostering writing and oral language continues to characterize many intervention programs.

A dramatic change has occurred, however, in the final area I examined, concern for adult literacy. In the mid- to late 1980s, focus on adult literacy was, for all practical purposes, absent from programs serving mixed to middle-class populations.

Concern for fostering language and literacy development was slightly evident in programs serving low-income populations (mean rating 2.5), but less common than more generic parenting issues, and not often inherent in educational services to adults. Since then, however, the government has initiated Project Even Start (see chapters 8, 9, 10, and 12) and even more remarkably, the phrase "family literacy" has emerged as a label that describes a whole new approach to providing services. Clearly we are in an era of rapid and important change so far as the provision of programs supportive of literacy is concerned. It is vital that we make optimal use of the current wave of interest in and funding for such approaches.

Issues That Need To Be Addressed

If optimal approaches to supporting the literacy development of children and families are to be found and institutionalized, a set of difficult problems must be addressed. I take as a given that our goal should be to provide services that meet the objectives of the program (e.g., improving literacy enough to enable parents to get jobs and read to their children) in the most cost-effective fashion. I refer to cost because, given the limited resources available and the enormity of the task confronting us throughout the world, we cannot afford to provide unneeded services to some while leaving many others devoid of help.

Who Is Being Served?

Of critical importance to program developers and researchers is information regarding exactly what segment of the population is being served and what are its needs, as determined by the agency as well as by themselves. The importance of this point is underscored by the results of Werner and Smith's (1977) massive longitudinal study of all the children born on the island of Kaui in 1955 ($n > 600$). Several strong predictors of children's ability to function as adults appearing as early as age two place some children at very high risk of long-term difficulty. Chief among these were biological insult at or near birth, maternal rating of the child as being socially unresponsive at age one, infant IQ ratings below 80 at age two, low maternal education, and limited economic means.

Thus, easily identifiable factors put children into high risk categories. Also, attention to gender and age is important because the importance of factors varies for boys and girls and the ability to predict subsequent problems increases greatly with age. Researchers of early childhood programs usually learn about only a few of these factors and, although service providers do have intake procedures, they could benefit from developmental work such as that of Werner and Smith (1977) to ensure that they learn as much as they should. More complete information for service providers could result in better targeting of limited resources; for researchers it could lead to better understanding of the complex interactions between the needs of children and families and program types.

Family programs and research would also do well to take the developmental history of the adults into consideration and to classify families in terms of their likelihood of engaging with the program in an effective manner. Toomey and Sloane (chapter 6) suggest one such possible classification system. Their work indicates that only certain families may be able to benefit from the kinds of services they provide. This theme runs throughout the programs described, which vary in intensity from those that provide full family support services (chapters 10, 12) to those that mainly provide books and encourage their use (chapters 3, 4). Remarkably, both types of program report successes, but different as these successes may be, it is worthy of note that programs so diverse in resources can be found to have beneficial effects. We need much better understanding of which kinds of programs are helping which kinds of families and children.

Finally, in addition to knowing how programs perceive the needs of families, we need to know how those families conceive of their own needs. As Ryan, Geissler, and Knell's description of Family Literacy programs makes clear (chapter 10), lacking input from the families, program developers may well fail to offer the kinds of services their target group values. Shimron's (chapter 4) discussion of the need to include children's preferences for classroom libraries, even when these preferences are in conflict with those of "experts," shows the importance of including the interests of those served in a different way.

Where Are Services Provided?

Another fundamental issue is finding the best location for a project. For literacy programs the options range from preschools to libraries to various community agencies. As Toomey and Sloane report (chapter 5), direct literacy support of families is considerably more expensive than delivering it through preschools yet may not be substantially more effective. The potential benefits of preschool-based work is also indicated by the fact that effects on the language and literacy development of low-income children is evident in well-run standard preschools (chapter 1), as well as in specially developed programs (chapters 2, 4, and 5). However, simply deciding that a program can be effectively provided through a preschool leaves open a host of complex problems related to the proper duration of the program, group size, and the unavoidable trade-offs between techniques that are "effective" and those that are merely "feasible" in standard preschools and schools (chapter 5).

If we can deliver effective literacy services through preschool and elementary schools, the economics of scale argue that we should pursue this approach. Once again, however, from the point of view of research, unless we know something about the families and children involved, we cannot know whether the observed effects pertain to all children or only to a subset of them. Some families may require highly personal contact with providers or parent educators (chapters 6, 7, and 8), whereas others gain just as much from viewing videotapes describing and illustrating strategies (chapter 5).

Though there are strong arguments for basing programs in existing agencies (schools, libraries, etc.), such a strategy raises many thorny issues. If programs are implemented through preschools and schools, they must be communicated in a manner that enables teachers to understand and continue them over an extended period of time. Karweit (chapter 2) describes a successful school-based program that requires major alteration of classroom routines (as opposed to simply providing an ancillary service such as a library), in which the teachers are part of a larger project and receive ongoing support. Preschool-based interventions that lack such enduring support can vary considerably in their implementation and continuation after the researchers leave (chapters 5, 6). Thus, as Snow points out (chapter 11), researchers and literacy providers must be concerned with finding ways to institutionalize effective programs.

Finally, there is a growing trend toward provision of services through collaborative ventures, partly as a result of governmental encouragement. As Nickse and Quezada make clear, such collaborations have much to offer, but the benefits come at the cost of time and energy (chapter 9). We know very little about the process of engaging in collaborations, and we do not understand the relative costs and benefits that may accrue as a result of collaborations. Once again, if we are to have complex collaborative programs that endure, we must understand the organizational dynamics of these projects better.

Assessing Program Effects

Assessing the effects of programs is a complex task that recently has begun to receive more sophisticated attention (chapters 9, 10, and 12; Weiss & Jacobs, 1988). One way to assess a program is to consider its impact on children's skills (chapters 1, 2, 5, and 6). A slightly broader focus occurs when the patterns of interaction intended to support the desired development are examined, for example, the program-related changes in the nature of interactions between mother and child or teacher and class during book reading (chapters 1, 5, 7, 8, and 10). Such an interactional focus seems critical for family literacy programs.

The fact that a number of programs have successfully demonstrated immediate effects on children and parents is heartening, but researchers interested in child and family literacy programs should not naively repeat the errors of evaluation made in the 1960s and 1970s (Jacobs, 1988; Weiss & Jacobs, 1988). An overly narrow definition of program effects fails to include consideration of the full range of a program's impact. One way to avoid this is to take the more institutionally oriented approach suggested by Jacobs (1988), as used by Ryan, Geissler, and Knell (chapter 10). Furthermore, the need to examine the impact of new initiatives on institutional dynamics is illustrated by Nickse and Quezada's discussion of the difficulties that arise as collaborations develop (chapter 9). Both of these research programs highlight the importance of including a broad range of issues in program evaluations.

The framework proposed by Jacobs (1988) is most appropriately applied to complex, multi-faceted programs (e.g., Even Start). But even those interested in tightly focused and relatively modest literacy programs would do well to open their evaluative lenses wider than the immediate actors in the program and for a longer time after the provision of program services than is often the case. Program effects may spread well beyond the original scope of the program. Projects described provide evidence of ripples spreading through communities as relatives and friends pass information along to one another (chapters 3 and 8). We witness what may best be called a tidal wave effect in Shimron's report of Feitelson's work (chapter 4), with a library program spreading to many thousands of classrooms throughout Israel. The huge effect of this project points to an additional noteworthy issue: the way in which educational programs are organized in different countries. Feitelson's work was vastly facilitated by the centralized control of education in Israel. Attention to the proliferation of programs in countries with different ways of controlling educational programs could provide important information for those wishing to disseminate effective models.

When long-term evaluations are possible, the added information may be qualitatively different from that garnered in short-term assessments. For example, a case study from Handel and Goldsmith (chapter 7) suggests that their reading program had a significant enduring influence on one woman's overall academic functioning and on her understanding of and interaction with her child. Moreover, the long-term follow-up evaluation of Segel's library-based program reveals effects on parents' use of libraries and children's literacy that were even more impressive than those seen in a short-term follow-up study (chapter 3). Accordingly, the longitudinal study of language and literacy reported by Beals, DeTemple, and Dickinson (chapter 1), promises to help elucidate both long-term effects of early experiences, and the complex interconnections among the factors that affect individual children.

In addition to looking for changes in behaviors, we also can look for changes in attitudes and beliefs, effects that might go well beyond the original aim of the intervention. Low-income parents traditionally tend to feel uneasy in schools and libraries – two public institutions obviously critical to children's literacy growth. In a recent discussion about the influence of class on parental patterns of involvement in schools, Lareau (1989) argues that less economically advantaged parents tend to view teachers as professionals and to see themselves as illequipped either to affect school practices and policies or to give their children the "right" kind of academic help. Such attitudes translate into reduced community involvement in schools and less parental support at home.

Several of the programs described in this book provide parents with the very knowledge they may feel they lack and thereby give them the confidence to help their children (chapters 5, 6, 7, and 8). This sense of empowerment is most clearly revealed in Edwards's description of her program, which culminated in parents critiquing training videotapes made by teachers. One can only wonder about the long-term impact on parents' patterns of interaction with teachers that resulted from this experience.

Changes in attitudes are an important aspect of Segel's program (chapter 3), which seeks to get low-income families to view the library as friendly instead of enemy territory. Thus they increase the low-income parent's access not just to books but also to a wide range of valuable information (e.g., about jobs, taxes, parenting strategies).

Overview of the Volume

In chapter 1, Beals, DeTemple, and Dickinson report results from the Home–School Study of Language and Literacy Development, a project following roughly 80 low-income children from the age of three until they complete the fourth grade. This chapter is the only one that describes the impact of naturally occurring experiences on literacy development, namely, the effects of book reading and other oral language experiences at home (meal time) and school (small teacher-led groups) on children's language at the ages of three and four and their literacy skills at the age of five. This attempt to look at children across places and times is rare yet critical. This chapter has two messages of special importance: 1) Particular kinds of experiences in both home and preschool have long-term effects on language and literacy development; and 2) the settings of importance include those where rich oral language is being used whether or not books are involved.

Part 2 describes programs based in schools and libraries that focus on the child. In chapter 2 Nancy Karweit describes the STaR reading program that she developed and now uses in classrooms that participate in the larger reform effort, Success for All. She goes into some detail, including information about the program's challenges and the data indicating its effectiveness in boosting language comprehension. Karweit also provides case studies that illustrate important points related to program evaluation: the need for qualitative individualized assessments and for careful observation of individual children's patterns of behavior.

In chapter 3 the focus shifts to library-based programs. Elizabeth Segel describes three programs designed to increase low-income families' use of libraries and frequency of reading. One of them involves minimal staff time, but the other two require library staff to work with groups of parents. These programs have received national attention both because they are innovative and because they are among the few library programs to be carefully evaluated. The range of programs devised serves as a challenge to libraries everywhere: With energy, ingenuity, and some additional funding libraries can do much to help low-income families.

In chapter 4 Joseph Shimron provides an overview of the remarkable work of Dina Feitelson in preschools, schools, and libraries. Dina would have been a contributor to this volume had she not tragically died before she could write her chapter. We all miss her ongoing insights about theory and practice, but we are fortunate to have Shimron's cogent overview of her work, some of which has never appeared in English. Certain features of Feitelson's work are especially significant. She calls our attention to the problem of development: Because literacy changes with age, new programs need to be developed for children who have moved past the earliest phase of reading growth. Feitelson also emphasizes the importance of language and culture to literacy, and her work demonstrates the potential of research to affect practice in a way that serves children from language and cultural minorites. Finally, Shimron offers considerable data supporting Feitelson's optimistic belief that institutions such as schools and libraries can have a powerful positive effect on the problems that immigrant and low-income populations face.

Part 3 shifts the focus to programs that provide services that include the participation of parents. Some facet of each program is based in a preschool or school. In chapter 5 Arnold and Whitehurst report about the important line of research done by Grover Whitehurst in the area of child-focused literacy interventions. They describe the dialogic reading method that has been in operation for nearly a decade and review studies examining its effects on different social classes and different linguistic and cultural groups (American, Mexican), in different settings (homes, preschools), and with different types of training (videotapes, trainers, graduate students). What is especially noteworthy about this research program is that it has moved beyond the simple demonstration of its success as a method to a consideration of such issues as its impact on children of different ages and social backgrounds, the effectiveness of different training approaches on different parents, and the relative merits of preschool-based as opposed to parent-focused programs. Finally, the authors point out that a direct causal relation between book reading programs and literacy has not been proven except via correlational studies, and call for controlled experimental work to reveal the route from early book reading to later literacy more fully (see chapter 1 for consideration of related issues).

In chapter 6, Derek Toomey and Joanne Sloane report about their work in West Heidelberg, Australia, since the mid-1980s. Like Arnold and Whitehurst they worked in preschools and homes and documented the results of their work by means of an experimental design that includes treatment and control groups. Their program is somewhat more broad-gauged than that of Arnold and Whitehurst, and at times included considerably more contact with parents. They propose a typology of parents based on their intimate contact with families that seems helpful in predicting parental involvement in programs and that could stimulate future investigation. Their discussion also treats issues related to the interaction between program type and family type, raising the possibility that not every program is suited for all families.

In chapter 7, Ruth Handel and Ellen Goldsmith describe their Family Reading program, an approach they have used for over five years in an urban technical college and in elementary schools. This program is the one on which Segel and her staff modeled their library-based Read Together program. As is the case for other programs in this section, the project strives to teach parents new strategies for reading with their children and to enhance their literacy skills by having them engage with other parents in discussions of children's books. Reflecting this concern for the growing literacy skills of adults, they assess their program in terms of its impact on parents. They present strong evidence that the program is well received by parents and that it can have powerful and enduring effects both on parents and on their children.

Chapter 8, the closing chapter in this section, by Patricia Edwards, deals head-on with an issue that simmers whenever intervention programs with minority or lower-income parents are discussed, that is, the question of whether or not it is appropriate for "outside experts" to "tell" parents how to raise their children. Speaking from her perspective as an African American, Edwards builds a strong and passionate argument that, not only are such programs appropriate, they are urgently needed and desired by many parents. She outlines in detail her year-long project with a small group of mothers and teachers on book-reading techniques. Her chronicle provides concrete details of programmatic interest, and her rich transcript data afford insight into the shifting attitudes and behaviors that occurred among the mothers and the teachers. What emerges is strong evidence that considerable work needs to be done to change the way mothers like the ones who worked with Edwards read to their children.

In part 4 the focus widens from the effects of programs on parents and their children to include broader institutional features of complex family literacy programs. Even the description of program types within this domain of collaborative ventures is a challenge. In chapter 9 Ruth Nickse and Shelly Quezada outline Nickse's framework for describing family literacy programs and use it to explain the functioning of a joint enterprise that was spearheaded by the Massachusetts Board of Library Commissioners. They also outline the range of difficulties that arise when such projects are attempted and suggest directions for future work. Finally, they present early results from Project Even Start, the large federal family literacy program that mandates collaborations, and they indicate points where programs funded by Even Start may be grappling with some of the challenges that they discuss. They conclude by suggesting future directions for research and calling for new approaches to training personnel who serve in community agencies.

In chapter 10, Katherine E. Ryan, Barbara Geissler, and Suzanne Knell present the most complete data available to analyze a variety of Family Literacy programs. They report results from an ongoing assessment of programs found throughout Illinois. Of special interest is their use of Jacobs's (1988) five-tiered approach to program evaluation. They use case studies to illustrate how evaluation can occur at each of these tiers and provide examples of how different kinds of programs evaluate program effectiveness. They also stress the importance of including the needs expressed by parents with the needs perceived by the service providers and note the recurrent finding that the viewpoints of men are grossly underrepresented and male participation is extremely low in the area of literacy.

The final part of the book emphasizes diverse aspects of the foregoing projects. Catherine Snow, in chapter 11, focuses on themes that distinguish programs and others that connect them. She also insists that literacy is a social, language-based activity and that the deepest challenge is not to discover techniques that "work" but to find ways to institutionalize effective programs. In chapter 12, Sharon Darling and Susan Paul report impressive results from another important Family Literacy program, the Kenan Family Literacy Project. Their results demonstrate the potential impact that broad-based, intensive programs can have on parents and children who face many hardships. After discussing how various programs can serve the needs of children and parents, they discuss the issue of how to evaluate complex programs. Finally, pointing to the deeply rooted problems many families face, they call for broad-based, collaborative Family Literacy programs that meet the needs of both parents and children. In chapter 13 I briefly synthesize key practical and theoretical insights gleaned from the programs described and suggest some directions for future work.

The programs described in this book represent what we hope are just the first generation of literacy intervention efforts. They make clear that many different approaches can have beneficial effects on families and children. However, the number of questions that have not even been addressed systematically is far larger than the number that have. Enormous amounts of practical and theoretical work remain to be done, but the research reported here indicates that we have at least begun.

References

Dickinson, D.K. (1987). Oral language, literacy skills, and response to literature. In J. Squire (Ed.), *The dynamics of language learning: Research in the language arts* (pp. 147–83). Urbana, IL: National Council of Teachers of English.

Dickinson, D.K. (1988). *An examination of programs that involve parents in efforts to support children's acquisition of literacy*. Final Report Submitted to the W.T. Grant Foundation.

Goldfield, B.A. & Snow, C.E. (1984). Reading books with children: The mechanics of parental influence on children's reading achievement. In J. Flood (Ed.), *Understanding reading comprehension* (pp. 204–18). Newark, DE: International Reading Association.

Harste, J.C., Woodward, V.A. & Burke, C.L. (1984). *Language stories & literacy lessons*. Portsmouth, NH: Heinemann.

Heath, S.B. (1982). What no bedtime story means: Narrative skills at home and school. *Language in Society, 11*, 49–76.

Heath, S.B. (1983). *Ways with words: Language, life, and work in communities and classrooms*. NY: Cambridge University Press.

Heath, S.B. & Branscombe, A. (1986). The book as narrative prop in language acquisition. In B.B. Schieffelin & P. Gilmore (Eds.), *The acquisition of literacy: Ethnographic perspectives* (pp. 16–34). Norwood, NJ: Ablex.

Jacobs, F.H. (1988). The five-tiered approach to evaluation: Context and implementation. In H.B. Weiss & F.H. Jacobs (Eds.), *Evaluating family programs* (pp. 37–71). New York: Aldine DeGruyter.

Lareau, A. (1989). *Home advantage*. New York: The Falmer press.

Mason, J.M. & Allen, J. (1986). A review of emergent literacy with implications for research and practice in reading. In C.Z. Rothkopf (Ed.), *Review of research in education* (Vol. 13, pp. 3–48). Washington D.C.: American Educational Research Association.

Snow, C.E. (1983). Literacy and language: Relationships during the preschool years. *Harvard Educational Review, 53*, 165–89.

Sulzby, E. & Teale, W. (1991). Emergent literacy. In R. Barr, M. Kamil, P. Mosenthal & P.D. Pearson (Eds.), *Handbook of reading research* (*Vol. II*) (pp. 727–58). New York: Longman.

Weiss, H.B. & Hite, S. (1986). A report from a national program survey conducted by the Harvard Family Research Project. *Family Resource Coalition – FRC Report, 3*, 4–7.

Weiss, H.B. & Jacobs, F.H. (1988). Introduction: Family support and education programs – Challenges and opportunities. In H.B. Weiss & F.H. Jacobs (Eds.), *Evaluating family programs* (pp. xix–xxvii). New York: Aldine DeGruyter.

Wells, G. (1985a). *Learning, language and education* (pp. 74–99). Philadelphia: NFER-Nelson.

Wells, G. (1985b). *The meaning makers*. Portsmouth, NH: Heinemann.

Werner, E.E. & Smith, R.S. (1977). *Kauai's children come of age*. Honolulu, HA: University Press of Hawaii.

Zigler, E. & Weiss, H. (1985). Family support systems: An ecological approach to child development. In R. Rapport (Ed.), *Children, youth, and families: The action-research relationship* (pp. 166–205). NY: Cambridge University Press.

Part 1

Preschool and Home Experiences
Affecting Literacy Development

1 Talking and Listening That Support Early Literacy Development of Children from Low-Income Families

Diane E. Beals, Jeanne M. De Temple, and David K. Dickinson

Intervention programs designed to support the development of literacy skills of children and adults typically focus on book reading. This focus is clear in the programs described in this volume, and the impact of these programs shows that efforts to increase children's exposure to books and improve the quality of the interaction that occurs while they read can have a significant influence on emerging literacy and on literacy-related language skills. Important as these intervention efforts are, maximal benefits will be achieved only when we fully understand what children are learning as they become literate and we identify the impact of different experiences on specific literacy skills. Intervention programs and experimental studies provide information critical to the theoretical work that helps provide guidance to those developing programs. However, if we are to understand the multiplicity of influences on literacy development, we also need to chart its course in the absence of intervention efforts.

Observational studies of literacy development reveal its relation to naturally occurring patterns of interaction thereby identifying potentially beneficial settings (e.g., book reading). Additionally, studies that describe the quality of interactions can help identify the types of interactions within these settings that are most likely to foster development. Of course, there have been many observational and correlational studies of home experiences during the preschool years pointing to the benefits of book reading and suggesting that high levels of interaction while reading are most beneficial (e.g., Heath, 1982; Wells, 1985;

in this volume see also chapters 2, 5, and 6). Surprisingly enough, there have been few attempts to describe how book reading is organized in preschools (but see Cochran-Smith, 1984; Dickinson & Keebler, 1989; Teale & Martinez, 1986), and prior to our project no efforts to examine long-term effects of naturally occurring variations in how books are read in group settings on children's language and literacy development.

In this chapter we present data from an ongoing long-term study of language and literacy development with low-income children and the various ways in which home and preschool experiences affect their emerging literacy skills. Because the study is based on a theory that emphasizes the importance of oral language skills, we examine settings that include but are not limited to book reading; we describe book reading in homes and preschools, mealtimes in the home, and teacher–child interactions throughout the day in preschools. We also report links between variations in the type of interaction in these settings and children's emerging literacy skills in kindergarten. These portraits should be of interest to program developers because they reveal patterns of interaction that exist prior to intervention efforts. Home data point to the potential richness of conversations in homes during meals and while reading books, but they also highlight the huge variability found among low-income families. Likewise school data reveal the rich potential of classroom experiences but show that this potential is not always realized.

We have three major points to make: 1) Literacy draws upon oral language abilities as well as print-specific skills; 2) literacy skills are nurtured both in homes and in preschools through events that include but are not restricted to book reading; and 3) homes and preschools differ in the kinds of support they provide for early literacy development.

Oral Language Contributions to Literacy

Children's oral language begins to blossom in the preschool years; they acquire sophistication using language at many levels, from articulation of sounds to construction of extended discourse. They also learn to use language for an ever-increasing number of purposes. In addition to discovering the power of language to make requests and demands in more subtle and powerful ways, children also begin telling stories about personal experiences and communicating information and ideas. Amidst this bewildering array of emerging competencies, we may well ask what skills contribute to literacy development;

and, if such skills can be identified, what experiences contribute to their appearance?

To date the clearest answers to questions about the linkage between language skills and reading come from research on the smallest speech unit – the phoneme. The results consistently demonstrate strong links between reading and phonemic awareness (i.e., the ability to focus consciously on the individual sounds that make up words) (for recent reviews see Gough, Juel & Griffin, 1992; Liberman & Shankweiler, 1991; Tunmer, 1991). The emphasis on phonemic awareness mirrors the traditional interest shown by researchers and teachers of reading in early decoding (the process of mapping sounds onto letters). Although phonemic awareness certainly plays a pivotal role in early reading, considerable evidence also suggests that it is greatly aided by early reading instruction (e.g., Ehri, 1991).

Our research expands the range of oral language abilities seen as crucial to literacy to include spoken vocabulary and discourse-level skills. To understand the importance of these skills we need to look beyond the simple texts that children encounter when they first begin reading and consider the challenges they face after they have become reasonably competent decoders. At about the third or fourth grade, children begin to read longer texts that tell about places and times outside their experience. At the same time, they begin to encounter vocabulary in books that expands beyond what they employ in everyday conversations. Of course, even before they begin talking, children learn new information through conversation, but in typical conversations people rely heavily on prior shared information: they use gestures and intonation to make their messages clear, they take relatively brief turns when they speak, and they deal with misunderstandings through back-and-forth exchanges. These conversational supports to meaning construction are not always available in reading or writing. Children can develop skill at constructing meaning that is relatively explicit when similar limitations are imposed (e.g., explaining ideas and points of view, telling stories about events not experienced by others).

Supportive settings.   Using this framework for thinking about the oral language precursors to literacy skill, we can see several reasons why book reading is of such value. With books children encounter a broader range of words than they do in typical conversations. Also, they can construct imaginary worlds using the text and pictures as a springboard, and when discussing books they get a chance to reflect on language and to develop skills interpreting and constructing extended discourse. Thus, while some benefits are likely to accrue simply from exposure to books, the full value of reading can only be realized if the adult and child engage in conversations that support meaning construction (see chapter 5).

Important as book reading may be, it is not the only setting conducive to development of language skills. Routine events in the home when people may share experiences, such as mealtimes, provide opportunities to explain events and actions and discuss opinions. Such conversations may involve new vocabulary and extended talk about novel places and events, thereby challenging children's abilities to build understandings based purely on verbal information.

Book reading and small teacher-led groups in preschool classrooms also provide opportunities for nurturing literacy-related oral language skills (Dickinson, in press). As teachers help children with art projects, they may introduce new words and use extended discourse to teach the children how to do new things. When interacting with children in small groups teachers are more likely to engage children in such complex extended talk than at other times (Dickinson, 1991; Dickinson & Smith, 1991).

In the following sections, after discussing the larger study, we describe mealtime conversations and book-reading sessions in the home, followed by descriptions of book reading and teacher–child interaction during small group activities in preschools. After describing home and preschool settings when the children in our study were three and four years old, we report analyses of the relationships between early experiences and aspects of children's literacy development near the end of kindergarten.

The Home–School Study

The Home–School Study of Language and Literacy Development is following 84 children from low-income families from age three through their early school years, dividing them into two cohorts, with the first cohort including 39 children who received home visits. Because the children in this study are generally at higher risk for retention in grade and placement in special education than children from middle-class homes, they represent a wide range of potential school outcomes. The study is longitudinal in design and has collected numerous samples of talk from children's homes and schools over the years.

The home visits to children in the first cohort took place when the target children were ages three, and four, to collect samples of mother–child interactions. Mothers were asked to look at two books with the child, and at the end of the visit, they were given a tape recorder and asked to record a typical mealtime. Children were also tape recorded in their preschool classrooms via small back packs that teachers and children wore, group book reading sessions videotaped, and teachers interviewed. For the first cohort we transcribed and analyzed these records to isolate types of talk that we believe to be supportive and predictive of certain features of literacy development. At age five, the target children were given a series of tests that assessed language skills thought to inform literacy development and print-related knowledge. In the sections that follow are descriptions of the interactions that took place within each setting.

Home Observations

Book Reading at Home

When mothers read picture books with their children they can simply read the text. Through intonation and rhythm, they can make the activity very vivid and involving. In our observation of 38 mothers reading to their preschool-age children, however, they tended to take a different approach. Most mothers engaged their children through questions and comments interspersed throughout the story. When reading favorite books or a new book provided by the experimenter, mothers asked questions to focus their children's attention, to check comprehension, and to elicit labels for objects and descriptive attributes, such as color, size, and mumber. They asked children for or provided explanations of behavior, predictions, and connections between events or objects in the story and those in the child's own life. The basic format for book-reading conversations consisted of the mother reading the text, making comments, and asking the child questions about the text and its connections to his or her own life (De Temple & Beals, 1991). Though there was great variation in the amount of talk during book reading as well as the frequency with which the reader stopped to interject a question or comment, mothers, on average, inserted 34 comments and questions per session, indicating that much more was happening than a simple reading of the text.

We analyzed book readings for the type of questions that were asked and answered, and coded each utterance to indicate whether the comments and questions were immediate or nonimmediate. Immediate talk restricted the mother and child to what they could see in the immediate physical context (i.e., the book). Nonimmediate talk allowed them to move away from what they could see on the page before them – to explain the behavior of characters and the meaning of words, to make connections between the story and the child's world, and to make predictions and draw inferences from the text or illustrations. The nonimmediate category of discourse, because it is more explicit and less reliant on shared context, appears to anticipate the skills that children will require later for successful literacy and school achievement. The following example contains numerous nonimmediate utterances by both mother and child:

Ethan:	Why she going to eat Hansel and Gretel?
Mother:	Because she was hungry.
Ethan:	Why was she hungry?
Mother:	Because she didn't have any food.
Ethan:	But that's not food.
Mother:	I know it's not food.
Mother:	But she was a mean old witch and she ate little girls and boys.
Ethan:	But – but there's no – the witch in here.
Mother:	There's a witch in this book.
Ethan:	Not in here.
Mother:	Yeah – no not here!
Mother:	There – witches are only make believe.
Ethan:	But I like 'em.

In this example, Ethan is taking the lead in asking questions about the story of Hansel and Gretel. He seeks to understand the witch's motive for eating the children. The mother responds, but also points out that witches are only make believe, taking Ethan beyond the immediate context of the story.

Table 1 presents the amount of nonimmediate talk by the mothers, the percentage of nonimmediate talk by both mothers and children during book reading, and the information index for both the unfamiliar (experimenter-provided) and the familiar books at both home visits for children at ages three and four. The information index is the number of times the child gives information regarding the story (either spontaneously or following a question or comment) divided by the number of times the mother requests information from the child. This measure gives us an indication of how much responsibility for the discussion the child takes on. An information index of 1 means that the child is simply responding to the mother's requests. An index greater than 1 indicates that the child is providing additional information, beyond the mother's requests. And, an index less than 1 suggests that the mother has to request information more than once in order to get a response from the child.

On average, the proportion of nonimmediate talk for children at

Table 1 Mother–child talk about an unfamiliar and a familiar book

Nonimmediate talk about unfamiliar book	Age three[a]		Age four[b]	
	Mean	Range	Mean	Range
Mother's number of utterances	4.4	0–12	3.8	0–15
Total (%)	10.5	0–23.8	12.7	0–37.5
Information index	1.4	0–4	1.6	0–5
Nonimmediate talk about familiar book				
Mother's number of utterances	4.4	0–24	5.1	0–28
Total (%)	10.4	0–41.2	16.1	0–42.9
Information index	3.1	0–29	2.7	0–21

[a] $n = 38$–39
[b] $n = 36$–38

four years old is greater than that for children at three. Although the total proportion of nonimmediate talk seems to increase with age in the reading of both types of books, the actual number of utterances of this type by the mother increases only slightly with the familiar book. When the mother read *Very Hungry Caterpillar*, the unfamiliar book that was supplied, to a child of four, she seemed to use less nonimmediate talk than she had when reading the same book the previous year. The higher proportion of nonimmediate talk may be accounted for by an overall decrease in the amount of talk during reading from age three to age four. A slight increase in such talk occurred when mothers and children read their own book together. The actual numbers, however, are a reminder of how rarely this type of talk occurs even with a familiar book. Although the children were older than four and a half years old at this visit, more than 80 percent of the talk about the book is either irrelevant to the content of the book (e.g., comments about other activities going on in the home or talk to others not engaged in the reading) or about concrete, immediately available information. The skills of the child that enable talk about the past, the meaning of words, and the interpretations of motives or feelings are being tapped less than 20 percent of the time.

The information index suggests that with the unfamiliar book children do little more than answer their mothers' questions. Although the book became somewhat more familiar by the second home visit and many children reported having read it at school, their involvement does not increase. On the other hand, the familiar book triggers twice as much talk from the three-year-old than the new book and a little less than that from the four-year-old. This difference in response between books suggests that familiarity makes it easier for the child to converse and comment spontaneously about the story or illustrations.

These book readings were situations that we set up for the purpose of our study. One question that our analysis often raises is: Do these mothers read books to their children at other times without our prompting? Hence, we conducted an interview with each mother on our first home visit to address the child's literacy experiences in the home and her own involvement in them. Questions included whether she or anyone else ever read to the child, and, if so, how often; whether or not the child pretended to read to her or anyone else, or pretended to read while playing alone; whether or not she knew if the child had a favorite book, could write any letters of the alphabet, or had any children's books in the home; and whether or not the library was used as a source of books. We also asked the mother if she ever read for pleasure, and to name her own favorite author. These questions helped us to gain insight into family experiences with reading and writing, and to gauge the level of interest in and value placed on literacy in the home. We then created a composite score for literacy environment based on the answers we received, with possible scores ranging from 1 to 14.

All mothers said that they read to their children. The literacy-environment score was associated with the amount of nonimmediate talk spoken by the mother when she read the unfamiliar book to her child. Though there was wide variation in reading style for mothers with literacy environment scores in the middle range, those with the highest reported literacy environments (scores of 10, 11, 12, and 13) used the most nonimmediate talk while reading, and those with the lowest scores (2, 3, and 6) used very little nonimmediate talk (De Temple & Snow, 1992).

The interview also addressed mothers' aspirations for their child's education. When asked whether they thought their children would quit school at 16, finish high school, or go on to higher education, only one expected her child to quit at 16. The mothers' educational expectations for their children were related to their use of nonimmediate talk while reading. Mothers who expected their children to go on to higher education (70%) produced an average of 4.5 nonimmediate utterances while reading the unfamiliar book (range 0–12), whereas those choosing high school as the highest level of education (30%) produced an average of only 3.0 utterances of this type (range 0–6). Even at this early age, we see that mothers' long-term aspirations for their children are related to how they talk to their children.

Mealtimes

Mealtimes seem to hold special power in American families. The popular media decries the decline in frequency of families who eat dinner together as portending a bleak future for the child, the family, and the nation. The culture has, historically, seen mealtimes as occasions for family members to work out their relationships, pass on family values and lore, and acquaint children with social and cultural norms. Because many families still vest mealtimes with this sort of power, the conversations that take place can be a valuable source of insight into their inner workings.

Because we were particularly interested in how preschool children acquire literacy skills, we coded mealtime conversations for the presence of two types of talk that we consider to be precursors of the kinds of discourse commonly used by children, teachers, and texts in classrooms later on, narrative and explanation. Talk was coded as narrative when the topic was a past or future event and as explanation when it sought to clarify some logical connection between objects, events, concepts, or ideas (Beals, in press). We hypothesized that a child's exposure to narrative and explanatory talk would support the development of discourse abilities that are crucial for success in school. The following is a sample of narrative talk in Todd's family when he was three years old. He and Elaine (age four) join in telling a story about their exciting experience earlier in the day. Their audience is their older sister and mother, who had not been with them at the time.

Elaine:	Darcy know what? They made me look in Scott's yard. Know what they saw under the table?
Darcy:	What?
Elaine:	A dead mouse.
Todd:	And we saw the blood!
Elaine:	And the heart.
Mother:	Okay okay we're eating.
Elaine:	No! We only saw the heart.
Mother:	Yeah Elaine.
Darcy:	Oh.
Elaine:	I hated it.

Next is an explanation that occurred in Karin's family when she was four years old. She is providing evidence for an assertion she has made.

Karin:	Sally had gym today.
Mother:	Sally had gym?

Karin: Uh huh. 'Cause I saw her coming out of the gym.
Mother: Oh you did?
Karin: Mm hm.

Kurt (age four) inquires into the definition of the word "servant." His mother initially assumes the task of giving the definition, but later the children begin proposing what a servant might be required to do.

Kurt: Mom what does that mean? To be a servant?
Mother: You have to do everything. They ask you to make some breakfast – you have to make breakfast; they ask you to get a newspaper – you have to get a newspaper.
Sister: Who?
Mother: A servant. Does everything you want them to do. Cooking . . . cleaning.
Sister: Or calling somebody? Or getting the food out?
Mother: Mm hm.
Sister: Or making coffee? Or a cup of tea?
Mother: Whatever.
Kurt: Or going out for a walk? Is [unintelligible] like that?
Mother: Taking the dog for a walk, whatever.
Kurt: How about kitty for a walk?
Mother: Whatever the kind of animal.

Narrative talk at meals is similar to the talk that occurs during book reading at home and at school. The books that mothers and teachers tend to read to children are generally narrative in nature, for example, *The Very Hungry Caterpillar* from our study. We hold that narrative texts and narrative talks both foster the development of a child's narrative ability.

Likewise, we also notice similarities between mealtime explanations and certain kinds of nonimmediate talk in book reading, such as the analysis of characters' motives, of connections between the child's world and the story, and of word meanings and use. Both kinds of talk support a child's growing capacity to explain and understand things.

Nonetheless, the purposes of mealtimes and book readings are different and thus have different ways of helping a child learn to deal with narrative and explanation. Mealtime conversations between mother and child, and among other family members as well, were more informal giving us the opportunity to listen in on intimate patterns of interaction.

We recorded how much narrative talk and explanatory talk each

Table 2 Inclusion of narrative and explanation in conversation during mealtimes

	Age three		Age four	
Narrative talk	Mean	Range	Mean	Range
Number of narratives	3.85[a]	0–15	3.26[a]	0–11
Percentage of narrative talk	15.4[a]	0–42.8	8.7[a]	0–29.5
Percentage of narrative talk by child	27.5[b]	0–71.4	30[c]	0–71.4
Percentage of narrative talk by mother	40[d]	0–100	45.9[e]	0–100
Explanatory talk				
Number of explanations	16.9[a]	2–45	15[a]	0–27
Percentage of explanatory talk	17.3[a]	3.4–30.7	15.3[a]	0–35.1
Percentage of explanatory talk by child	27[f]	0–50.5	28.7[f]	0–66.7
Percentage of explanatory talk by mother	47.3[a]	13.3–91.7	47[a]	21.4–73.8

[a] $n = 27$
[b] $n = 24$
[c] $n = 22$
[d] $n = 23$
[e] $n = 21$
[f] $n = 28$

family member, especially mothers and target children, was responsible for and computed the results as percentages of the total talk (in number of utterances) within mealtime conversations.

Table 2 presents the means and ranges of the frequency and proportion of mealtime talk that is narrative, the frequency and proportion of mealtime talk that is explanatory, and the proportion of the narrative and explanatory talk that is produced by the target child and the mother for each home visit.

The first and second meal times show roughly equivalent amounts of explanatory and narrative talk on average. Mothers and target children accounted for approximately 75 percent of explanatory and narrative talk at both meals. Children, even at the ages of three and four, are very involved in explanatory and narrative talk, contributing from 27 to 30 percent of the utterances in segments of such talk. Other family members, including fathers, siblings, and grandparents, were relatively infrequent contributors on average.

Preschool Experiences

Book Reading

Book reading is a routine event in nearly every preschool classroom. Though it is only one of several activities which comprise a group meeting, teachers make it a point to read one or more books to the entire group. When we interviewed preschool teachers we asked them to estimate about how many books they read to children each day. Combining the responses from over 130 interviews with teachers of three- and four-year-olds, we found that teachers report reading approximately nine books a week to children. If the average preschool is in session for about 32 weeks, children are read nearly 300 books each year.

Teachers vary in how they read and discuss these books with children (Dickinson & Keebler, 1989; Dickinson & Smith, in press). Some teachers tend to treat book reading as a performance, reading with few interruptions of the text. Often these teachers engage children in conversations about the stories after they finish the book. Other teachers engage children in conversations about the book as they read. The content and timing of the questions tends to vary from one teacher to the next, but individual teachers tend to be consistent in their strategies (Dickinson & Keebler, 1989). Thus, given that the same teacher tends to read to the group each day, during the course of a year children hear many book readings with a standard format.

Book-reading data in school have been coded in a manner similar to that used for book reading at home, enabling us to compare results from the two settings. School book-reading situations are quite different in character from those at home, involving a large group of children rather than a single child. Thus, group management is a prominent feature of school book readings, especially before the actual reading begins. Most teachers, however, also pause during reading to ask the children questions, to elicit their reactions, or to allow them to "chime in" on familiar portions of text, in a way that resembles some of the patterns observed in the home. We coded interaction during school book readings for many of the same categories of talk as for home book readings (Dickinson, De Temple, Hirschler & Smith, 1992). In addition, we developed an extended coding system that described more specific categories of talk (Dickinson & Smith, in press). In both home and school contexts, we were especially interested in interactions that required children to move beyond the text in their responses (coded as nonimmediate talk). The interactions that typified this kind of talk (also referred to as analytic talk) induce the child to analyze characters' personality traits and motivations, to speculate about causes of behavior or events, to predict upcoming events, and to directly discuss vocabulary. The following exchange occurred in a classroom of four-year-olds. The class had been reading Mercer Mayer's *There's a Nightmare in My Closet*, and the teacher has just pointed silently to one of the pictures.

Jed: He's sad, he's sad.
Teacher: Why do you think he's sad Jed?
Jed: He's sad because he wants the teddy bear.
Teacher: You think so?
Jed: Yeah.
Teacher: But how can you tell he's sad?
Jed: By his face.
Teacher: Oh, his face is telling you?
Jed: (nods in agreement)

The teacher used the child's spontaneous observation, "He's sad, he's sad", to extend the discussion into reasons and evidence for the sadness, leading the children to analyze both the text and the pictures.

A teacher's efforts can also serve to help children analyze vocabulary, focusing especially on their phonemic awareness. Here the class is reading a simple rhyming book entitled *Fred and Ted*.

Teacher: (reads text) "We can walk and talk".
Sue: Walk and talk.
Teacher: Do you hear lots of rhyming sounds in there? rhyming words?
Sue: Yeah.
Teacher: Listen: "Let's take a walk and talk." Here's one, "We can walk and talk." Which sounds rhyme?
Sue: Talk and walk.
Teacher: Talk and walk.

Like the preceding discourse, this one demonstrates a teacher's willingness and a child's ability to analyze texts in a manner that moves beyond the immediate context of the book.

Table 3 presents our analysis of school book-reading talk. (Note that these are classroom variables, not individual-child variables.) During

Table 3 Number of selected child and teacher utterances during book reading in school

Child utterances	Age three[a]		Age four[b]	
	Mean	Standard deviation	Mean	Standard deviation
Immediate topic comments	8.21	10.62	9.68	8.36
Nonimmediate topic comments	3.58	4.52	7.68	7.94
Organizational comments	3.59	4.46	2.88	2.86
Total	17.47	16.50	23.16	16.04
Adult utterances				
Immediate topic comments	7.37	7.76	9.60	8.20
Nonimmediate topic comments	5.53	8.87	9.59	9.79
Organizational comments	11.63	13.38	10.20	7.51
Total	32.79	32.44	42.08	27.64

[a] $n = 19$
[b] $n = 25$

both our school visits teachers tended to make more nonimmediate comments than children did in the book-reading situation, not surprising given the amount of talk by teachers. However, a greater proportion of children's talk was made up of nonimmediate comments because teachers engaged in more kinds of talk. Children's nonimmediate comments were both spontaneous and prompted by the teacher. There is an age-related trend: Both teachers and children make more nonimmediate comments when the children are 4 years old than they do when the children are 3 ($t(38) = -2.20$, $p = .03$). Thus, across a number of preschool classrooms, we see that children make proportionally more nonimmediate comments than their teachers and, in contrast to what was seen in the homes, the number of such comments increases with children's age.

Small Group Sessions

When we interviewed teachers we asked them how they typically allocated their time each day. Most teachers reported that they spend some time in small group activities. Using the total amount of time available each day, we calculated that on average, according to teacher reports, teachers are available to children in small groups about 13 percent of the time. If we figure conservatively and assume that children are in half-day programs only 32 weeks a year, we can estimate that teachers spend over 60 hours in small group settings. Of course, because only a selection of children can join in such activities at a given time, a particular child may participate in only some of these teacher-led sessions.

In contrast to book reading, utterance-level coding of the interactions within small groups has not been completed, though some small-group sessions have recently been transcribed. Because of their significance for long-term development, we describe examples of the kinds of interactions that seem to be typical. Small group time tends to be devoted to art projects. During these activities there are exchanges between teachers and children that enhance vocabulary and help children deepen their understanding of phenomena. For example, the following interactions occurred in a classroom that one of the children in our study was attending when he was four. The children have pictures of dinosaurs that they are coloring.

Teacher: Are you ready for this dinosaur? He's huge, he's gigantic, he's tremendous, and what kind is he?
Child: A brontosaurus.
Teacher: A brontosaurus.
Teacher: He's a. . . . Is it a girl or a boy?
Child: His shoes are on.
Teacher: His shoes are on?
Child: Is that a shoe?
Teacher: I think that's his foot.

Note that during this interchange the teacher used a variety of descriptive vocabulary, the child felt free to ask a question that exposed her confusion about the picture, and the teacher was able to respond to the child's curiosity.

Small group sessions often include descriptions of procedures to be followed and practice with skills such as naming colors and counting. We see such didactic interchanges in the following:

Teacher: Now what I'm gonna do . . . (overlapping talk by child)
Child: I made brown, see?
Teacher: I'll give you a popsicle stick and then you can draw a design in there, okay?
Child: Helen (the teacher's first name), I made brown.
Teacher: Okay? Here, go. Go for what you know. That looks great. Oh, nice.

Child: Helen, I made brown.
Teacher: You certainly did. Brown and what?
Child: And green.
Teacher: Green.

Note that once again the teacher is responsive to the child, but this time she is also directive, giving the children verbal nudges and posing questions, the answers to which she already knows (i.e., "Brown and what?").

Thus, though small group sessions cannot always accommodate every child, when they do occur they allow teachers and children to engage in extended discussions during which teachers can respond to children's interests, some of which remove the topic of conversation beyond the present.

Long-term Effects of Home and School Experiences

In the introduction to this chapter, we argued that verbal interaction in early childhood is a precursor of later cognitive and linguistic activity. The Home–School Study has developed a series of tasks, administered at age five, that serve as measures of the child's independent language and literacy skills in kindergarten. Various analyses of the relationships between these measures and the book reading and mealtime measures have been undertaken (Beals, 1991; Beals, De Temple, Tabors & Snow, 1991; Beals & Smith, 1992; De Temple & Beals, 1991; De Temple & Snow, 1992; Dickinson, Cote & Smith, in press; Dickinson & Smith, 1993; Dickinson & Tabors, 1991). They range from those based on simple correlational explorations to more complex regression analyses, reflecting different rates of analysis for different portions of our data.

Outcome Measures

Among our measures was the Peabody Picture Vocabulary Test (PPVT) (Dunn & Dunn, 1981), a standardized test of receptive vocabulary, which is widely used and known to be correlated with verbal intelligence tests and school achievement. A story comprehension task, in which the experimenter reads the children's book *The Snowy Day*, by Ezra Jack Keats, and asks questions about it, taps into the child's knowledge of the world and inferential capability. Also included is a narrative production task, in which the child is asked to tell a story about a group of bears shown in three photographic slides that the experimenter cannot see. The purpose of this task is to evaluate the child's ability to produce a narrative, for someone who does not share the same visual field. We also administered the Early Childhood Diagnostic Instrument: The Comprehensive Assessment Program (CAP) (Mason & Stewart, 1989) which assesses a child's print skills, such as the recognition of environmental print (e.g., names of candy bars, words on signs, etc.) in and out of context, the identification of the alphabet, the comprehension of story and print concepts, as well as phonemic awareness and writing skills.

Home Results

Mealtimes. In the correlational analysis, we found both the proportion of explanatory talk and the number of narratives (both of which are whole-family measures) at the age-four meal times to be associated positively with children's PPVT scores (percentage of explanatory talk: $r = .61$; $p < .001$; number of narratives: $r = .45$; $p = .05$). The more exposure to explanatory and narrative talk that four-year-olds in our study received, the greater was their receptive vocabulary at age five. Also, the higher the number of narrative utterances and larger the proportion of narrative to nonnarrative talk in meal times at age four, the better was their score on the story (listening) comprehension task ($r = .51$; $p < .05$). These findings suggest that children do not necessarily need to be offering their own explanations and narratives; they also benefit from from hearing them, requesting them, and putting in their two cents whenever appropriate.

Book reading. Both the amount and proportion of nonimmediate talk in book reading at age three are correlated with the child's performance on the CAP, the test of early print skills (amount: $r = .41$; $p < .05$; proportion: $r = .44$; $p < .01$). The mother who makes book reading a rich and cognitively challenging event is also helping her child to develop a familiarity with how books work and what you need to do to read one. But nonimmediate talk also supports the more sophisticated skills of story comprehension and story production, as two relationships that we found demonstrate: (a) The amount of nonimmediate talk in book reading at age three correlates with children's ability to tell the bear story ($r = .42$; $p < .05$), (b) and a higher information index (i.e., ability to provide information without assistance) indicates better story comprehension ($r = .49$; $p < .01$).

School Results

Book reading. Book reading data from the school also suggests the particular kinds of language experiences during preschool that affect children's emerging literacy. Similar to what we found in the home, analyses of our book-reading data from the four-year-olds' classrooms reveal a strong positive correlation between the amount of non-immediate talk at age four and story comprehension scores at age five (r = .49; p < .005). The early experience with cognitively challenging talk about books and stories carries over to story comprehension a year later.

We have even more striking results concerning vocabulary. The amount of nonimmediate talk at age four also correlates strongly with PPVT scores (r = .60; p < .0005). The strength of this association is underscored by regression analyses that enable us to take into account the fact that teachers who read to children in interesting ways most likely also provide other rich opportunities throughout the day. Using regression analyses we removed the links between other beneficial features of preschool classrooms that we identified in our interviews, observations, and audiotaping in order to determine how much impact book reading in itself had on children's PPVT scores. We found that the amount of time teachers and children engage in analytic discussions during book reading still accounts for 20 percent of the variation in children's kindergarten vocabulary scores.

Thus, teachers who spend more time talking about words and analyzing story lines (e.g., character motivations, cause and effect sequences) are most effective at enhancing vocabulary learning. It is important to note that the specific content of the talk, not the overall amount of talk, is what counts; total amount of talk about the book at age four is unrelated to vocabulary or to story comprehension scores.

Small group sessions.   Recently completed analyses relating preschool experiences for our entire sample demonstrate the importance of time spent in small groups and, as is the case with home data, the benefits of rich adult–child interactions to various aspects of early literacy development. The amount of time teachers reported scheduling for small teacher-led groups for three-year-old relates positively to kindergarten literacy skills (r = .41; p < .001) and receptive vocabulary (r = .39; p < .01). The amount of time we observed four-year-old children participating in small teacher-led groups relates significantly to story understanding (r = .31, p < .02), receptive vocabulary (r = .31; p < .02), and emergent literacy (r = .25; p < .05).

We also attempted to determine the impact of particular kinds of teacher–child interactions on children's language and literacy growth, especially what we call "cognitively challenging" conversations, talk about non-present topics (narratives about past experiences, plans for the future, etc.), talk that encouraged children to think deeply about issues, and talk about print. We assessed the effect of cognitively challenging talk using regression analyses that statistically control for other factors that could also affect outcome variables. These analyses reveal that children who experience cognitively challenging interactions at the age of three do better on kindergarten tests of storytelling ($t = 3.04$; $p < .01$).[1] For children of four such interactions correlate with better kindergarten scores in the following areas: storytelling ($t = 5.07$; $p < .001$), emergent literacy ($t = 3.25$; $p < .01$), and receptive vocabulary ($t = 3.45$; $p < .001$). Thus, at both ages talk deemed "cognitively challenging" has positive bearing on print skills, receptive vocabulary, and storytelling (e.g., the bear story). Such talk may occur any time throughout the day, but it thrives in small group settings in which teachers make special efforts to foster it. It encourages children to use language to build conceptual models of their world and reflect on language and the printed word.

Discussion

The purposes that people bring to any given interaction will necessarily shape the conversation. We have examined four different interactional settings, each with different purposes, each with different forms, and each with different outcomes.

In book reading situations at home, a few mothers simply read the text to their children; most of them, however, interject comments and questions about the text and illustrations, drawing their children into the story more deeply To some extent school book reading situations have a similar purpose: Teachers are attempting to bring the child into the world of the story. But because a number of children are present at any book reading, some of the teacher's talk is inevitably devoted to managing behavior. Children may have fewer opportunities to respond to the teacher's comments and questions than they do at home, but they do have the advantage of their classmates' responses and input.

Mealtimes often present a free-flowing conversation among family members about all kinds of topics. Children are full-fledged participants in these conversations, asking for and giving explanations, and joining in the reporting of past events and the planning of future ones. Small group sessions in preschools also provide opportunities for free-flowing conversation, but exchanges during these times conform more typically to the demands at hand and the instructional agenda of the teacher.

Consistent with our theory of literacy development, we find that the language interactions of young children with adults are important determinants of their literacy development. Too often it is assumed that one or two kinds of knowledge gained through a limited field of verbal interaction can cover all the necessities for literacy and school performance. But once we understand that literacy is not a single activity, but a conglomeration of interconnected skills and abilities, it follows that the skills and abilities a child needs to learn can be (and may need to be) learned in a wide variety of interactive settings.

We have just begun to show that the variety of settings and activities with specialized interactional styles that can support the development of different aspects of language and literacy. Each of the settings we have described has some influence on our literacy scores for kindergarten children. But different settings make their individual contributions to the development of component skills that, as a whole, constitute the cognitive background that we believe kindergarteners need when they encounter the literacy demands of the elementary school years.

Despite this heterogeneity of settings, there is a certain consistency in the most beneficial kinds of interactions. Rich, cognitively challenging talk at mealtimes (i.e., explanatory and narrative talk), book reading at home and in school (i.e., nonimmediate talk and analytical talk), and small group activities all support varied aspects of children's emerging literacy skill. What is common to talk in all these situations is that it takes children away from the here and now, distancing them from their immediate physical and social contexts. Because one essential purpose of literacy in Western technological societies is to enable communication with others from different places and times by means of the written word, exposure to and practice with such kinds of talk helps prepare children to acquire the requisite skills.

Our analyses are still at an early stage; ongoing work will enable us to identify more links between particular kinds of early experience and later literacy development. At this stage our work underscores the need to create as many opportunities as possible for language to be freely exchanged in homes and in schools.

Notes

We would like to thank Project Head Start and the Spencer Foundations, who currently support this research, and the Ford Foundation, who provided the funds to start it. We also thank the many research assistants who helped collect, transcribe, verify, and code the data. Of special commendation are Miriam Smith for her coding and analysis, and Petra Nicholson for her collecting and organizing. Finally, we thank the teachers, preschool directors, children, and families who allowed us to use their experiences to help us understand literacy development.

1 For each regression result the overall model must be taken into account. The values reported for three-year-olds reflect the significance of cognitively challenging talk after controlling for amount of time the child engaged in verbalized pretend play. Values for the four-year-olds reflect the significance of cognitively challenging talk without much prior control.

References

Beals, D.E. (1991). *"I know who makes ice cream": Explanations in mealtime conversations in low-income families of preschoolers.* Unpublished doctoral dissertation, Harvard University.

Beals, D.E. (in press). Explanatory talk in low-income families' mealtime conversations. *Applied Psycholinguistics.*

Beals, D.E., De Temple, J.M., Tabors, P.O. & Snow, C.E. (1991, April). *Reading, reporting, and repast: Three R's for co-constructing language and literacy skills.* Paper presented at the biennial meeting of the Society for Research in Child Development, Seattle, WA.

Beals, D.E. & Smith, M.W. (1992, April). *Eating, reading, and pretending: Predictors of kindergarten literacy skills.* Paper presented at the annual meeting of the American Educational Research Association, San Francisco, California.

Cochran-Smith, M. (1984). *The making of a reader.* Norwood, NJ: Ablex.

De Temple, J.M. & Beals, D.E. (1991). Family talk: Sources of support for the development of decontextualized language skills. *Journal of Research in Childhood Education, 6* (1), 11–19.

De Temple, J.M. & Snow, C.E. (1992, April). *Styles of parent-child book reading as related to mothers' views of literacy and children's literacy outcomes.* Paper presented at Conference on Human Development. Atlanta, GA.

Dickinson, D.K. (1991). Teacher stance and setting: Constraints on conversation in preschools. In A. McCabe & C. Peterson (Eds.), *Developing narrative structure,* 255–302. Hillsdale, NJ: Lawrence Erlbaum.

Dickinson, D.K. (in press). Features of early childhood classrooms that support development of language and literacy. In J. Duchan (Ed.), *Pragmatics: from theory to practice.* Englewood Cliffs: Prentice-Hall.

Dickinson, D.K., Cote, L. & Smith, M.W. (in press). Preschool classrooms as lexical environments. In C. Daiute (Ed.), *The development of literacy through social interaction.* In *New Directions in Child Development.* San-Francisco, CA: Jossey-Bass.

Dickinson, D.K., De Temple, J.M., Hirschler, J. & Smith, M.W. (1992). Book Reading with Preschoolers: Co-Construction of Text at Home and at School. *Early Childhood Research Quarterly, 7,* 323–46.

Dickinson, D.K. & Keebler, R. (1989). Variation in preschool teachers' book reading styles. *Discourse Processes, 12,* 353–76.

Dickinson, D.K. & Smith, M. (1991). Preschool talk: Patterns of teacher-child interaction in early childhood classrooms. *Journal of Research in Childhood Education, 6* (1), 20–9.

Dickinson, D.K. & Smith, M.W. (1993, March). *Contributions of specific preschool experiences to emerging literacy skills.* In G. Williamson (Chair), *Ready to Learn: Sources of Influence on Growth of Early Literacy.* Symposium presented at the annual conference for the Society for Research in Child Development, New Orleans, LA.

Dickinson, D.K. & Smith, M. (in press). Long-term effects of preschool teachers' book readings on low-income children's vocabulary, story comprehension, and print skills. *Reading Research Quarterly.*

Dickinson, D.K. & Tabors, P.O. (1991). Early literacy: Linkages between home, school, and literacy achievement at age five. *Journal of Research in Childhood Education, 6* (1), 30–46.

Dunn, L.M. & Dunn, L.M. (1981). *Peabody picture vocabulary test – revised.* Circle Pines, MN: American Guidance Service.

Ehri, L.C. (1991). Development of the ability to read words. In R. Barr, M.L. Kamil, P.B. Mosenthal & P.D. Pearson (Eds.), *Handbook of reading research: Vol. II* (pp. 383–417). New York: Longman.

Gough, P.B., Juel, C. & Griffin, P.L. (1992). Reading, spelling, and the orthographic cipher. In P.B. Gough, L.C. Ehri & R. Treiman (Eds.), *Reading Acquisition* (pp. 35–48). Hillsdale, NJ: Erlbaum.

Heath, S.B. (1982). *Ways with words: Language, life and work in communities and classrooms.* New York: Cambridge University Press.

Liberman, I.Y. & Shankweiler, D. (1991). Phonology and beginning reading: A tutorial. In L. Rieben & C.A. Perfetti (Eds.), *Learning to read: Basic research and its implications* (pp. 3–17). Hillsdale, NJ: Erlbaum.

Mason, J. & Stewart, J. (1989). *Early childhood diagnostic instrument.* Iowa City, IA: American Testronics.

Teale, W.H. & Martinez, M. (1986). Teachers' storybook reading styles: Evidence and implications. *Reading Education in Texas, 2,* 7–16.

Tunmer, W.E. (1991). Phonological awareness and literacy acquisition. In P.B. Gough, L.C. Ehri & R. Treiman (Eds.), *Reading Acquisition* (pp. 105–20). Hillsdale, NJ: Erlbaum.

Wells, G. (1985). *Learning, language and education* (pp. 74–99). Philadelphia: NFER-Nelson.

Part 2

School- and Library-Based Programs
Working with Children

2 The Effect of Story Reading on the Language Development of Disadvantaged Prekindergarten and Kindergarten Students

Nancy Karweit

Background

Shared storybook reading is strongly related to the language growth and literacy development of young children (Adams, 1990; Burroughs, 1972; Chomsky, 1972; Clay, 1979; Smith, 1979). A modest body of research isolates specific features of shared storybook reading that promotes language development of young children (Ninio & Bruner, 1978; Peterman, Dunning & Mason, 1985; Morrow, 1985; Teale, 1986). The interactions between the adult and child that enable the child to actively construct meaning from the story are particularly important for the development of vocabulary, understanding of the function of print, and comprehension of the story.

The research on shared story reading focuses primarily on one-on-one book reading. Relatively little attention has been given to the benefits of shared story reading in group situations, such as in day care or classroom settings. This paper focuses on the effects of storybook reading in the classroom setting.

Many differences exist between the one-on-one and classroom settings that can affect the benefits derived from story reading. In the first place, there is an intimacy and closeness of book and reader in the one-on-one situation that is difficult to replicate in the group setting. The print and the illustrations in traditional storybooks are typically too small to allow clear visibility for all children in a group reading. Oversized books with large print or individual copies of the book can overcome the visibility problem, but do little to facilitate one-on-one interaction. In a group setting, it is usually difficult for the teacher to personalize the story, to address individual questions and to allow individual comments.

The role and function of story reading is also different in the two settings. In classrooms, story time is often designed as a transitional activity or a management strategy. Children are expected to sit down, put their hands in their laps, be quiet, and listen. They are not expected to interact, question and talk about the story – the very types of behaviors that are argued to be responsible for beneficial effects in one-on-one story reading. Shared story reading at home is likely to be interactive; story reading in school is likely to be passive.

Although there are numerous differences between story reading in a one-on-one and in a group setting, this later difference in the extent and quality of interaction between reader and listener is argued to be particularly important. The interactions and conversations about the story are seen as instrumental in generating positive effects on language development. Consequently, we expect that for group story reading to have the same type of benefits as one-on-one reading, it must generate active student involvement with and interactions about the story.

This chapter reports on efforts to design, implement, and study such an interactive classroom story-reading program and discusses three main areas: (a) the development of an interactive story reading program, STaR (Story Telling and Retelling); (b) the effects of the interactive story-reading program on young children's language development; and (c) an examination of the nature of student interaction during interactive story reading.

Development of an Interactive Story-reading Program

We began the development of the interactive story-reading program STaR in 1986 as part of a larger school improvement and restructuring effort, Success for All (see Madden, Slavin, Karweit & Livermon, 1989; Madden, Slavin, Karweit, Dolan & Wasik, 1991; Slavin, Karweit & Wasik, 1994). Success for All was piloted in Baltimore City at one school in 1987–8 but is now in place at over fifty schools throughout the nation.

Success for All is a complex program, incorporating many elements, including a specific reading curriculum and tutoring program, cooperative learning strategies, family support teams, and staff development. All students and teachers from prekindergarten through grade three participate in the Success for All program whenever a school adopts it. The reading curriculum consists of three major components, roughly corresponding to prekindergarten/kindergarten, Beginning Reading (first grade or so), and Beyond the Basics (second and third grade).[1] Children are placed into the Beginning Reading and Beyond the Basics on the basis of tested reading level.

The prekindergarten/kindergarten curriculum follows an emergent literacy approach.[2] The content of the curriculum is organized into integrated learning units, which the reading and writing activities support. Specific language arts activities that often take place daily in prekindergarten and kindergarten classes include shared writing, shared book experiences, STaR (interactive story reading), individual writing, and individual reading (Karweit, 1988).

In the pilot year of Success for All (1986–7), we worked with the prekindergarten and kindergarten teachers to develop the story reading program. In the summer, I led an in-service training for the prekindergarten and kindergarten teachers and assistants focusing on interactive story reading. The in-service training demonstrated the use of strategies for group retelling of a story, including dramatization and use of sequence or story cards, and procedures for individual students to retell stories.

At the beginning of the pilot year, then, the teachers and their assistants had a general awareness of the importance of shared story reading, and had a general knowledge about how to conduct an interactive story session. However, classroom observations revealed that general awareness does not reliably translate into instructional practice; the story reading still tended to be a pretty one-sided, teacher-led activity. Several obstacles appeared to contribute to this lack of implementation. First, selecting and locating appropriate stories proved difficult for teachers. Teachers were either unaware of appropriate stories or could not locate them. Second, making supportive materials and developing activities to foster student involvement proved to be excessively time consuming. For example, preparing puppets or flannel board figures to illustrate a story could take as much as several hours. Third, even when these first two obstacles were overcome, teachers tended to ask primarily factual, routine questions to which students could give one or two word responses.

As a result of these observations, we decided that we needed more specific examples illustrating what was meant by interactive story reading. We (the Hopkins staff and the prekindergarten and kindergarten teachers) developed specific examples, including materials, and suggested activities that illustrated interactive story reading. We built story kits that contained (a) a storybook, (b) a teacher guide sheet (called a STaR sheet), that provided suggestions for discussion and retell activities, and (c) specific manipulables, such as sequence cards or flannel board figures to help the student retell a story. These story kits became the basis for the STaR program.[3]

We developed materials for over 110 different stories, including hand-drawn sequence cards depicting major events in the story, questions to use as prompts for retelling stories, and activities for dramatization of the story.[4]

Operation of STaR

Several features distinguish shared storybook reading in classrooms using STaR from typical story reading. First, stories are read on a consistent and frequent basis. Two stories are read and become the basis for discussion in a five-day period.[5] Then, there are strategies and materials available that provide opportunities for active involvement of the students, specifically in conversations about the story. This active involvement is generated by focusing on ways to involve children before, during, and after the story reading. The activities are designed for a whole-class format with a teacher and a classroom aide, and the program takes about 20 to 30 minutes per day.

STaR includes five main activities: (a) introducing the story, (b) reading the story, (c) reviewing the story, (d) retelling the story in a group, and (e) retelling the story individually. Typically, the story is introduced, read, and reviewed on the first day and then briefly reviewed and retold on the second day.

The introduction links the story to the theme under investigation and establishes what the children know and what they would like to find out about the story. For example, in a unit about water in which *Make Way for Ducklings* is read, the teacher asks what the children know about ducklings, especially about migration and life cycle patterns. She also determines what students would like to know about the topic and provides the concepts and vocabulary that are needed to understand the story. Hence, the teacher might discuss molting or migration of birds as conceptual background for this story and where feasible, use such concrete objects to illustrate it as an actual feather, if *feather* were one of the words to be discussed. Students are also encouraged to make predictions about what they think the story will be about, using information they have discussed and illustrations on the cover of the book.

Once the actual story reading is under way, teachers provide a running commentary to summarize the main points of the story, which amounts to brief recapitulations and consolidations. The teacher usually assumes a "reader" voice while reading and her "teacher" voice when offering a running commentary. Although some may argue that the story should be read straight through without these digressions, this supportive, running commentary appears to be very helpful, especially for students who have had limited experience with stories and print. In essence, the teacher is modeling comprehension strategies for the student.

About half way through the story, the teacher may ask children if they want to revise their predictions or make new predictions about how the story will turn out and then write the responses on chart paper along with the individual student's name. When the reading of the story is finished, students briefly summarize the story events, and the teacher forecasts the next day's activities, in which students will retell the story as a group or engage in a dramatization of it.

On the second day when the story reenactment/retelling takes place, either in the form of a dramatization or play, or with the use of colorful laminated (or sequence) cards to portray the story events, the goal is to involve all students and to allow them to talk about the story in their own words. In the case of a dramatization of *Three Little Pigs*, all the children would have parts, not just the main characters; the supporting cast might take the role of the straw or the bricks or the twigs. If the teacher is using the sequence cards, individual children may take turns describing what is happening on a particular card.

A conference with the classroom assistant provides an opportunity for individual students to have a more elaborate discussion about the story. This activity takes place during group retelling activity in a separate area, and because the individual conference can take from five to ten minutes, usually there is time for only three students or so to have one for each story. The aide begins the session by offering the just read book to the child and asking him or her to read the story. In almost all cases, students promptly begin to behave like readers, turning the pages of the book and often incorporating the exact language in the book, but if they are reticent, as four-year-olds can be, especially at the beginning of the year, the aide will prompt them with questions about the part they liked best and urge them to find that part in the book. The aide records what individual children do and say during these sessions on a form and if appropriate, asks them specific questions about their versions of it. Children also receive a STaR certificate to take home to their parents, indicating the name of the story that they retold and suggesting that parents might like to hear the child retell the story too. In some classrooms, a copy of the book goes home with the child when he or she has had a conference about it.

Older students, such as kindergarteners at the end of the year, may be paired for retelling activity using the sequence cards or the books. Some teachers utilize tape recorders for story retelling when an aide is not available. One school successfully utilized fifth grade buddies as listeners for story retelling. There are a variety of formats by which students can actively participate in recounting the story in their own language.

Evaluation of STaR

Success for All has been carefully evaluated across multiple years and multiple sites by means of a design that matches control schools with the Success for All schools and individual students within the schools according to their scores on standard achievement tests, such as the Comprehensive Test of Basic Skills (CTBS) or Metropolitan Achievement Test. At the end of the year, individual assessments of the control and experimental schools are made.

In examining the specific effects of STaR, we face the difficulty that after the first year of the program, many other components were put into place in addition to STaR. We added many of the elements of an integrated language arts curriculum to the prekindergarten and kindergarten, and Beginning Reading, which has a strong focus on phonics, was also incorporated in many of the kindergartens toward the end of the year. Moreover, many first grade teachers began utilizing STaR as a program at the beginning of the year.

The evaluation of the 43 students in the prekindergarten classrooms of Baltimore, conducted at the end of the pilot year (spring, 1988), provides the most straightforward evidence of STaR's effects. When children entered prekindergarten, they were given The Boehm Test of Basic Concepts (1971), a measure of general concept development in the areas of space, quantity, and time, as a screening instrument for placement. At the end of the school year, they were given the Sentence Imitation scale, a measure of expressive language, and the Picture Vocabulary scale, a measure of receptive language skill, both from the Test of Language Development (TOLD; Newcomer and Hammill, 1988), and the part of the Merrill Language Screening Test (Mumm, Secord, and Dykstra, 1980), in which children must answer five questions about a story read to them to assess their comprehension of it.

The measure of difference between the control and the STaR groups that we utilize is the effect size (ES), which is computed as the difference between group means, divided by the standard deviation of the control group, and gives the difference between the two groups in standard deviation units. An effect size of .3 is generally regarded as significant. Table 1 contains the results of this comparison.

Table 1 Comparison of STaR and control children test scores in prekindergarten Success for All 1987–8

	Control scores[a] (mean values)	STaR scores[b] (mean values)	Effect size
Boehm (pretest)	21.5 (5.7)[c]	20.6 (5.9)	−.11
TOLD (vocabulary)	8.5 (3.9)	10.6 (3.8)	.51
TOLD (sentence imitation)	4.5 (2.9)	6.4 (5.2)	.73
Merrill	2.5 (1.4)	3.2 (1.4)	.52

[a] $n = 43$.
[b] $n = 43$.
[c] Numbers in parentheses are standard deviations

The first row provides the results of the pretest and indicates that the two groups were not statistically different from each other (ES = −.11). The effect sizes for the assessments at year's end indicate positive results for the program, in the range from a half to almost three quarters of a standard deviation. The largest effects are on the Merrill story comprehension test. Similar results have been obtained for evaluations in other years and in other Success for All sites (Madden, Slavin, Karweit & Livermon, 1989; Madden, Slavin, Karweit, Dolan, and Wasik, 1991; Slavin, Karweit, and Wasik, 1994).

One of the most consistent findings across the various assessments at the kindergarten and prekindergarten levels are the pronounced effects on story comprehension as documented by the Merrill. These effects could come about by a number of means. For one thing, it is likely that kindergarten and prekindergarten teachers in STaR simply read more stories to their students. The availability of books with appealing supporting materials may greatly facilitate the incorporation of stories into the classroom. Moreover, the very nature of the reading aloud event in the STaR classroom should be quite different from that of the regular classroom. The emphasis in STaR is on promoting active student involvement in the story and providing models of reading behaviors that can facilitate student comprehension.

To address this issue of the *why* of program effects adequately requires detailed observation and assessment in control and STaR classrooms. Unfortunately, limitation in access to the classrooms of the control schools made it impossible for us to carry out such a comparison. We were not able to observe students in the control classrooms or to ask teachers about their practices related to story reading. One compensating strategy, although not ideal, is to examine variations in interaction within a STaR classroom in order to relate them to actual story comprehension.

Interactions During Story Reading and Comprehension/Recall

Given our inability to observe interactions in regular classrooms during story reading, we report here on student interaction within a STaR classroom and its relation to story comprehension. The purpose of this examination is to better understand the role of interaction during story reading in promoting comprehension.

We recorded and videotaped one story-reading session in a STaR kindergarten classroom in Baltimore. The story reading took place in February in a kindergarten class taught by Mrs. T. The class had twenty-one children and a classroom aide. The kindergarten classroom was a large, well equipped, and cheerful room with a carpeted area for story time. Mrs. T. and the children had an easygoing, smooth rapport, in which disciplinary remarks were infrequent to nonexistent. The classroom climate was warm, supportive, and busy. Mrs. T. and all the children in the class were African Americans. The school is in one of the most poverty-stricken areas in Baltimore, serving children from a nearby housing project.

For the story reading, the children sat in a semicircle, with Mrs. T. seated in a chair at the open end. While I videotaped the session, two assistants recorded interactions verbatim during the story reading, and at the end of it, the three of us interviewed the students to assess their recall and comprehension of the story.

The teacher read *Snow Lion* by David McPhail. The class had been investigating winter under the general theme of environment, and this book, as well as Ezra Jack Keats's book *The Snowy Day*, was selected to complement it. *Snow Lion* is the story of a lion who lives in a jungle where it is too hot for him to enjoy the things lions typically do, such as chasing zebras. The lion seeks relief from the heat by traveling to the cool hills far away. There the lion finds something white and fluffy that he packs in his suitcase to show his friends, the elephant, baboon, giraffe, and snake. When he returns to the jungle, Lion opens his suitcase only to find it empty! His friends do not believe that something "cold, fluffy, and white" was ever inside. They decide to follow

Lion through the jungle and into the cool hills to see for themselves. They travel for a long time, but once in the hills, they all do indeed see the white fluffy snow. All are amazed at the snow and delight in slipping and playing in it, and they make a statue of Lion out of snow to thank him for taking them to the white, fluffy stuff.

Prior to the story reading, Mrs. T. used large pictures of the animals in the story to help familiarize the children with their names and characteristics. The children freely made associations ("we saw that at the zoo" or "we read about that snake in the book the other week"). Except for the animal words, Mrs. T. did not go over any other vocabulary or concepts prior to this reading.[6]

The children showed very different patterns of responding to the story as they listened to it. A few made no responses; one child constantly responded and elaborated on the story (30 responses by this one child). The typical pattern involved the teacher reading a passage or page, providing a summary or consolidating questions, and allowing children to ask questions for clarification. The story reading lasted about 45 minutes. The easy give-and-take between the teacher and students generated interest and clarified confusions but still maintained the story line.

At the end of the session, we asked the children to recall the title of the story, the main characters and the major events in the story. Most of them knew the title of the story and frequently were able to point it out on the cover of the book because the teacher always pointed out the title, author, and illustrator as a part of the story introduction. "Do you want me to show you where it says *Snow Lion*?" was a frequent response to this query. Other titles given by some were *Lion Snow, Snow Tiger*, and *Snowy Day*.

Concerning the main characters in the story, we either let the child indicate who was in the story, or we directly asked, "Who was in the story?" or "Who was the story about?" Recall of this factual data was accurate; 11 of the 21 children remembered four or more animals. All the children recalled at least one animal name. One child who was not able to recall the animal's name (giraffe) did refer to it as "the one with the long neck."

When asked why the lion was sad, the majority of the children (14) replied he was sad because he was too hot. Two children responded that the lion was sad because the snow had melted in the suitcase. One child explained instead why the lion was happy ("because he had a good idea to tell animals to follow him on the way to the frosted stuff"). Two students gave answers that indicated they didn't know why the lion was sad ("was sad 'cause" and " 'cause was in his face"). Two other students simply restated the question as the response ("The lion was sad because he was sad"). Altogether, 17 of the 21 students appeared to understand this central problem in the story.

Another question was, "What happened to the snow that Lion put in his suitcase?" Almost all (19 of 21) knew the answer and recounted vividly how the lion packed snow in his suitcase, returned to the jungle, and found it had melted. One child indicated that there was water and snow. Another gave no response.

We next asked where Lion took his friends. Again, 19 of the 21 children indicated that they understood the story line by saying such things as, "to where the snow at, so they could see some snow." The interesting part of the responses to this question, however, is their incorporation of the actual language used in the story. The sample responses to follow repeat phrases and words, and one even recounts in detail.

> "Somewhere in the snow. They said, 'Yahoo – slide all on the snow!' "
>
> "To the fluffy stuff."
>
> " 'Hey, I have an idea, let's go where it's nice and cold.' At first they didn't want to follow but they did and they threw snowballs and made statues and said, 'This is for you Lion for bringing us here.' "
>
> "To look at the fluffy stuff."
>
> "So they could play with the light fluffy stuff."
>
> "With him to5 the white, fluffy stuff."

Finally, the children recounted their favorite part of the story. Most became animated when talking about the fun the animals had playing and sliding in the snow. Again, many repeated the text verbatim at this point, especially where the lion says, "Yippee!"

Interestingly, the number of comments and responses by the children was not related in a predictable way to how well they recalled or understood the story. The two children who responded during story time most often (30 and 19 responses, respectively) were also quite verbal and responsive in our interviews. That is, their responses during the story were related to their comprehension of it later in a predictable way. However, several children who were very quiet during the classroom reading were able and eager to converse about the story in a one-on-one situation.[7] At the same time, one very quiet child and one very loquacious child were the two students least able to tell us about the story.

We examine the responses of one talkative child ("D.") in more detail. This boy sat next to the teacher and paid (for the most part) rapt attention to the story, staring intently at the book as the story unfolded. In the retelling activity, however, this child did not recall or seem to understand the main idea in the story. He seemed confused about everything except his favorite part (the making of the lion statue). Looking back at his responses and questions during the story reading revealed that D. asked the following seven questions about the illustrations and language in the story:

"Why he make snowballs?"

". . . jungle?" [said in response to the teacher reading that the lion lived in a jungle]

"Why's the snow on his head?"

"What's that snake on the tree?"

"Look at that!" [pointing to illustration]

"What's that elephant got on his nose?" [tusks]

"Why's he jumping at the snow?"

D. paid attention to details on each page in the story, inquiring about those he didn't understand. He was awash in information but did not seem to understand why or how it made sense. Note that the questions D. asks are primarily about the illustrations, not about the story as read.

Mrs. T. indicated that attention to detail at the expense of the big picture was a characteristic problem for D. She also explained that he could be impulsive, rarely thinking before answering or asking a question. We suggested that D. be given more opportunities for individual retelling to help determine if his confusion about this story was contingency or part of a more consistent pattern. For example, if he simply did not understand the meaning of a "jungle" (as his second query implies), the meaning of the whole story could have been lost to him.

For most of the children, however, the give-and-take with the teacher was adequate to keep the story line alive and to address their questions. The questions Mrs. T. asked provided a framework for children to make sense of the story; that is i.e., they served to indicate what was essential to the story. We note that in D.'s case the exchange did not successfully focus his attention. Instead, he continued to focus on idiosyncratic, though to him critical, sidelights of the story.

The interview with the children after this first reading of the story was informative for several reasons. First, even in conducting story reading with a group of approximately 20 children, the recall of story details and understanding of story line was high. For the most part, the children were able to understand a fairly complex story after the initial reading. A number of children incorporated language used in the story directly or even assumed the role of the lion in their responses. Many delighted in the expressive language used in the story ("Yippee!")

and were still uttering catchy phrases ("tip of his tail") in other settings later that day and in subsequent days.

Children's responses to stories can indicate anything from understanding to enjoyment to utter bewilderment, just as their lack of response can indicate anything from complete lack of understanding to a high degree of mental, although not verbal, involvement. One implication for practice from this brief look at a single classroom is that teachers should pay strict attention to particular patterns of responses to stories as indicators of comprehension. Students who consistently ask questions that miss the mark or students who fail to respond at all are obvious candidates for frequent close scrutiny during individual story retelling.

Summary and Discussion

We developed STaR to address specific difficulties encountered in prekindergarten and kindergarten classrooms. The typical way stories are told in classrooms tends to limit interaction and make story reading more passive than active. Believing that conversations and interactions surrounding the story generate documented positive benefits for story reading in one-on-one situations, we created a method of group storytelling that encourages the active involvement of students and the modeling of comprehension strategies by the teacher.

The program provides several important lessons that may be of general significance. First, simply providing a general framework for teachers does not ensure practice faithful to it. Thus, we developed story kits that concretely incorporate these general ideas. Second, selecting books, devising teacher guide sheets, and creating supportive art work are time-consuming and expensive. Teachers and schools may find it difficult to come up with such materials given their resources and schedules. Third, making any such materials widely available is problematic as well. Art work or other manipulables created to support already published materials may infringe on specific copyrights or other authorship rights (though individual teachers can certainly use and create such art work or books without difficulty). The issue then is how to copy these materials and ideas and share them with other teachers and other schools. We find that providing kits with materials and suggested activities supports and does not impair, teacher creativity. The kits provide a base on which teachers can build ideas, not a script that constrains their creativity or infringes on others'.

Using a matched control–experimental group design, we noted

positive and meaningful effects for STaR on children's vocabulary, expressive language, and story comprehension at an urban school serving a large proportion of disadvantaged prekindergarten children. Although we could not tell from this study whether these effects arise from more frequent story reading or from specific elements of the interactive story reading, we did explore this issue in a limited way by focusing on the relationship between student responses to a story and comprehension of it for one group story reading in a kindergarten classroom. This examination suggests that the appropriateness of children's responses may be a valuable indicator of their comprehension, but it also suggests that both very verbal and very quiet children are capable of exhibiting little story comprehension.

Work exploring the differences in the frequency of story reading and the nature of the interactions during and after story reading between classrooms with and without STaR still remain to be done. The specific role of the rolling dialogue by the teacher as a means to model comprehension also needs to be examined. So far, these strategies have been examined exclusively in classrooms serving disadvantaged children who enter school with limited exposure to print and books. Additional work in classrooms serving more diverse student populations needs to be conducted. Positive results are apparent in schools serving students with English as a second language, but systematic observational work in these classrooms has not been done.

In designing the prekindergarten and kindergarten program, I drew upon my observations of reading preparation in kindergarten classrooms in the mid-1980s. I saw that the biggest task was to create a context in which language use is a meaningful activity for children. Stories seem to be perfect vehicles for this goal, engaging children's imaginations and hopefully providing them with the motivation to learn to read. To a large degree, the use of stories as central features in classroom literacy instruction increases children's listening comprehension and their ability to take meaning from text. Whether this technique is more beneficial to disadvantaged children's literacy acquisition than a simple phonetic one is not clear. Limited research contrasting different combinations of approaches to beginning reading (Stahl and Miller, 1989) suggests the appropriateness of more holistic attitudes.

Debates about this topic will likely never be settled to everyone's satisfaction. In the meantime, third grade classrooms all over the United States, in all kinds of schools and with all types of children, are peopled with a substantial number of children who still do not know how to read or who read at a low level. One main lesson of intervention research is the importance of sustained effort over time (Slavin, Karweit and Wasik, 1994). The timing and continuity of services for children experiencing difficulty may be equally as important as the method employed. Such tasks as organizing instruction to guarantee continuing support for children with difficulties may not be as exciting as debates about the merits of different philosophical approaches to literacy training, but they are consequential nonetheless in children's lives.

Appendix A.   STaR Book List

Title	Author	Publisher
Alexander and the Terrible, Horrible, No Good, Very Bad Day	Viorst, J.	Macmillan
Amelia Bedelia	Parish, P.	Harper & Row
Arthur's Christmas	Brown, M.	Little, Brown & Co.
Arthur's Eyes	Brown, M.	Little, Brown & Co.
Arthur's Loose Tooth	Hoban, L.	Harper & Row
Arthur's Thanksgiving	Brown, M.	Little, Brown & Co.
Arthur's Valentine	Brown, M.	Little, Brown & Co.
Ask Mr. Bear	Flack, M.	Macmillan
Babar and Father Christmas	Debrunhoff	Random House
A Bargain for Frances	Hoban, R.	Harper & Row
The Bear's Toothache	McPhail, D.	Puffin Books (1982) Atlantic Monthly Press (1988)
Bedtime for Frances	Hoban, R.	Harper & Row
Blueberries for Sal	McCloskey, R.	Harper & Row
The Boy Who Didn't Believe in Spring	Clifton, L.	E.P. Dutton
Bread and Honey	Asch, F.	Parents Magazine Press
Bread and Jam for Frances	Hoban, R.	Harper & Row
Caps for Sale	Slobodkin, E.	Harper & Row
Carrot Seed	Krauss, R.	Harper & Row
Chicken Soup with Rice	Sendak, M.	Scholastic
Christmas Moon	Cazet, D.	Macmillan
Cloudy with a Chance of Meatballs	Barrett, J.	Macmillan
Clyde Monster	Crowe, R.L.	E.P. Dutton
Corduroy	Freeman, D.	Viking
Curious George Goes Sledding	Rey, M. & H.A.	Houghton Mifflin
Curious George Rides a Bike	Rey, H.A.	Houghton Mifflin
Dandelion	Freeman, D.	Viking
Danny and the Dinosaur	Hoff, S.	Harper & Row

Title	Author	Publisher
Dear Garbage Man	Zion, G.	Harper & Row
Ernest and Celestine	Vincent, G.	Mulberry Books
Franklin in the Dark	Bourgeois, P.	Scholastic
Frederick	Lioni, L.	Alfred A. Knopf
Gilberto and the Wind	Ets, M.	Puffin Books
The Gingerbread Man	Schmidt, K.	Scholastic
The Giving Tree	Silverstein, S.	Random House
Green Eggs and Ham	Dr. Seuss	Random House
Gregory the Terrible Eater	Sharmat, M.	Scholastic
Happy Birthday Moon	Asch, F.	Simon & Schuster
Happy Birthday Sam	Hutchins, P.	Puffin Books
Harold and the Purple Crayon	Johnson, C.	Harper & Row
Harry by the Sea	Zion, G.	
Harry the Dirty Dog	Zion, G.	Harper & Row
Henny Penny	Galdone, P.	Clarion Books
How the Grinch Stole Christmas	Dr. Seuss	Random House
If You Give a Mouse a Cookie	Numeroff, J.L.	Scholastic
I'm Terrific	Sharmat, M.	
I Don't Care	Sharmat, M.	
Imogene's Antlers	Small, D.	Crown Publishers
Ira Sleeps Over	Waber, B.	Houghton Mifflin
Jack and the Beanstalk	Cauley, L.	G.P. Putnam & Sons
John Henry	Keats, E.J.	Harper & Row
Katy and the Big Snow	Burton, V.	Houghton Mifflin
Katy No-Pocket	Payne, E.	Houghton Mifflin
Leo the Late Bloomer	Krauss, R.	Simon & Schuster
A Letter to Amy	Keats, E.J.	Harper & Row
The Little Engine that Could	Piper, W.	Putnam
The Little Red Hen	McQueen, L. (illus)	Scholastic
Little Red Riding Hood	(no book) words to story included	
Make Way for Ducklings	McCloskey, R.	Puffin Books
May I Bring a Friend?	De Regniers, B.	Atheneum
Mike Mulligan and His Steam Shovel	Buton, V.	Houghton Mifflin
Ming Lo Moves the Mountain	Lobel, A.	Scholastic
Miss Nelson has a Field Day	Allard, H. & Marshall, J.	Houghton Mifflin
Miss Nelson is Back	Allard, H. & Marshall, J.	Houghton Mifflin
Miss Nelson is Missing	Allard, H. & Marshall, J.	Houghton Mifflin
The Mixed-Up Chameleon	Carle, E.	Harper & Row
Moongame	Asch, F.	Simon & Schuster
Mousekin's Thanksgiving	Miller, E.	Simon & Schuster

Title	Author	Publisher
Mr. Gumpy's Motor Car	Burningham, J.	Puffin Books
Mr. Gumpy's Outing	Burningham, J.	Puffin Books
Mr. Rabbit and the Lovely Present	Zolotow, C.	Harper & Row
A New Coat for Anna	Ziefert, H.	Alfred A. Knopf
Nobody Listens to Andrew	Guifoile, E.	Modern Curriculum Press
Norman the Doorman	Freeman, D.	Puffin Books
No Roses for Harry	Zion, G.	Harper & Row
Once a Mouse	Brown, M.	Macmillan
One Zillion Valentines	Modell, F.	Mulberry Books
Pardon? Said the Giraffe	West, C.	Harper & Row
Peter and the Wolf	Prokofiev, S. Carlson (trans)	Puffin Books
Peter's Chair	Keats, E.J.	Harper & Row
A Pocket for Corduroy	Freeman, D.	Puffin Books
Popcorn	Asch, F.	
The Princess and the Pea	Gackenbach, D.	Puffin Books
Really Spring	Zion, G.	Harper & Row
Rudolph the Red-Nosed Reindeer	Sambro, C. (illus)	
Runaway Bunny	Brown, M.	Harper & Row
Sand Cake	Asch, F.	Parents Magazine Press
Snow Lion	McPhail, D.	Parents Magazine Press
The Snowy Day	Keats, E.J.	Puffin Books
Stone Soup (1)	Brown, M.	Aladdin Books/ Macmillan
Stone Soup (2)	McGovern, A.	Scholastic
The Story of Ferdinand	Leaf, M.	Puffin Books
The Story of the Nutcracker Ballet	Hautzig, D.	Random House
Swimmy	Lioni, L.	Alfred A. Knopf.
Sylvester and the Magic Pebble	Stleg, W.	Simon & Schuster
The Tale of Peter Rabbit	Potter, B.	Scholastic
There's a Nightmare in My Closet	Mayer, M.	Dial Books For Young Readers
The Three Bears	Galdone, P.	Clarion Books
The Three Billy Goats Gruff	Galdone, P.	Tickner & Fields
The Three Little Pigs	Battaglia, A.	Random House
Tikki, Tikki, Tembo	Mosel, A.	Scholastic
Umbrella	Yashima, T.	Puffin Books
The Velveteen Rabbit	Willams, M.	Platt & Munk
The Very Busy Spider	Carle, E.	Putnam
The Very Hungry Caterpillar	Carle, E.	Scholastic
Waiting for Mom	Tyler, Wagner, L.	Scholastic

Title	Author	Publisher
Where the Wild Things Are	Sendak, M.	Harper & Row
The Wingdingdilly	Peet, B.	Harper & Row
Whistle for Willie	Keats, E.J.	Puffin Books
White Snow, Bright Snow	Tressalt, A.	Mulberry Books
Who Took the Farmer's Hat?	Nodset, J.	Harper & Row

At this time, JHU is able to provide artwork for the STaR stories in bold print.

Appendix B. Story Kit for *The Boy Who Didn't Believe in Spring*

Materials

Book
Sequence cards
STaR Sheet
Individual Retell Form

Vocabulary

spring   crops   vacant

Introducing the Story

Today's story is about a little boy named King Shabazz who did not believe in spring. What is spring? What kinds of things happen in spring? Do you believe in spring? What proof do you have about spring? Let's read about *The Boy Who Didn't Believe in Spring* and find out what King Shabazz learned about spring.

Reading the Story

Begin reading the story. Stop when appropriate to ask predictive, summative and inferential questions that will motivate children to interact with the story.

Page 1:   Why do you think King Shabazz did not believe in spring?
Page 5:   What were King Shabazz and Tony Polito trying to find? [spring]
          Where would you look for spring?
Page 9:   Where do you think King Shabazz lives? Why?
          Why do you think they are having difficulty finding spring?
Page 16: What did King and Tony find on their walk? [The boys found a vacant lot.]
          What do you think they heard?

Page 18:   What did King Shabazz and Tony find? [They found flowers grow-
ing in a crack in the stones.]
Page 21:   What other signs of spring did they see and hear? [Birds]
Page 23:   What did the boys find inside the car? [The boys found a bird's
nest.]
How did the boys know they had found spring?
How did finding spring make them feel?

Reviewing the Story

SC1 – King Shabazz did not believe in spring. When his teacher would talk
about spring he would whisper, "No such thing."
SC2 – One day King Shabazz and his friend Tony Polito decided to look for
spring.
SC3 – They passed the bakery, but did not find spring.
SC4 – King Shabazz was very doubtful that he would ever find spring.
SC5 – Suddenly the boys came to an old vacant lot and heard a noise coming
from inside a car.
SC6 – When they went closer to investigate the noise, they found flowers
growing.
SC7 – Then they looked in the car and found a bird's nest with four blue eggs.
SC8 – All at once. King Shabazz and Tony Polito realized that they had found
spring.

Discussion Prompts

Knowledge
What was the title of the story? [*The Boy Who Didn't Believe in Spring*]
Who were the story characters? [King Shabazz, Tony Polito, Teacher, Mother,
and Sam]
Where did King Shabazz live? [He lived in the city.]
What didn't King Shabazz believe? [King Shabazz did not believe in spring.]
What did King Shabazz and Tony Polito decide to do? [They went looking for
spring.]
Where did they finally find spring? [They found signs of spring in a vacant
lot.]
What signs of spring did they find? [They found flowers growing and a bird's
nest with eggs inside.]

Comprehension
Retell the story in your own words.
What was the main idea of the story?

Application
How are the flowers growing and the bird's nest examples of spring?
Why is spring Important?

Analysis

Outline the signs of spring King Shabazz found on his walk.
What proof did the story give King Shabazz for believing in spring?

Synthesis

How could you help someone believe in spring?
What other signs of spring have you observed?
What did King Shabazz learn about spring?

Evaluation

What did you enjoy most about this story?
What do you think about King Shabazz's discovery?

Story Extension Activities

Bird Nest: Collect string, twigs, and grass. With collected items, form nest in a margarine tub or bottom half of milk carton. Add cotton balls for eggs.

Hand Tulip: Hold fingers together on one hand. Place hand in brightly colored paint. Press hand onto paper. Dip side of hand into green paint and press onto paper to make stem. Repeat to make leaves.

Discuss: Discuss that spring is the season between winter and summer.

Outdoors: Take a signs of spring walk.

Planting: Plant seeds and discuss the parts of a plant.

Cooking:

Grassy Sandwich

1 avocado, mashed	1 teaspoon mayonnaise
$\frac{1}{2}$ teaspoon lemon juice	1 hard-cooked egg, diced

Mix above ingredients together. Spread over bread or crackers. If desired, sprinkle with alfalfa sprouts.

Poems and Songs:

Spring

Trees are budding.
The grass is green.
Flower blossoms I have seen.
The days are warm.
By evening it cools.
It's time to find the garden tools.

Five Pretty Flowers

See the five pretty flowers we planted near the door.
A little boy picked one and now there are four.
Four pretty flowers for everyone to see.
The dog stepped on one of them.
And now there are three.
Three pretty flowers, yellow, pink and blue.
The newsboy threw the paper and now there are two.
Two pretty flowers growing in the sun.
A caterpillar chewed the stem.
And now there is one.
One pretty flower with a smilling face.
I picked the pretty flower and put in a vase.

It is Springtime
(To the tune, *London Bridge*)

Leaves are growing on the trees,
On the trees, on the trees.
Leaves are growing on the trees.
It is Springtime.

(Other verses)
All the grass is turning green . . .
See the birdies build their nest . . .
Watch the flowers start to grow . . .

Appendix C.   Individual Story Retell Form

Student Name _ _ _ _ _ _ _ _ _ _ _ _ _ _ Date _ _ _ _ _ _ _ _ _ _ _ _ _ _ _ _ _ _ _

Teacher _ _ _ _ _ _ _ _ _ _ _ _ _ _ _ _ _ School _ _ _ _ _ _ _ _ _ _ _ _ _ _ _ _ _ _

The Boy Who Didn't Believe in Spring
by
Lucille Clifton

Questions for Individual Story Retell

1. Recall the name of the story. [*The Boy Who Didn't Believe in Spring*]

- -

2. Recall the story characters. [King Shabazz, Tony Polito, Teacher, Mother, Sam]

- -

3. What didn't King Shabazz believe in? [King Shabazz did not believe in spring.]

----

4. What did King Shabazz and Tony Polito do? [They went looking for spring.]

----

5. What signs of spring did they find? [They found flowers growing and a bird's nest with eggs.]

----

6. What do you like best about spring?

----

7. What was your favorite part of the story? Why?

Notes

1 Beyond the Basics is an adaptation of the CIRC program developed by Stevens, Madden, Slavin, and Farnish (1987). STaR and CIRC are also stand-alone programs that many schools utilize without adopting the entire Success for All model.

2 STaR is used both as a name to refer to the story reading program specifically and to the entire integrated language arts curriculum.

3 A listing of these stories and of all books currently in the STaR kindergarten program as well as a portion of one story kit are provided in the appendices.

4 We requested permission from the book publishers to use the supporting art work developed for future work in other schools. Of the 110 books originally chosen, we secured permission for about 40 only.

5 To my knowledge, there are no statistics currently available on the frequency of story reading in prekindergarten or kindergarten classrooms.

6 The teacher guide sheets suggest words that children may find difficult and which therefore may require discussion prior to the story, for example the word *jungle* in this story.

7   Children in this class would be used to interviews of this sort because in
the STaR program they have individual conferences with the aide in which
they retell the story.

References

Adams, M. (1990). *Beginning to read.* Cambridge, MA: MIT Press.

Boehm, A. (1971). *Boehm test of basic concepts.* New York: Psychological Corporation.

Burroughs, M. (1972). The stimulation of verbal behavior in culturally disadvantaged three-year olds. Unpublished doctoral dissertation, Michigan State University, Ann Arbor, MI.

Chomsky, C. (1972). Stages in language development and reading exposure. *Harvard Educational Review, 42,* 1–33.

Clay, M.M. (1979). Reading: The patterning of complex behavior. Auckland: Heinemann Educational Books.

Karweit, N. (1988). *STaR (Story telling and retelling): Teacher's manual.* Baltimore: Johns Hopkins University, Center for Social Organization of Schools.

Madden, N., Slavin, R., Karweit, N., Dolan, L. & Wasik, B. (1991). Success for All Baltimore: Johns Hopkins University, Center for Research on Effective Schooling for Disadvantaged Students.

Madden, N., Slavin, R., Karweit, N. & Livermon, B. (1989). Restructuring the urban elementary school. *Educational Leadership, 46,* 14–18.

Morrow, L. (1985). Retelling stories: A strategy for improving young children's comprehension, concept of story structure and oral language complexity. *Elementary School Journal, 85,* 647–61.

Mumm, M., Secord, W. & Dykstra, K. (1980). *Merrill language screening test.* New York: Psychological Corporation.

Newcomer, P.L. & Hammill, D.D. (1988). *Test of language development-2.* Austin, TX: Pro-Ed.

Ninio, A. & Bruner, J.S. (1978). The achievement and antecedents of labelling. *Journal of Child Language, 5,* 5–15.

Peterman, C.L., Dunning, D. & Mason, J. (1985). *A storybook reading event: How a teacher's presentation affects kindergarten children's subsequent attempts to read from the text.* Paper presented at the 35th annual meeting of the National Reading Conference, San Diego, CA.

Slavin, R., Karweit, N. & Wasik, B. (1994). *Preventing early school failure: Research, policy and practice.* Boston: Allyn and Bacon.

Smith, F. (1979). *Understanding reading.* (2d ed.). New York: Holt, Rinehart and Winston.

Stahl, S. & Miller, P.D. (1989). Whole language and language experience approaches for beginning reading: A quantitative synthesis. *Review of Educational Research, 59,* 87–116.

Stevens, R., Madden, N., Slavin, R. & Farnish, A. (1987). Cooperative integrated reading and composition: Two field experiments. *Reading Research Quarterly, 22,* 433–54.

Teale, W.H. (1986). *Emergent literacy: Reading and writing development in early childhood.* Paper presented at the annual meeting of the National Reading Conference, Austin, TX.

3 "I Got to Get Him Started Out Right": Promoting Literacy by Beginning with Books

Elizabeth Segel

In the early 1980s, as teachers of children's literature at the University of Pittsburgh and writers on the subject of children's books and reading, Dr. Joan Friedberg and I became aware of accumulating research evidence showing that the early years are crucial in establishing the habits and skills of literacy, and that the most effective way to prepare children to become fluent and enthusiastic readers is to read to them as early as their infancy (see Anderson, 1985). We recognized that not all parents were aware of the value of regular home storybook reading. In particular, low-income parents were less likely to have been read to themselves as children or to have age-appropriate children's books available at home. We believed that if communities could empower parents to provide their children with this valuable early experience, the distressing gap between affluent and less privileged children in reading achievement and overall school success could be reduced. Ultimately, if efforts to introduce daily storybook reading into the lives of young children were successful, these children would grow up to be parents who would in turn expose their young children to books and stories at an early age, thus interrupting the costly inter-generational cycle of illiteracy.

In the early years of our work, the evidence of older fluent-reader studies (Clark, 1976; Durkin, 1966) was supplemented by Shirley Brice Heath's articles about the experience of a teen-aged dropout learning to read to her son (Heath and Thomas, 1984; Heath, Branscombe, and Thomas, 1986) and Gordon Wells's longitudinal study of language development (1986). These provocative studies confirmed that listening to stories and scrutinizing picture book pages are the best preparation for success in learning to read. These activities also develop, Wells suggests, children's ability "to narrate an event, describe a scene, and follow instructions" (p. 157). Even more important, listening to stories apparently prepares children "to discover the symbolic potential of language" (p. 156), which is, of course, central to the learning process. The work of Heath and her collaborators (1983, 1984, 1986) was particularly heartening to us, for it suggested that nonmainstream parents and children could, when provided with a few appropriate books and a bit of encouragement, enjoy and benefit from this traditionally middle-class activity.

A preeminent goal of our programs has always been to put exciting and appealing children's books into the hands of low-income children and the adults who care for them. We knew that in the world of publishing, children's books had become the most rapidly growing sector. The boom in "baby books" – board books and others for infants and toddlers – was the most newsworthy trend in juvenile publishing, and each season brought exciting new picture book titles for preschoolers to add to the well-loved older titles. Yet we were aware that the great majority of children did not have a chance to pore over these books, to hear the fine stories while absorbing the engaging illustrations. Even if many would eventually be exposed to quality books in the grade-school classroom, they were unlikely to encounter and benefit from them in the formative preschool years.

For the one quarter to one third of the nation's children growing up in poverty, parents can rarely afford to buy books. When they do, they are likely to purchase a mass-market book from the supermarket or discount store. Those who value books and have heard about the importance of exposing their children to books early may stretch scarce dollars to join a children's book club, but the clubs they know about are unlikely to offer the kind of compelling, high-quality trade books that persuade a family to make story time a regular activity. For minority parents, dependence on the easily available mass market books is particularly limiting, for by definition, few of these books portray minority characters or culture.

Child-care centers for the children of low-income families may have a few children's books, but in our experience, their collections are small, mediocre in quality, and shabby. Though a story may be read as part of a formal daily "circle time," the books on hand do not entice either the children or the overtaxed caregivers into the side-by-side story sharing that is so beneficial to the young child.

Given these conditions, we founded Beginning with Books in 1984 and set out to develop ways to increase the number of children who grow up to be skilled and enthusiastic lifelong readers by increasing the number of children who are read to in the first five years of their lives. We get books into homes and child-care settings; we extend to

parents and other caregivers information, guidance, and encouragement on reading to children; we link low-income families to the library
system; and we recruit volunteers to read to children whose parents
cannot do so.

Core Beliefs of Beginning with Books

Several convictions underlie our efforts. In addition to believing that
good books introduced early are the most effective tool for preventing illiteracy, we believe that most parents want their children to be
successful in school, that they know reading ability is crucial to school
success, and that they are responsive to suggestions about how to
increase the chances their children will learn to read without difficulty
(Segel, 1986). We believe that the children's picture books available in
this country provide an affordable stimulus for enriched parent–child
storybook reading.[1] What is more, when children are able to listen to
repeated readings while viewing the corresponding text and illustration, the picture book constitutes the ideal instrument for helping
them develop an understanding of the relationship of oral to written
language.

Finally, we are convinced that, with a bit of guidance and a good
book, most parents and caregivers of very young children can be successful in making storybook sharing sufficiently enjoyable that both
child and parent will wish to repeat the activity with the frequency
recommended for maximum benefit (that is, on a daily basis). Thus,
an early intervention can have ongoing impact, as the intrinsic rewards
of the storytime experience motivate frequent repetition.

The Pilot Project

Working independently and part-time, Dr. Friedberg and I obtained a
small grant from the Pennsylvania Humanities Council in 1984 and
matching funds from local foundations to put children's books into
the hands of low-income parents who had little money to spend on
books and were not library users, and to share with them the facts
about the importance of reading to children. We decided to work
through an agency already serving such families (a key decision), our
county Health Department, whose well-baby clinics provide free health
care to many families of extremely limited means. In our pilot project,
we gave out packets of four free paperback picture books and a pamphlet of tips on reading to children to 1,000 families. In the clinic, our
first part-time employee talked with parents one by one while they

waited to see the doctor, encouraging them to try reading to their children every day and to visit their nearest library. A follow-up survey of 394 families, six months to a year after they received the books and counseling, showed a significant increase in time spent reading to children (the number reporting daily reading aloud rose from 47 to 69 percent) and in time spent by children looking at books (56 percent reported looking at books several times a day, as compared to the 21 percent who did so before receiving the gift books). Library use remained minuscule among this population, however. More than a few answered the question "Do you borrow library books for your child?" with the unexpected reply, "No, we have our own books," or "No, we belong to a book club" – as if the two were mutually exclusive.

As a result, we modified the packet to contain just three books and an attractive coupon to be redeemed for a fourth book at any branch of The Carnegie Library of Pittsburgh (or district library, if they lived outside the city), and began to stress in the parent counseling that the library belongs to everyone, that it is not a charity, and that once a child becomes a book lover, no home library is big enough to satisfy that child's hunger for books. We briefed librarians on the program's goals, so that once the coupon drew families into the library, library staff could work on getting them to return.

The survey of parents who received book packets in the pilot program invited comments on the books and the children's responses. Some of the answers, though by no means all, revealed parents with extremely limited literacy skills, and yet even in those cases, enthusiasm for sharing the books with their children was striking:

> "The packet of books is a great help especially when you don't have money. It's something for the child to learn on [get started]. It brings you closer to your child when you do things together."

> "I used to buy him coloring books. Now he wants reading books."

> "J. is handicapped and slow in developing. He loved *500 Words to grow on*. He is now able to point to nearly every item in the book and tries to pronounce the name." [from the mother of a four-year-old]

Affiliating with the Carnegie Library of Pittsburgh

We began to receive inquiries from other agencies serving low-income families who wished to obtain the gift-book packets for their clients. An expansion was clearly in order. At this point we entered into an affiliation with The Carnegie Library of Pittsburgh, an arrangement that has been beneficial to both parties. Beginning with Books gained credibility from the association with an established and highly respected institution. It has grown rapidly: The agency now employs six full-time and six half- to two-thirds-time employees to implement its four programs and to provide training and technical assistance to staff at other agencies, both local and national. From the Library's perspective, the affiliation made possible outreach to the underserved, low-income population that its limited funds had previously precluded. The library provides the program with free space, fiscal services, assistance with personnel matters, public relations, and graphics, and contributes a modest amount to staff salaries. Other sources of support are foundation and corporate grants, sales of family literacy publications, individual contributors, fees, and honoraria.

We recognize that our semiautonomous relationship with a public library makes us different from many literacy programs, and that most libraries would find it difficult to justify the expense of employing an experienced professional to deal only with literacy projects. Yet with the current interest expressed by both private and public funders in the areas of early intervention, children at risk, parent involvement in children's education, and literacy, we believe that support can be found for ongoing early intervention literacy projects. With an initial small commitment of staff and space, other libraries could eventually enjoy similar success in finding the resources to support significant child- and family-literacy programs and outreach to low-income families.

Benefits of Becoming Comfortable in Libraries

Libraries seem to us an ideal home for family literacy programming; their mission to serve citizens of all ages accords with the philosophy of family literacy. Even more important, libraries are where the books are, the irresistible children's books that are crucial to the success of any such efforts. All of our different programs entail giving away fine books, yet at the same time all our activities are geared to enticing families into the library where a free supply of the best children's books awaits.

Libraries have numerous resources that can benefit struggling families, such as information on jobs and consumer products, help with taxes, and reference materials for children's school assignments. Yet few of the families we work with had taken advantage of these resources before we reached them, because the library was alien territory to them. One of the most important benefits of library-based child or family literacy programs is their potential for transforming this alien territory into familiar and comfortable home turf.

Recent Growth

Since affiliating with The Carnegie Library of Pittsburgh, the Beginning with Books gift-book program has grown to the extent that each year we distribute 6,000–7,000 packets of books through two to three dozen agencies that serve low-income families: shelters for battered women and their children, teen parenting programs, Head Starts, kindergartens of economically depressed school districts, and many others. We now train staff at many of these agencies to do the parent counseling; at others, an employee of Beginning with Books speaks at a parent meeting on reading to children. We have also developed a manual that enables people in many communities to set up similar programs. A Beginning with Books pamphlet of tips for parents on reading to children and an attractive list of suggested children's books, both readable by adults with limited reading skills, are used by many family literacy programs across the country, providing a source of income for the agency.

Program Evaluation

In 1989–90, researchers at the School of Education at the University of Pittsburgh undertook a study of a small number of five-year-old children whose families had received gift-book packets from Beginning with Books four years earlier during the pilot program, when the youngsters were one year old. A control group was chosen from children who attended the clinic sites on days when book packets were not distributed or attended a clinic in a comparable neighborhood. Parents were questioned about literacy activities in the home and children completed various literacy tasks. Parents were asked to share a book with their child and this activity was assessed by a trained observer using a checklist. Teachers' perceptions of the child's literacy development late in the kindergarten year were solicited through a written questionnaire. The researchers concluded that the parents who had received Beginning with Books book packets and counseling provided more literacy experiences and reading materials in the home for their children than did the control group, and the parents visited the library more often. This latter finding seemed to contradict the finding of a survey conducted six months after the intervention. One explanation might be that, although parents of toddlers had not taken the suggestion that they visit the library, once they had established the habit of reading to their children and their children were a bit older, they were motivated to seek out library resources.

Perhaps the most exciting find in the University of Pittsburgh study was that the children who had been served by the Beginning with Books project were perceived four years later by their kindergarten teachers as having significantly higher reading and language ability than those who were not served by the program: Sixty-one percent were rated in top third of their class in reading ability, as compared to forty-six percent of the control group; sixty-five percent were judged in the top third of the class in language ability, compared to forty-two percent of the control children.

Books: The Key to Success

We believe that the quality of books and the process of book selection are crucial to the success of this brief and inexpensive intervention. A segment from an article we wrote for the newsletter of the Children's Book Council, a publishers' association (Segel & Friedberg, 1991), describes well our selection criteria and methods:

> Our selection process is designed to combine our children's book expertise with the judgment of those closely acquainted with the needs and interest of the families who will receive the books. We begin by selecting twenty to twenty-five appealing, high-quality books. Whenever possible, we limit our choices to books retailing for under $4. Then we schedule a meeting with staff members and representative parents at each agency, show each book and point out its special features, and ask them to select three of the books for their packets. This increases the chances that the books will be right for the recipient families, and in the process, the staff members and parents "buy into" the program.
>
> In making our initial selection, we look for those qualities that make any book special: attractive illustration and design, good reproduction, reasonably sturdy binding, interactive possibilities. Books where the illustrations both depict and extend the text help children become adept readers of picture language long before they can decode letters. In storybooks, we want a compelling narrative: touching, or funny, or exciting. We want distinguished writing: language that is fresh, playful, precise. We're always looking for the repeated phrases and rhythmic prose that young children love. We include engaging board books for the very young.
>
> We make a point of seeking out books that represent a variety of classes and cultures, as well as gender models. We always offer several books featuring African American characters, since the majority of the families we serve are African American. We include concept books, especially word-and-picture conversation-generating books for little ones, but strongly suggest that each packet contain at least one storybook.

A sizable number of the parents who will be taking home a packet of books are not confident readers, so we take care to offer some books with very little text and others with predictable elements.

Read Together

We realized from the beginning that some parents who received gift books were *unable* to read them to their children. Then we saw a survey of adult-literacy students that showed lack of child care as a major obstacle to attendance at literacy tutoring or classes. Consequently, when venture grants targeting children at risk were available from our local United Way in 1987, we conceived our Read Together program. This program trains volunteers to read one-on-one to children between the ages of 3 and 11 in the children's room of the library, while elsewhere in the building the parent or grandparent may be meeting with a tutor from an adult-literacy agency.

Read Together currently serves approximately 115 children, most of whom have a parent who is receiving literacy instruction, either in a group or individually, from 1 of about 12 adult literacy providers. In two families, parents are legally blind. Children come once or twice a week to one of eight branch libraries scattered around the city. Many families bring several children, siblings, or cousins. The majority of families are African American; about three quarters are receiving Public Assistance. We discovered some time ago that attendance fell off late in the month when welfare checks ran out; since that time we have found generous funders to underwrite bus tickets. In 1992 4,087 Read Together sessions took place.

Sessions last for 60 or 90 minutes, depending on whether the parent is being tutored simultaneously (tutoring sessions are 90 minutes long) and on the age of the child. Volunteers, who range from high school students to retirees, are trained, then matched with a child. Reading to the child is the first priority, but other literacy-related activities supplement the reading. Games, puppets, writing and drawing materials, and puzzles are provided at each site, and ingenious volunteers add activities of their own invention. Children receive three books a year to take home. Though Beginning with Books does not actually provide literacy instruction to parents, we have been able to develop a family literacy component for our adult-literacy partner agencies. Thanks to a Bell Atlantic–American Library Association Family Literacy grant, we have written a tutor training module introducing the concept of family literacy, suggesting how and why to use children's books as tutoring materials for adult students who wish to read to children, and introducing a small library of predictable books recommended for adults with limited reading skills because of the predictability of their texts from their pictures and rhyming patterns. The Greater Pittsburgh Literacy Council, for whom the training was developed, now incorporates it routinely into its tutor training, and the module has been shared with other local literacy providers as well. We also encourage Read Together parents to share books with their children as their own skills improve. This involves giving them, when they enter the program, a Beginning with Books gift packet containing very simple books and gently encouraging them to try a daily family story time.

Read Together is more expensive in time and dollars than a gift-book distribution, of course, but it offers much more intensive help to a family. Parents, children, and volunteers are enthusiastic. Parents tell us, "My kids won't let me cancel." A young mother of preschoolers reports, "I'm reading to them every day. I think that's why my own reading's getting better." Though "no-shows" on the part of families are common when children are first enrolled, once the routine of Read Together sessions is established, parents transcend daunting obstacles to bring their children to the library. One mother has brought her four school-aged children to Read Together for more than four years. At one point she was given custody of her sister's infant and toddler, both born addicted to crack. Still she managed to get to Read Together, bringing all six children to the library on the bus and caring for the little ones while four volunteers read to her own children. She even managed to get to the library when she lost her apartment and was moving from one neighborhood to another, staying first with friends, and then in a homeless shelter. Her youngest child, who was four when he entered the program, is a Maurice Sendak aficionado and a very good student. The session records filed by his volunteer are nearly always heartening. "We alternated reading," she wrote when he was seven. "He is becoming more fluent with phrasing. He was focused and enthusiastic throughout today's session. We read for the entire session." More poignant was her report from the time when the family was at the homeless shelter: "I asked J. about reading at home and he said 'my mom reads to me when I can't sleep at night, and next thing I know I'm snorin'!' " It had been years before this mother would let her children borrow library books; the bedtime story represented a true breakthrough in this family.

Recognizing that our impressions of the Read Together program's value are subjective, based as they are on anecdotal records and the comments of parents, we are currently undertaking a descriptive evaluation of Read Together.

Read-Aloud Parent Clubs

One of the most gratifying of the programs developed by Beginning with Books is the Read-Aloud Parent Club. Each club consists of a series of family literacy workshops aimed at promoting regular home storybook reading. We use the term *club* because the intent is to provide a relaxed social atmosphere in which parents can enjoy getting to know other parents and learn how to support their children's literacy learning as well. Typically, a group of twenty parents or parent surrogates (grandparents, foster parents) meet at a library weekly for six to ten weeks. At each meeting, members receive a free children's book, hear a fluent reading of it, discuss topics, such as how listening to stories benefits a child, how to read aloud effectively and enrich the story-time experience, how to understand emergent writing, etc. Parents consider such issues as limiting television, teaching children to respect and care for books, and finding time to read to children. Parents are encouraged to read daily to their children for 15 minutes or more and are given a special calendar on which to draw (or have their child draw) a smiling face for each day they are able to do so. They also receive a clothbound blank book in which to write about their experiences reading to their children. Each weekly meeting begins with a discussion of how children responded to the previous week's gift book.

Clubs usually meet at a library. At the first meeting, participants are given a library tour and encouraged to apply for library cards for themselves and their children. If the group meets at a school or site other than a library, a field trip to the nearest library is quickly scheduled. Lots of library books are displayed and briefly described at each meeting, and parents are encouraged to borrow from among them to supplement the gift book. This program was originally intended for Head Start parents and continues to serve that population, but it has been adapted for residents of a public housing community, for Adult Basic Education students, for Even Start parents, and for kindergarten Chapter 1 families.

The idea for the clubs derived from the early stages of Ruth Handel's and Ellen Goldsmith's Parent Reader Program, which was designed for parents in a college-level developmental reading class (see chapter 1). Because of the different populations served and the range of parents' reading skills, we do not teach formal reading strategies, as in the Parent Reader Program, but rather model enriched storybook reading and provide informal suggestions to promote effective home literacy experiences and encourage parents to be responsive to their children's reactions and interests. Each group contains some parents who are fluent readers and others who initially believe they cannot read well enough to read to their children. The latter are encouraged to try reading the gift book to their child; in most cases they feel confident enough to do so after having heard the group leader or a fluent parent read the text aloud during the club meeting. A few of the parents prove to be effective oral readers, most are perceptive, articulate participants in the group discussions. Writing skills, however, prove to be marginal in nearly all cases. The majority of parents say they did read occasionally to their children before attending the clubs, but very few report doing so regularly.

In most cases, parent participants immediately begin reading to their children nearly every day and return to the group eager to describe their young listeners' enthusiastic and perceptive responses to the stories. Group discussion quickly establishes that different children have different favorites among the gift books and react differently when listening. The leader can build on this foundation to develop the idea that young children's learning is best fostered by following the child's lead, tapping into the child's eagerness to learn, and seizing "the teachable moment," rather than by following any set of inflexible rules on how to conduct a read-aloud session. Parents believe that they are their child's first teacher, but their limited understanding of how young children learn often frustrates their good intentions. Coming to understand that they can help their children enormously just by reading to them excites and empowers most parents, and they complain less about insufficient seatwork in their child's Head Start or kindergarten.

Evidence of Program Effectiveness

Discussion at club meetings is lively, with parents getting ideas from each other as well as from the group leader. During a session on the importance of encouraging emergent writing, when one parent was skeptical about taking home markers and paper for her four-year-old, another parent said, "Just tape a length of butcher paper to the wall. My kids know they can write and draw there and they never mess up other places." One group discussed dialect in children's books with as much insight as any college students we have known. The culmination of this animated exchange was an African American grandmother opining that the dialect McKissack uses in *Flossie and the Fox* was to her ears like a Scottish or Irish brogue – "pretty and fun to hear" – with others nodding in agreement. Parents' comments at the end of the six or ten sessions include:

"I'm into buying books for my kids now; I'm proud of myself."

"The parents who didn't sign up are stupid! They missed so much."

"The more books we got, the less I had to holler at [my daughter], 'cause she was always in 'em."

Our most recent group vowed to continue meeting because members enjoyed the chance to talk with other parents about their children and parenting issues so much.

Follow-up telephone calls and a six-month reunion of some club groups show that in most cases, the parents still read aloud as regularly as they did while they were attending (five days a week or more). We also see an impact on the parents' personal reading patterns, even though the program does not focus on parents' own literacy needs (except to refer them when appropriate to adult-literacy programs). One parent wrote at the end of her journal, "I enjoyed the class very much and looked forward to Monday's. The reading lessons started me to read the newspaper every day now, I was never to interested before. I started reading some of my paperback books, I had put aside." A father wrote us a letter which he brought to the last session. It ended: "As this program has help [my daughter] in wanting to try to read herself, it has also make me see some of the weak points of my learning skills. So this program will help us both learn together for the rest of are life."

This letter also typifies how this literacy program reaches beyond the immediate families represented. The man and his mother regularly care for four preschool cousins of his daughter while the other adults in the family attend choir practice. These children also enjoyed the books, he reported, and began asking their parents to read to them. An elderly participant, foster mother at the time to five small children, went from never having read to her children to instituting story time as a nightly bedtime ritual. "We went to church and dident get home untill after bed time," she wrote in one journal entry, "but that dident save me we still had to have a story." The night before (after three club meetings) she had written: "We are having more and more fun with the books each night they ask to be read to which is better than me telling them."

We realize that this program reaches parents and surrogate parents who are already committed to furthering their children's learning and who have sufficient energy and self-esteem to come out to meetings. The clubs do not benefit those whose parents are addicted, abusive, neglectful, or simply too discouraged by life to take advantage of the opportunity. Yet we believe that those we do reach through their parents are a very important audience. Many of them, we contend, are children who start out life eager to learn and who would very likely learn to read. However, if they were to start school lacking the precedence of regular home reading as well as a love of books, they would not read often enough during their primary school years to become fluent readers. These are the children who begin to slip behind in the third or fourth grade, when their schoolwork requires more frequent and difficult reading, and who may well fail to complete high school. Lisbeth Schorr, in her haunting book *Within Our Reach: Breaking the Cycle of Disadvantage*, argues that one does not have to remove all of the risk-factors a child faces to make a difference – very possibly a critical difference – in that child's future. When parents and children share books with excitement and appreciation, instead of viewing this activity as marginal to their lives, they help to overcome a major risk-factor for failure at school.

Nearly a decade of working closely with low-income families has convinced us that there is no shortage of parents ready and willing to help their children succeed. As I was leaving the library one day after the first meeting of a Read-Aloud Parent Club for Head Start parents, a father, accompanied by a little boy, was asking at the front desk where the parents were meeting. It turned out that he had missed the bus and had to wait an hour for another one. I told him I was sorry he had missed the meeting and come all this distance for nothing. He assured me that he knew he would be too late, but he wanted to come anyway so that he would know where the next meeting was held. "I'm so glad you didn't get discouraged," I said to him. "Oh, I can't get discouraged, ma'am," he said, looking from me to his son. "I got to get him started out right."

Nor can practitioners afford to get discouraged about the obstacles that must be overcome to establish effective family or child literacy programs. Too much is at stake for the children of poverty in our communities and for the parents and surrogate parents who desperately want a better future for them.

Note

1   A significant number of top-quality paperback picture books can be obtained for approximately $2.00, thanks to publishers' standard discounts of 40–60 percent for customers who do not resell the books and do not require the right of return. Contact the Special Sales department of any publisher for further information.

References

Anderson, R.C., Hiebert, E.H., Scott, J.A. & Wilkinson, I.A. (1985). *Becoming a nation of readers: the report of the commission on reading*. Champaign, IL: National Academy of Education, Center for the Study of Reading.

Clark, M.M. (1976). *Young fluent readers*. London: Heinemann.

Durkin, D. (1966). *Children who read early*. New York: Teachers College Press.

Heath, S.B. (1983). *Ways with words: Language, life, and work in communities and classrooms*. Cambridge, England: Cambridge University Press.

Heath, S.B. & Thomas, C. (1984). The achievement of preschool literacy for mother and child. In H. Goelman, A. Oberg & F. Smith (Eds.), *Awakening to literacy* (pp. 51–72). Exeter NH: Heinemann.

Heath, S.B., Branscombe, A. & Thomas, C. (1986). The book as narrative prop in language acquisition. In B.B. Schieffelin & P. Gilmore (Eds.), *The acquisition of literacy: Ethnographic perspectives*. Norwood, NJ: Ablex, 16–34.

Schorr, L. & Schorr, D. (1989). *Within our reach: Breaking the cycle of disadvantage*. New York: Doubleday.

Segel, E. (1986). Pushing preschool literacy: Equal opportunity or cultural imperialism? *Children's Literature Assoc. Quarterly, 11* (2), 59–62.

Segel, E. & Friedberg, J. (1991). The search for irresistible first books. In *Features* (newsletter). New York: Children's Book Council.

Wells, G. (1986). *The meaning makers: Children learning language and using language to learn*. Portsmouth, NH: Heinemann.

4 The Making of Readers: The Work of Professor Dina Feitelson

Joseph Shimron

The untimely death of Professor Dina Feitelson brought to a sudden end a 40-year career of research and development devoted mostly to the cultivation of literacy among children in Israel. With Dina's departure, we lost a friend, a colleague, a teacher, and, in our efforts to foster literacy, one of our most resourceful navigators.

From the beginning of her career to its end, Dina's greatest strengths were in analyzing concrete educational situations. Her eagle eye enabled her to place triumphs and failures in correct perspective. Her critical mind and her experience as a teacher made her unusually sensitive to the difference between armchair speculations or research for the sake of research, and work of consequence to the classroom teacher. Indeed, she was the right person for telling "facts from fads."

Yet Dina never stopped at diagnosing an educational situation. She always came up with a prognosis and a treatment – initiatives that she carried out without delay. When she found an ill-designed program of instruction, she developed an alternative program of her own. When she realized how impoverished the language of disadvantaged children was, she found means to enrich their linguistic experience.

Indeed, Dina did not leave us empty-handed – her ideas are well articulated in books and articles; her research is carefully documented, and some of her projects are still running. In this chapter, I will describe Dina's latest work at some length. But let us start with some background, which, I believe, is needed to understand Dina's approach and motivation.

A Teacher First

Dina Feitelson started her career not as a reading expert, but as a teacher in elementary school. After a few years of teaching, she enrolled in the Department of Education at the Hebrew University in Jerusalem. Two years after the founding of the state of Israel, then a graduate student in the School of Education, she was employed as an independent researcher by the Szold Institute in Jerusalem to find out why elementary school students were failing. She chose to analyze instructional methods. In carrying out this task, she benefited from her teaching experience and from her acute intuition as to what works in the classroom and what does not.

It was then that Dina detected the difficulties of many children in learning to read by the "whole-word" method (Feitelson, 1952). She claimed that (a) the whole-word method is ill-suited to the teaching of Hebrew writing, and (b) that it is particularly unsuitable for teaching children from literarily impoverished homes – homes where reading or literacy skills are not actively encouraged. In retrospect, the practical implications of these claims proved fruitful, even though the rationale for them may require amendment. It now appears that the whole-word method is ill-suited to the instruction of reading in many languages that have characteristics quite unrelated to the idiosyncrasies of Hebrew and that the only languages that may benefit from the whole-word method are those that have an extremely high proportion of orthographically simple single-syllable words (having no consonant or vowel clusters). In such languages, the whole-word method may even be better. Dina herself used single syllable words in her primer.

Notwithstanding this reservation, the practical (pedagogical) implications of Dina's observations are that (a) the whole-word method should be replaced with a phonic or eclectic method that emphasizes code learning, and (b) that the educational system should look for means by which to enrich the linguistic experience of students brought up in a literarily deficient environment. I shall return to these implications later on.

Educating the Children of New Immigrants

A major concern of Israeli educational researchers in the early fifties was how to accommodate the children of new immigrants from Asia and Africa into the general educational system. Dina was among those who felt that what hampered these children was not just the language barrier (indeed they did not know Hebrew when they arrived in Israel), but their ability and the ability of their families, as well as that of their community as a whole, to adjust to modern education and modern schooling.

Reading and writing were not alien to these new immigrants. As

religious Jews they practiced a 2,000-year tradition of educating the
male children in order to prepare them for assuming their roles in the
religious rituals and daily practices of the Jewish (orthodox) way of
life (cf. Shimron, 1990). Yet most new immigrants were relatively unprepared to accept reading and writing for secular usage, that is, as an
avenue to art and science and as a central tool of self-development
and self-expression.

Accommodating the new immigrants into the existing educational
system involved substantial cultural changes, a risky process even if
undertaken with the consent of the people involved. It is all too easy
to undermine traditional values but tremendously difficult to find
functional replacements without irreversibly hurting the identity of
the individual and the infrastructure of the family and community.
To minimize the risk, one must become familiar with the traditional
culture, its values, and its practices.

Dina's dissertation was written with these understandings in mind.
The dissertation was an anthropological study of new immigrant children from Kurdistan, the northern part of Iraq, in their new settlements
near Jerusalem. Dina fully understood that in order to help these
children to become accomplished students capable of coping with
school demands, she would have to understand how they were reared
and how they lived in their community. School learning, she was
convinced, relies on prior learning at home.

What Dina found in her observations (Feitelson, 1954, 1955) was
highly relevant to the concerns of teachers in Israeli schools. Most of
the Jewish families from Kurdistan had a large number of children.
The mother was limited in her ability to pay attention to each and
every child. The young child was well cared for as far as feeding was
concerned, but the mother, like other adults in the family, spent almost no time talking to the children or playing with them. The children were left to fend for themselves around the house, often with an
older sister looking after them. Although children were not forbidden
to be in the company of adults, their interaction with adults was kept
to the minimum. In fact, when adults were with them, children were
expected to remain silent.

Dina found the small amount of verbal exchanges in these families
particularly disturbing. Talk was limited to mundane affairs such as
food, sleep, and clothing; the parents had few conversations even
between themselves (cf. Feitelson, 1957). Dina found that the children
she observed did not learn to ask questions. In fact, children were not
expected to ask questions. Thus, spontaneous curiosity was discouraged, and strategies of verbal interactions were not developed. As a
result, children knew few names of objects in their surroundings –

even color names were not fully acquired. Ironically, these children did not present any discipline problems in their first days in the school. They were well behaved and quite obedient in the main. But their good behavior in school did not reflect real participation in learning, for which they were poorly prepared.

Very early in her career, Dina realized that in order to facilitate the learning of these children it would not be sufficient to improve instructional methods. The educational system would have to find better ways to compensate for early neglect of intellectual development. The compensation, she thought, could not be restricted to linguistic experience or reading. Following up her hunch, for several years she studied the effect of play on the intellectual development of young children (cf. Feitelson, 1972, 1977; Feitelson & Ross, 1973). The findings were important to the development of her theories. Because of space restrictions, however, I will not deal with these contributions in this chapter.

Learning to Read a New Language

The Reading of Novel Words

New immigrants in every school grade encounter novel words from their first day in school. Learning to read is difficult for them regardless of the method of instruction. In the whole-word method, learning to read a new word amounts to connecting a string of random letters with a blend of random speech sounds. In methods emphasizing code-learning, relating letters to sounds is by definition more lawful, but nonetheless still difficult. For one thing, associating letters with sounds in unknown words is a meaningless exercise. More important, even a strictly "phonic" method cannot be said to teach the child the exact pronunciation of a word that he or she has never heard before, because the associations between letters and speech sounds, as acquired by code-emphasis methods, are necessarily generative and abstract. The fricative *s*, for example, has innumerable pronunciations in different words. Even if the child's knowledge of grapheme-to-phoneme correspondence is perfect, he or she may not be able to guess the exact pronunciation. Indeed, in teaching reading via the code-emphasis method we presume that children learn words whose meaning and pronunciation they already know.

It is, therefore, generally true that we should avoid teaching novel words through reading, which, unfortunately, has not been the case in teaching reading to children of new immigrants or to children of impoverished literary backgrounds. The sensible solution, as Dina realized, is not to teach reading of just the words these students know but to direct efforts toward increasing their word knowledge and familiarity with written texts.

Familiarity with the Language of Books

As is evident from the foregoing, the children of new immigrants from Asia and Africa were not read to at home. Thus, when they arrived in school, they were totally unprepared for the language of written texts. Indeed there was a considerable gap between the text these children found in a school textbook and the language that they heard at home. Written texts in most languages contain more infrequent words than spoken language does. But this gap was particularly wide in learning to read Hebrew in the early fifties in Israel. Texts given to children often included infrequent words drawn from the Bible, the Mishna, and the prayer books. In addition, a considerable discrepancy existed between the morphology and syntax of the textbooks and those of the spoken language at home or on the street.

Hebrew is a highly affixed language. At the core of all verbs and most nouns is a root that normally consists of three consonant letters and is differently affixed and voweled to form the variety of words in the Hebrew lexicon. Several function words, the equivalents of *to, from, the, and, in/at, which/that,* and *when/while* are indicated by prefixes attached to nouns or pronouns. Some of these may also be expressed by independent function words.

A large class of Hebrew nouns is derived from the same roots as verbs. These nouns are classified into forms (or patterns or *mishkalim*) that sometimes provide a general indication of the noun type, for example, a location or an occupation. All nouns may be affixed to indicate plural. They also may be inflected to indicate possession of object or objects by either the first, second, or third person (although possession may also be indicated by independent words). Verbs may be conjugated in about seven forms (*binyanim*). A verb form is a pattern of conjugation that entails syntactic and semantic properties. The conjugation of each verb form is accomplished by varying the vowels of the root and by attaching affixes which indicate tense, voice, number, person, and gender.

Remembering these characteristics of Hebrew morphology, we can appreciate the difference between Hebrew written texts and the spoken language. One difficulty children have with written texts appears to derive from the extensive use of affixes. Highly affixed words are more typical of written texts than of spoken language. For example, one Hebrew word, *velixsheyishakeni,* is expressed in English in the six words, "and when he will kiss me." However, it may also be phrased in four words: *ve-ka'asher hu yishak li.* Compared with the single word, the longer expression replaces some affixes with discrete words and introduces some redundancy. Nonetheless, the four-word paraphrase, although informationally equivalent, seems to be much easier to comprehend than the single word, perhaps for two reasons. First, highly affixed words are rather infrequent. Second, the decomposition of the multiaffixed words may exact a high cost in processes of comprehension.

Another factor that may account for some of the difficulties in written texts is the order of the sentence constituents. As in English, the simple declarative Hebrew sentence in the active voice has a subject-verb-object (SVO) word order. But unlike English, Hebrew allows for more flexibility in word order. For example, the English sentence, "David broke a window," does not tolerate changes in word order, but any change of word order in the Hebrew equivalent is also grammatically correct. Characteristically, deviations from SVO order are more frequent in written texts than in spoken language, and as in many other languages, compared to spoken language, the written text in Hebrew is likely to have longer and more complex sentences.

Bridges to Literacy

The Three Phases of Reading Development

Dina Feitelson (1988) portrayed the development of reading with a three-phase model: prereading (before reading), decoding acquisition (formal reading instruction), and postdecoding acquisition (free unending reading development). Dina's greatest impact on the instruction of reading in Israel is related to the second phase of reading development, decoding acquisition. Her leading role in this domain resulted in the replacement of the whole-word method of instruction with code-emphasis methods of one kind or another in most Israeli schools. Dina argued emphatically that the educational approach in this phase must be radically different from that in the first and the third phases. Decoding, she believed, must be taught in a systematic and structured manner. As with the teaching of any other complex skill, nothing should be left to chance. In the basal reader she produced, the introduction of every letter was carefully planned and prepared.

Dina's own book *Facts and Fads in Beginning Reading* as well as many articles reported and exemplified the story of this effort. I will not elaborate on it in this chapter. Instead, I will expand on Dina's recent work in the prereading phase, in which intervention programs purport to compensate for early neglect of literary skills, and in the postdecoding acquisition phase, the development of leisure reading. To date part of this work has been published only in Hebrew.

Interventions in the Prereading Phase

The first and the third phases have much in common. They are content-oriented; they aim at reaching meanings through texts. They are designed to satisfy and build on the curiosity of the child, rather than to impose obligatory, externally structured learning. The obvious difference between the first and the third phase is that in the first children are read to, and in the third they read on their own.

Dina thought that adults have important roles in the first phase. She believed in "mediated" instruction (Cochran-Smith, 1984; Heath, 1982, 1983) for mainly two reasons. On the one hand, the emotional ties between adult and child create opportunities for intellectually stimulating activities that facilitate cognitive development. Moreover, many books introduce the child to unfamiliar knowledge domains that adults can help explain and exemplify; and adults can take a substantial role in simplifying difficult texts and defining novel words.

The adult in this predecoding phase does not necessarily have to be a parent. Dina believed in the compensatory power of the educational system, including kindergartens and prekindergarten institutions. In a series of studies with Jewish kindergarteners, conducted by Dina with her students (Eshel, 1979; Reshef, 1984), Dina found that reading regularly to kindergarteners positively affected not only the comprehension of these children, but also their active use of spoken language and "book language." In addition, their attention span was demonstrated to increase. In general, with the proper programs of intervention, the educational system can make up for the lack of prereading activities at home.

Some of the activities carried out by Dina and her associates in the first, predecoding phase were continued experimentally during the first year of elementary school, in parallel with decoding instruction. In one study (Feitelson, Kita & Goldstein, 1986), children who were read to as a whole in class during the last twenty minutes of the school day for six months outscored a control group on measures of decoding, reading comprehension, and active use of language. It is worth noting that this intervention was actually carried out by the regular school teachers within classroom settings and that the books from which the stories were selected were part of a 15-volume series of tales, known to be popular among children of this age, and accessible to all in the trade-book market.

Story Reading to Arab Kindergarteners

In a study carried out by Dina, Zehava Goldstein, and Jihad Iraqi, a former student of Dina (1992), an intervention program similar to the one described above with Jewish kindergarteners was attempted with Arab kindergarteners. What makes this study particularly interesting is that in the Arab population the distance between the spoken language and the language of books is far beyond the common difference between a low and a high style or register. Spoken and written Arabic are in many ways two different languages, with different vocabularies, different phonologies, and different syntaxes. The language of books (called *Foos'ha*) is used for writing as well as for certain formal speech situations. The spoken language (called *Amiyah*) is used for daily (oral only) communication. It has no written form.

Thus, Arab children beginning to learn to read are taught to read *Foos'ha*, the book language, despite the fact that all speech directed to them prior to school entry is in *Amiyah*. Since *Foos'ha* differs from *Amiyah* in every respect, the children in effect learn to read a language they do not know. Once again the question raised was what can education do to alleviate the difficulty?

An educational intervention among Israeli Arabs could either involve an attempt to write *Amiya*, the spoken language, or to teach *Foos'ha*, the language of books. In reality, writing *Amiyah* would amount to defying a sacred tradition. Also, since no books are written in Amiyah, learning to read Amiyah would provide an access to no books at all, not even children's books. Thus the more practical alternative for an educational intervention was to familiarize the Arab children with *Foos'ha*. The more familiar these preschoolers were with *Foos'ha*, the more they would be prepared for school learning.

The parents could also participate in the teaching of *Foos'ha* by reading stories to their children in *Foos'ha*, and acting as mediators, explaining the *Foos'ha* when needed. However, a study investigating the ways almost 300 families of Arab kindergarteners used books (Iraqi, 1990) revealed that less than 2 percent of them read to their children from books and, story telling was not a daily practice in about 75 percent of them. When parents did tell stories to their children, almost 60 percent of them reported telling stories from memory. The remaining 40 percent reported that they used books, although they did not read from them directly. Apparently, they were telling stories from children's books written in *Foos'ha* in *Amiya*, without introducing the *Foos'ha* words.

The other direction to turn for help in preparing Arab preschoolers for the language of books was the school system, which under Israeli law mandate one preschool (kindergarten) year. In their study, Dina and her associates asked Arab kindergarten teachers to read stories in *Foos'ha* to their students on each school day for about six months. As in the study with Jewish children described above, the aim was to read stories to which children were attracted. The control group was instructed with a language development program produced by the Israeli Ministry of Education.

An examinination of the children after the six months found that those in the experimental classes outperformed their peers in the control classes in measures of comprehension and active use of language and that they had incorporated literary language into their daily speech. Once again Dina demonstrated the compensatory power of the school system.

Note that successful as it was, this intervention did not radically alter the situation in which children's first encounter with *Foos'ha* was in school. The ultimate solution, it seems, will come either when the gap between *Foos'ha* and *Amiya* is considerably narrowed (e.g., when *Foos'ha* and *Amiya* share more elements) or when *Foos'ha*, as a second language, is introduced much earlier in the children's life. Both parents and educational authorities will have to collaborate to bring about such a change.

Leisure Reading in the Postdecoding Acquisition Phase

In recent years, Dina and her associates devoted much of their effort to the third, postdecoding, phase of reading development. This last series of studies began with a survey of patterns of book-ownership and reading to young children in lower-class and middle-class populations (Feitelson & Goldstein, 1986). Most of the observed lower-class homes consisted of families of immigrants from Asia and Africa where parents and grandparents had scant education or none at all. On the average, lower-class children had ten times fewer books at home than middle-class children. Sixty-one percent of the lower-class homes did not have any books, and of the ones they did have, many were reference books (e.g., encyclopedias), books that children may need for preparing homework but not books for leisure reading. The survey also revealed that 96 percent of the children of middle-class homes were read to daily (in 45 percent of the homes, for at least half an hour a day), whereas 61 percent of the children of lower-class homes were not read to at all.

The Effectiveness of School Libraries

Confronting the results of this survey, Dina examined what could be done in the school system to compensate the children of literarily impoverished homes for the lack of prereading experience. Following Bamberger (1969, 1976), Dina suspected that many children do not read well because they do not read enough, and that consequently, the problem, simply put, was how to get them to read more. The most appropriate agent for help within the school system was, naturally, the school library. Most schools in Israel have a library and employ a librarian on a part-time basis. But what did these libraries do to foster reading? To find out, Dina conducted a second survey on school libraries in Israel (Feitelson, Rahat & Dolev-Shamir, 1985) to study the use of the school library by third and fourth graders. This population seems a proper target for intervention programs that aim at increasing reading rate. Most of these children have already passed the decoding acquisition stage, and to some extent should be able to read on their own. Moreover, the homeroom teacher in these grades is still in control of most of the class schedule and thus able to introduce new classroom activities.

The survey centered on twenty elementary schools in northern Israel serving various sectors of the Israeli population, namely, Kibbutz schools, Arab schools, and urban schools, of which half were classified as middle-class and the other half as lower-class. Seventy percent of the schools surveyed had a library from which children could borrow books. Some of the schools also had classroom libraries of one sort or another.

The surveyors were graduate students from the School of Education at the University of Haifa. They observed children engaged in reading or in exchanging library books; they interviewed teachers, librarians, and school principals; and they also examined the activity of school libraries through reading records, library catalogues, and library inventories.

Most of the libraries (75 percent) were found to be well equipped, not only as libraries but also as reading rooms for students and teachers. Though the number of books available ranged from four to seven books per student, the number that could actually be offered to the students for leisure reading – reading for fun and enjoyment – was much smaller. The libraries were equipped predominantly with reference books donated to the library from a variety of sources, not the kind of books children are likely to open if left to themselves. Furthermore, the survey found that school librarians tended to base their purchases of new books on lists compiled by the Ministry of Education and thus reflected the attitudes of educational administrators in Jerusalem. These recommendations were not necessarily bad or tasteless, but they were not sensitive to the interests of young readers.

Nor was the placement of the books on the shelves of the kind that invited students to find the books they like. In many libraries, books were not sorted according to either levels of difficulty or subject matter. The most frequent ordering of books was alphabetical, by author's name. Opening hours in most of these libraries were restricted to certain days of the week, certain hours of the school day, or to recesses. In a few schools, the library opened for each class at a different time.

In all schools, one person was assigned to manage library operations. Sometimes this person was one of the teachers on the staff, who became a librarian to supplement his or her income. In only half the schools was the librarian specifically trained for the job. During opening hours some librarians were assisted by homeroom teachers or by student volunteers. Much of the librarian's time was spent on secretarial and managerial duties – ordering new books and keeping track of the books in circulation. Only a quarter of the librarians knew their readers well enough to counsel them in their choice of books, and less than a quarter attempted class discussions on book reading (except for one introductory meeting at the beginning of the school year). No data were collected about the reading progress of individual students. As often happens in individualized activity (Shimron, 1976), the students who received most of the librarian's attention were often those who read the most and needed more time to get new books. Little time was left for those students who read few books or none.

The trouble with readers (alas, like the trouble with horses) is that you can bring them to the books but you cannot make them read. Dina Feitelson argued that school authorities must understand that in order to develop reading skills, they need to be attentive to readers' desires. A case in point was a study in Israel (Bergson & Levy, 1984) that found that elementary school children were more than willing to read (or hear) adventure stories, especially if they appeared in serial form. Some of these series may seem like "fast food." They are emphatically not the first choice of literary adults. Yet they were just the ones that seduced children to read. As we all know, the most difficult pages to read in a book are often the first ones. We have to let ourselves be carried away by the author into new worlds. As in other situations of uncertainty, reading involves some excitement and some fear of the unknown. Children's preference for series seems to indicate that they take comfort in returning to familiar settings and familiar protagonists.

Classroom Libraries

The survey found classroom libraries in six of the twenty schools studied. On the average, these libraries could offer one to two books per student. In some classes the main library refreshed the collection of books once or twice a year. Books were loaned at regular class hours, once or twice a week, though in one classroom books could be borrowed every school day. Unlike in the main library, books were kept in a cupboard, to which only the teacher had access. Thus, keeping records of books on loan was much simpler.

Because all the classroom libraries in this survey received most of their books from the school's main library, the school librarians (or actually the Ministry of Education) were still the ones who determined the kinds of books available for reading. On rare occasions, a homeroom teacher asked for particular books to be purchased on students' request or donations from students' families supplemented the collections.

The potential advantage of the classroom library became apparent in one class where the teacher asked each student about the book he or she was returning, and every Friday had two or three students report extensively on the books they had read. Yet, to the surveyors' surprise, the number of books loaned in the six classroom libraries was not significantly higher than the number of books loaned in the main library. Dina and her associates suggested that as long as students themselves have no say in selecting books, their enthusiasm for reading remains low.

In concluding their study, Feitelson, Rahat, and Dolev-Shamir (1985) identified two major requirements in the attempt to encourage reading for pleasure. First, as noted above, the acquisition of books must consider children's motivation to read, and second, the books must be made available every day, on open shelves no higher than the children's eyes. Finally, the books should be circulated by a person who is familiar with the children, that is, a teacher or a classmate.

One implication of these requirements is that school libraries may not be the best instigators of book reading. They are rarely open every day and if they are, they are likely to be accessible mainly during recess. Children then face a difficult choice between playing in the schoolyard or going to the library. If they do choose the library, they may find it jammed with children from other classes, children perhaps older than they are, and they may not be able to find the books they want amongst the many shelves. Furthermore, children frequently have to deal with a librarian they do not know, at least not enough to dissolve their anxieties. As a result, they may be too weak to resist a proposition to read a book they do not want to read. If so, they invite embarrassment a second time when they return it unopened.

Dina Feitelson considered the classroom library a better setting for the encounter between children and books. There the children are surrounded by people they know well. They can borrow a book during class hours from open shelves stocked mainly with their own selections and examine the books available under no external pressure. Circulation procedures in the classroom library can be short and simple. When records are unnecessary, they can be avoided altogether. Finally, in the classroom library, homeroom teachers can assist children in their choice of books and monitor their progress and the advanced readers of the class can assist them in this role.

The Classroom Library Pilot Study

To test these expectations, Dina initiated a pilot study at six schools in northern Israel (Feitelson & Rahat, 1985) that aimed at examining the potential of the classroom library. One or two classes in every school, for a total of eight, participated in the study. Among these, six were in schools where Hebrew was the language of instruction, and two were in schools where Arabic was the language of instruction. Half of the classes were from the middle grades of elementary school – the third and fourth grades – and the other half were from upper grades. The students in five of these classes came from a lower-class population, and the students from the other three came from an upper middle-class population. The postgraduate students of the School of Education at the University of Haifa who conducted the study also held teaching jobs or were school principals at the time of the study.

The objective was to assess the change of reading rate as a result of establishing a classroom library under the following conditions:

1 If possible, the class is to determine book selection exclusively; that is, the library collection is to be comprised of the favorite readings of the students participating in the study.
2 Books are to be highly accessible; that is, books are to be loaned every school day, at all times, provided that the book exchange does not interrupt other class activities.
3 The procedures of circulation and record keeping are to be simplified to the point where the students can exchange books by themselves and record their own book loans.

To fulfill the first condition, an arrangement was made between the schools participating in the experiment and the students' families to the effect that for the three-month period of this study, the students would be allowed to bring to class their favorite books from home.

To fulfill the other two conditions, special procedures were devised to allow exchanging books and keeping records of books in circulation as smoothly as possible. For example, owing to the small size of the library, one method invented for recording circulation consisted of drawing a matrix on a large sheet of paper where the columns marked the books' titles, and the rows marked students' names. All that was needed for record keeping was to write the date of the loan and the date for returning the books in the right cell, at the intersection of the book's title and the student's name. The table was posted near the book shelves, so that record keeping could be done by the readers themselves. The advantage of this method, besides its simplicity, was that the reading progress of every student could be seen at once.

Feitelson and Rahat's study was carried out in three phases. In the first phase, the teachers who conducted the study were to reach an understanding with all the parties involved: principals, librarians, homeroom teachers, parents, and students. Understandably, some librarians approached the study with anxiety. Although they admitted that the reading rate in their library could be improved, they questioned the wisdom of establishing an alternative library. The response of the families, however, was generally favorable. Only one letter from the school was needed to get their cooperation. When all parties agreed, the homeroom teacher conducted a class discussion about the goals of the experiment and the procedures for running the class libraries. A certain space and some shelves were designated for the library. When the books arrived, the students usually welcomed them with enthusiasm, and many students volunteered to register the books, have them wrapped, and prepare the library for its operation.

In middle-class schools it took less than a week to collect a sufficient number of books to allow the opening of a classroom library with at least one book per student. One middle-class classroom accumulated 70 books toward the end of the first month (about 2.5 books per student). At the end of the second month, the number of books increased to 103 (about 3.6 books per student). There was no need to remind the students or to encourage them to bring books to class. Most students donated at least two books. In one class, students' enthusiasm led them to raise money, sometimes from their weekly allowances, to buy books for the library.

In lower-class schools, particularly among the Arab students, the collection of books was achieved with some difficulty. Many homes had no books to donate. In some schools, classes decided that children who did not bring at least one book to class would not be allowed to take books out of the library. In such classes children urged their parents to buy a book for them so that they could borrow books from the class library as the rest of the students did. In some-lower class schools in which the school's main library transferred some of its books to the classroom library, the expansion of the library was very slow and, evidently, the collection of books less attractive.

The second phase of the study examined methods of classroom-library management. In most classes the students assumed responsibility for operating the library. They took turns supervising the circulation and keeping inventories of the library books. As noted, in some classes sudents developed methods of recording their own book loans, making the job of the students in charge of the library a much easier one. All classes were in agreement that a student could take out no more than one book at a time but that books could be borrowed everyday. One class arranged a library card for each individual student, another class arranged readers' cards, and yet another kept no record of circulation at all – students exchanged books or placed and replaced them on the library shelves much as we do with our books at home. In some classes the teacher devoted five to ten minutes of one class hour daily for book exchange.

In most classes, the most popular books changed hands without ever reaching the library shelves, in a kind of informal circulation, sometimes without any record of book movements. This arrangement made it difficult for some students to get hold of them. When that was brought to the attention of the teacher, she had to stop this informal circulation, and to establish some kind of waiting list for the more desired books.

The third phase of this study was not actually planned. As noted above, the planned study was to be terminated by the end of the third month. However, the suggestion from the teachers of four classes that the students take the books home and close down the library, met with such vehement opposition from the students that the library kept on running to the end of the school year. In the other four classes, teachers did not suggest ending the project, and no student or parent complained. Thus, all the libraries remained open until the end of the school year.

In the last week of the school year, teachers asked their students to take their books home. In two classes, however, the children asked for a class meeting in which they suggested contributing the books to the school for use during the next year by other students.

Frequency of Book Loans

At the end of the planned period of this study the teachers involved were asked to assess the changes in book-reading habits of their students. When teachers compared the new book loans with the preintervention school library records, the changes in frequency were quite remarkable. The increase was three to six times the previous rate. In two classes of a lower-class school, children had borrowed less than one book per month on the average from the main library, and four and a half books a month from the class library. Some advanced readers borrowed a different book every school day; apparently their reading had been severely restricted prior to the classroom project. As for the slow readers, no class reported students who borrowed no books at all: Most students borrowed at least one book a week.

"Fringe Benefits" of the Classroom Library

With the establishment of the classroom library, several additional activities were reported. Some classes created a "reading corner" in which new books were displayed or announced, together with students' recommendations of books they liked. Some classes offered oral reports on books during the class discussions. Of particular interest were informal discussions among students about their own readings. Another "fringe benefit" of the a classroom library was its aid to individualized instruction. When students completed their individual assignments, they could turn to the library and spend their time reading until the end of the hour.

Concluding Remarks

To a large extent, the development of a literate person depends on such practical matters as the availability of proper reading materials and the arrangement for book loans. Yet, these prerequisites are obviously not sufficient to produce good readers. Unlike the attainment of many school objectives, literacy cannot be successfully achieved by prescribing school assignments. Much depends on creating an environment in which an individual can discover that reading is interesting and fun and in which it is considered a virtue to be a "reader." The formation of classroom libraries seems to serve these purposes in the elementary school.

One change introduced by classroom libraries was making reading a collective issue. When every student was involved in establishing the library and making it work, book reading became a topic of social interaction, and the advanced reader was recognized, perhaps admired, for his or her excellence. It is likely that class enthusiasm for the library swept up even those who did not count reading among their favorite activities.

Teachers have a subtle role in this venture. Though they are usually not needed for the ongoing operation of the library – this responsibility they can delegate to the students themselves – they can influence the motivation by how they read to the class and participate in the collective experience of establishing the library and monitoring its operation. The contribution of the teacher is particularly important in encouraging the slow readers.

Creating a classroom library is perhaps most advantageous to students from literarily impoverished homes. The goal is to help them and their parents appreciate the roles of books in modern life. In the traditional perception of many immigrant parents, books were almost exclusively perceived as sacred texts. After settling in Israel, these parents realized that reference books (dictionaries, lexicons, encyclopedias, etc.) were instrumental as sources of knowledge for preparing school assignments, but books that tell stories, books read for pleasure, were the last to be recognized as important household items.

This attitudinal change is a sign of the narrowing cultural gap. It also shows a growing awareness of what makes children successful in a literate civilization. In this study involving the parents in buying storybooks may have helped to transform the traditional outlook into one that acknowledges the developmental value of having books to read at leisure in the home. As Dina Feitelson's innovative work bears out, only with that condition met can the making of readers then begin.

Work in Progress

In the summer of 1986 the Israeli Ministry of Education authorized Dina Feitelson to establish classroom libraries for the second and third grades of five schools (totaling 11 classes in each grade) in the northern part of Israel. With one exception, two classes of each grade participated in the project in every school. During the summer and throughout the year, special seminars acquainted the teachers and the principals involved with the goals and the principles of the project as well as its implementation procedures.

Unlike in the pilot study, the children in these classes were not asked to bring books from home. The Ministry of Education financed the purchase of 120 books for the two classes of every grade, each class receiving a different collection of 60 books. Dina and the project coordinator (Yael Ofir) were free to select the books of their choice, which were those most popular with the participants of the pilot study, including several published in a series. The classes agreed that they would exchange their collections toward the middle of the year so that every student would have at least 120 books to choose from.

The teachers were asked to place the books on open shelves or on desks in a manner that would make them accessible to the children. The children were encouraged to pick up the books and to leaf through them at their convenience whenever they were free. The teachers were asked to read to their students from a selected book (or a series) every day for at least fifteen minutes at a time of their choice. The project coordinator visited the classes from time to time in order to guide the teachers and to monitor the library operations.

The procedures for lending books and keeping record of the circulation were similar to the ones developed in the pilot study. Second graders could become class librarians and borrow books on their own initiative, without the help of an adult.

To enable an evaluation of the effect of class libraries on the rate of book loans, the total books loaned in the project classes were compared with the total loaned from central libraries in five other schools, and the respective students compared for their reading comprehension scores in regional tests. An analysis of the data made in the middle of the school year revealed that the number of books read by the project classes was on average about four times higher than the number at the control schools.

Classroom observations disclosed that some students in the project classes arrived at school early in the morning to finish a book or to borrow a new one. One principal reported that one day when a teacher had failed to show up in a class, the students arranged a reading hour, and no one noticed that the class was working without a teacher. Some teachers reported that some children expressed their concern about having books to read during vacation. Consequently, teachers organized a trip to a public library where children could borrow books on their vacations. Again, it was found that the teacher's daily readings to the class seemed to encourage the students to read the books introduced in this way and that the preferred readings tended to be books from a series.

In the second year of the "Feitelson Project," as it is called by educational practitioners in Israel (1987/1988), the project included ten more schools (61 classes), and it has grown exponentially every year since then. Today, only six years after its initiation, the project encompasses

1,300 classes throughout the country. It is not impossible that in few more years there will be a class library in every elementary school classroom in Israel.

References

Bamberger, R. (1969). The joy of reading. In R.C. Steiger & O. Anderson (Eds.), *Reading: A human right and human problem*. Newark, DL: International Reading Association.

Bamberger, R. (1976). Literature and development in reading. In I.E. Merit (Ed.), *New horizons in reading*. Newark, DL: International Reading Association.

Bergson, G. & Levy, A. (1984). A study of leisure reading of students in 4th, 6th and 8th grade. *Sifrut Yeladim Vanoar*, 39–40, pp. 7–14 (Hebrew).

Cochran-Smith, M. (1984). *The making of a reader*. Norwood, NJ: Ablex.

Eshel, M. (1979). *Improving language skills of low SES kindergartners through tutoring*. Unpublished master thesis, University of Haifa (Hebrew).

Feitelson, D. (1952). Teaching strategies in a class of under achiever children. *Megamot, 3*, 212–37 (Hebrew).

Feitelson, D. (1954). Childrearing practices in the Kurdish community. *Megamot, 5*, 95–109 (Hebrew).

Feitelson, D. (1955). Changes in the educational patterns of Kurdish Jews. *Megamot, 6*, 275–97 (Hebrew).

Feitelson, D. (1957). Some aspects of the social life of Kurdish Jews. *The Jewish Journal of Sociology, 1*, 201–16.

Feitelson, D. (1972). Developing imaginative play in preschool children as a possible approach to fostering creativity. *Early Child Development and Care, 1*, 181–95.

Feitelson, D. (1977). Cross-cultural studies of representational play. In B. Tizard & D. Harvey (Eds.), *Biology of play* (pp. 6–14). London: Heinemann.

Feitelson, D. (1988). *Facts and fads in Beginning Reading: A cross language perspective*. Norwood, NJ: Ablex.

Feitelson, D. & Goldstein, Z. (1986). Patterns of book ownership and reading to young children in Israeli school-oriented and nonschool-oriented families. *The Reading Teacher, 39*, 924–30.

Feitelson, D., Goldstein, Z., Iraqi, J. & Share, D.L. (1992). Effects of listening to story reading on aspects of literacy acquisition in a diglossic situation. *Reading Research Quarterly, 28*, 70–9.

Feitelson, D., Kita, B. & Goldstein, Z. (1986). Effects of listening to series-stories on first graders' comprehension and use of language. *Research in the Teaching of English, 20*, 339–56.

Feitelson, D. & Rahat, R. (1985). Establishing class lending libraries: An experiment. *Ma'agalei Kriah, 13/14*, 115–25 (Hebrew).

Feitelson, D., Rahat, R. & Dolev-Shamir, Y. (1985). School libraries as a mean for encouraging leisure reading. *Ma'agalei Kriah, 12*, 5–25 (Hebrew).

Feitelson, D. & Ross, G. (1973). The neglected factor – play. *Human Development, 16,* 202–23.

Heath, S.B. (1982). What bedtime story means: Narrative skills at home and school. *Language in Society, 11,* 49–76.

Heath, S.B. (1983). *Ways with words: Language, life and work in communities and classrooms.* London: Cambridge University Press.

Iraqi, J. (1990). *Reading to Arabic speaking kindergartners compared to alternative enrichment activities as a means of improving reading comprehension and language skills.* Unpublished Master Thesis, University of Haifa (Hebrew).

Reshef, O. (1984). *Daily reading to kindergarten children as a way to improve verbal skills and comprehension.* Unpublished masters thesis, University of Haifa (Hebrew).

Shimron, J. (1976). Learning activities in individually prescribed instruction. *Instructional Science, 5,* 391–401.

Shimron, J. (1990). Time perception and time as an organizer in teaching reading in Israeli parochial schools. In M. Ben-Peretz & R. Bromme (Eds.), *The nature of time in schools.* New York: Teachers College Press.

Part 3

Programs Working with Parents and Children in Preschools and Schools

5 Accelerating Language Development through Picture Book Reading: A Summary of Dialogic Reading and Its Effects

David S. Arnold and Grover J. Whitehurst

The first part of this chapter summarizes the theoretical basis and evaluations of a shared picture book program called *dialogic reading,* which was designed to accelerate the language development of pre-school children, with the ultimate goal of targeting children at risk for later academic failure. The model that underlies our research is that dialogic reading and other book-related activities during the preschool period enhance language skills, which in turn help children learn to read when they begin school. In the second part of this chapter we present an overview of the extent to which this model is justified by the research literature, summarizing what is known and what remains to be learned about the long-term effects of early shared picture-book reading.

Picture Books and Language Development

Picture book reading provides an ideal context for learning language. Adults often approach shared reading with an intent to teach language to their young children. For example, Ninio and Bruner (1978) conducted an extensive case study of a mother and her child, and found that 76 percent of the mother's object labeling occurred during picture-book reading. Also, the mother consistently corrected incorrect labels and reinforced correct labels in this setting. A large set of

Preparation of this report was supported by grants to Whitehurst from the Pew Charitable Trusts, a private foundation that prefers not to be identified publicly, and The Administration for Children and Families, United States Department of Health and Human Services.

studies suggests that these instructive behaviors may have an impact on children's language ability. For example, children's novel linguistic forms often emerge via imitations of storybook text (Cornell, Senechal & Broda, 1988; Elley, 1989; Leung & Pikulski, 1990; Moerk, 1985). Thus, it is not surprising that correlational studies have shown that the frequency with which children are exposed to picture books is related to language skills. For example, Wells (1985) found that the amount of time that children listened to stories at ages 1–3 is associated with teacher ratings of language skills at 5 years of age. Further, home reading variables (frequency of oral reading, number of books owned, and library membership) predict levels of language skills above and beyond economic status (Raz & Bryant, 1990; Share, Jorn, MacLean, Matthews & Watterman, 1983). Thus early picture-book experiences are reliably correlated with language development.

Though these studies are widely cited as demonstrating the importance of early shared reading, they are correlational and so consistent with other interpretations. For instance, preschool experience with books may be a marker of differences between children without playing a causal role in academic achievement. Alternatively, the relations between early experience with books and language development may be an example of a child effect: Children who are more interested in books during the preschool period may generate more shared book reading with parents and teachers. The same underlying abilities and proclivities that generate more interest in books may also foster rapid language development independently from the early book-reading experience. Thus, experimental studies are needed to establish the direction of effects. We have developed a shared reading program aimed at increasing stimulation of children's language skills via interactive picture-book reading and have experimentally evaluated the program's effects in a number of contexts.

Dialogic Reading: Rationale and Description

Theoretical Principles

Our program, dialogic reading, is based on three general principles: (a) *Evocative techniques* are used to encourage the child to take an active role during story time. For example, asking a child a "what" question is preferable to straight text reading or asking the child to point. This principle is based on evidence that active learning is more effective than passive learning, and that language, like other skills, benefits from practice (Wells, 1985). (b) *Parental feedback* is encouraged in the form of expansions, modeling, corrections, and praise. There is an abundance of data demonstrating the importance of providing children examples of slightly more advanced language than their own. Scherer and Olswang (1984) manipulated mothers' use of expansions to their two-year-olds and found that they increased children's spontaneous imitations and productions. (c) *Progressive change* in adult standards for the child are encouraged so that the parent or teacher is constantly encouraging and enticing the child to do just a bit more than he or she normally would. This principle is based on the assumption of a zone of proximal development (Vygotsky, 1978). For example, the child should know an object's label before being asked about the object's function. Several studies have demonstrated such a naturally occurring progression in interactional patterns (see Moerk, 1985, for a review). Dialogic reading is based on the premise that language development may be accelerated if the boundaries of the proximal zone are pushed further than they might be spontaneously.

The specific reading techniques of dialogic reading require that parents gradually reverse the typical pattern of storybook reading to permit the child to become the teller of the story and the adult the active listener – prompting, expanding, and rewarding the child's efforts to talk. The program for two- and three-year-olds is presented in two segments, each lasting two–three weeks.

Assignment 1 for Two- and Three-Year-Olds

Adults are taught the following seven points in assignment 1:

1. *Ask "what" questions.* Practicing language helps children to learn, so ask *what* questions that evoke speech from child. For example, point to a fire truck and ask "What is this?" Such questions are much more effective than pointing questions, which do not require any speech from the child. Similarly, yes/no questions are not very effective at increasing the child's language skills. Asking "What is this?" while pointing to a fire truck encourages more speech from a child than asking "Is this a fire truck?" or asking the child to point to the fire truck.

2. *Follow answers with questions.* Once the child knows the name of a pictured object ask a further question about the object. For example, ask questions about aspects of the object itself, such as its shape, its color, or its parts. Or ask what the object is being used for or who is using it. Any question that asks the child to talk about the object is helpful. If a child correctly labels a wagon, you might point to its wheel and say "Right, what is this part of the wagon called?"

3. *Repeat what the child says.* Reinforcing the child's correct responses

by repetition provides encouragement and lets the child know when he or she is correct. So if the child answered "frog," you might say, "That's right; it is a frog."

4. *Help the child as needed.* A child's inability to anwer a question provides a good opportunity for teaching. Provide the child a model of a good answer, and see if the child will repeat what you said. For instance, say "Those are roller skates. Can you say roller skates?" Children eventually get into the habit of repeating without being asked.

5. *Praise and encourage.* There are many ways to provide feedback and praise when the child says something about the book, such as "Good talking," "That's right," or "Nice job."

6. *Follow the child's interests.* Children learn very quickly when they are learning about the things that interest them. At this age it is not important to read all of the words on a page or talk about every picture. It is important to talk about the things that the child likes. When the child points at a picture, or begins to talk about part of a page, use this interest as a chance to encourage the child to talk.

7. *Have fun.* The most important thing to remember about this program is to make reading fun. We have found that children generally enjoy an active approach to story time, particularly when adults take a game-like, turn-taking approach. If the child seems to be getting tired, read a few pages without questions, or take a break from reading. Try to keep these two phases in proportion by simply reading to the child part of the time. One way is for you to read a page and then for the child to read the next.

Assignment 2 for Two- and Three-Year-Olds

During the second assignment, adults are taught the following:

1. *Ask open-ended questions.* In part one the child was asked specific questions about objects and their attributes. In part two ask less structured questions – questions that ask the child to pick something on the page and tell about it. Examples of these open-ended questions are "What do you see on this page?" or "Tell me what's going on here." These questions are more difficult than specific questions. At first the child may be able to answer very little. Encourage any attempts, and provide models of good answers. When the child doesn't know anything else to say about a picture, provide a multiword description and try to get the child to repeat it: "The duck is swimming. Now you say, the duck is swimming." After a few days practice, the child should begin to offer multiword phrases spontaneously in response to the request, "Tell me about this." After the child gets used to answering this type of question, you may be able to ask two or three such questions

on a page. When the child says something about a page, praise him or her, and then ask what else the child can tell you. When the child runs out of things to say, add one more piece of information and try to get the child to repeat what you said.

2. *Expand what the child says.* When the child says something about the book, encourage this language, and use it as an opportunity to model slightly more advanced language. Repeat what the child says and add a bit more information or one or two more words. For example, if the child says "Duck swim," you might say "Right, the duck is swimming." If the child says "Wagon," you might say "Yes, a red wagon." You can expand on what the child has said by adding parts of speech or by supplying new information. Later, you might ask a question about the information you have provided, such as "What color is the wagon?" When you expand the child's utterances, make sure you add only a little information, so that the child will be able to imitate you. If your expansions are too long, the child is unlikely to be able to repeat what you say. If you encourage the child to repeat your expansions, he or she is more likely to use longer phrases spontaneously.

3. *Have fun.* Use your judgment in adjusting this program to make it fun for the child. Do not expect the child to do all of the talking about a book. You should talk about some of the pages, or take turns describing a picture. Many children find turn-taking to be like a game.

Evaluating Dialogic Reading for Two- and Three-Year-Old, High-SES Children

We originally evaluated the effects of the dialogic reading program with a group of middle- to upper-SES (socioeconomic status) mothers and their two-year-olds (Whitehurst et al., 1988). Half of the families were randomly assigned to an experimental group and received training in the reading assignments described above. Mothers in this group received two half-hour training sessions two weeks apart. Each training session consisted of three components: (a) *didactic instruction* in which the techniques were described to the mother by the trainer; (b) *modeling* of the techniques in which the trainer gave a demonstration of the techniques and role-played a reading session with a trained research assistant; (c) *direct feedback* in which the trainer pretended to be a child and had the mother practice the techniques, providing feedback about her performance. The other half of the families were assigned to the control group. These mothers read to their children with equal frequency in their typical manner. Mothers in both groups tape-recorded reading sessions across the four-week study.

Analyses of the audiotapes revealed that experimental mothers employed the dialogic reading techniques, whereas control mothers primarily read the text. Over the four-week intervention period the program produced significant increases in mean length of utterances (MLU) of children in the intervention condition. Effects of the intervention were also assessed with three standardized tests of the children's language skills: the Expressive One Word Picture Vocabulary Test (One Word), the verbal expression subscale of the Illinois Test of Psycholinguistic Abilities (ITPA-VE), and the revised Peabody Picture Vocabulary Test (Peabody). The One Word and the ITPA-VE are tests of expressive language, the former asking children to say the names of pictures and the latter assessing children's verbal fluency in describing common objects. The Peabody measures receptive language ability, asking children to point to a picture from an array of four choices. We chose these tests because they assess the language skills targeted by the intervention. Results are presented in figure 1. Children who received the dialogic reading intervention exhibited a 6-month gain on the One Word, and an 8.5-month gain on the ITPA-VE, which were maintained at a 9-month follow-up assessment. Results on the Peabody favored the intervention group but were not statistically significant.

These expressive language gains are both statistically significant and clinically meaningful. They represent the first experimental verification that reading ordinary picture books in the home can have a causal effect on the development of language skills. Perhaps more important, given the magnitude of the effects obtained with upper-middle-class children whose language development was already quite advanced, the results raise the possibility that dialogic reading might also improve the language skills of children whose language development is delayed.

The largest group of children with below normal levels of language development comes from low-income families. These children exhibit disproportionately high rates of academic failure and are in particular

---

Figure 1. High-SES children. Means for the three tests of language at posttest and nine-month follow-up for children in the experimental (EXP) and control groups. The plotted variable is corrected language age, that is, language age (LA) minus chronological age (CA). Results are depicted for the Expressive One Word Picture Vocabulary Test (One Word), the Illinois Test of Psycholinguistic Abilities expressive subscale (ITPA-VE), and the Peabody Picture Vocabulary Test – revised (Peabody).

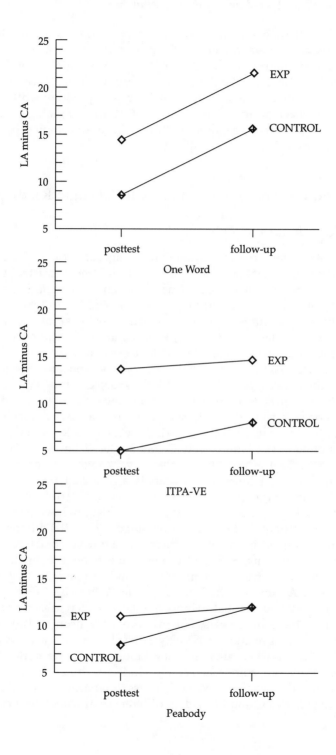

One Word

ITPA-VE

Peabody

need of effective, early shared reading experiences. According to the 1991 Carnegie Foundation report, *Ready to learn: A mandate for the nation*, 35 percent of children in the United States enter kindergarten unprepared to learn, with most lacking the vocabulary and sentence structure crucial to school success. These children are predominantly from low-income backgrounds. Our most recent studies of dialogic reading have focused on these children, with the aim of developing practical interventions.

Early Educational Intervention with Dialogic Reading

High Risks in Low-SES Groups

Social-class differences in the language usage of preschool children are widely documented. Underprivileged children consistently perform more poorly than middle-class children on standardized tests of verbal ability (e.g., Lesser, Fifer, Clark, 1965; Moore, 1982) and on other diverse measures of verbal production. For example, compared to their middle-class counterparts, these children possess smaller vocabularies, produce less complex sentence structures, use less varied speech functions, are less verbally responsive, and are less able to express their ideas verbally (e.g., Black, 1966; Gordon, 1984; Lesser et al., 1965; Ward, 1971). Social-class differences in language production are present from the early stages of language development; differences in children's vocabulary size are detectable as early as 18 months of age (e.g., Ninio, 1980; Olson, Bayles & Bates, 1986).

Children raised in poverty are also at very high risk for later illiteracy and school failure. When schools are ranked by the median socioeconomic status (SES) of their students, SES correlates .68 with academic achievement (White, 1982). The National Assessment of Educational Progress (1991) has documented substantial differences in the reading and writing ability of children as a function of the economic level of their parents. SES is also one of the strongest predictors of performance differences in children at the beginning of first grade (Entwisle & Alexander, cited in Alexander & Entwisle, 1988, p. 99), and there is also substantial stability in relative differences in performance across the school years. For instance, Stevenson and Newman (1986) found a correlation of .52 between a child's ability to name the letters of the alphabet when entering kindergarten and performance on a test of reading comprehension in grade 10. Thus, school achievement covaries with social class, social-class differences exist at the very beginning of school, and individual differences in school performance are relatively stable from kindergarten to high school. Children from low-income families typically start school behind and stay behind.

One factor contributing factor to the early language deficits in many low-SES children may be a lack of effective, early shared reading experiences. Consistent with the hypothesis that early shared reading affects language development, low-SES children receive very little exposure to literary materials. McCormick and Mason (1986) demonstrated large social-class differences in the availability and use of printed materials in the home. Forty-seven percent of public-aid parents of preschoolers reported having no alphabet books at home, compared with three percent of professional parents. Feitelson and Goldstein (1986) found that 60 percent of the kindergarteners in neighborhoods where children did poorly in school did not own a single book; in neighborhoods characterized by good school performance, kindergarteners owned an average of 54 books each. Perhaps most astounding, by one estimate a typical middle-class child enters first grade with approximately 1,000 to 1,700 hours of one-on-one picture book reading, while the corresponding child from a low-income family averages 25 such hours (Adams, 1990).

Other lines of research suggest that mothers of lower-SES groups tend to engage in fewer instructive behaviors during story time (Ninio, 1980). Low-SES mothers are less likely than their high-SES counterparts to label object attributes and actions, and are less likely to initiate reading cycles with *where* or *what* questions. Low-SES mothers are also less responsive to changes in their children's language abilities (Valdez-Menchaca, 1990), adjusting their own language style less than high-SES mothers in response to increases in their children's language skills. Low-SES mothers consistently differ from middle-class mothers in the extent to which they respond to children's language, produce verbalizations that are contingent on children's language, and request verbal productions from their children. Because these are the areas we target for dialogic reading, the dialogic reading program may be ideally suited for this group of children.

Mexican Day Care

We extended dialogic reading techniques to two-year-old children of low-income parents attending a public day-care center in Mexico (Valdez-Menchaca & Whitehurst, in press). We chose day-care centers for our intervention because they provide a convenient way for us to reach large numbers of high-risk children. The families in this study had a mean income of $192 per month. The linguistic ability of the children was in the retarded range as measured by standardized assessments, even though they were developmentally normal in physical and motor development. We matched children by language test scores and then assigned them randomly to an experimental or control group. The intervention program consisted of ten-minute one-on-one dialogic reading sessions with each child and a graduate student teacher every weekday for six weeks, for a total of approximately 5 hours of intervention per child throughout the course of the intervention. Children in the control group engaged in a similar schedule of such non-book-related, one-to-one activities with the teacher as building with blocks and doing puzzles.

We first assessed the effects of the dialogic reading intervention through measures of children's spontaneous verbalizations to an unfamiliar female adult who asked specific and open-ended questions during a reading session. The children in the intervention group produced significantly more utterances, longer utterances, and more complex utterances than the control group. They also used more diverse language than the control group and were more likely to provide answers, to initiate topics, and to continue conversations. These effects encompass the domains of syntax, semantics, and pragmatics, and are perhaps the most general and extensive ever to have been demonstrated for a language intervention.

We also used standardized tests to evaluate the impact of dialogic reading (see figure 2). The experimental group was ahead of the control group by 29 language quotient (LQ) points on the ITPA-VE and 7 LQ points on the Peabody (language quotients are standard scores of language ability measured on the same scale as IQ). Two months after the intervention, the One Word was given. The experimental group was 8 LQ points ahead on this test. These results are both clinically and statistically significant.

While these findings suggest that dialogic reading has an impact on high-risk children, the format of the intervention raises implementation issues, because the teacher in this study was an advanced doctoral student who met with subjects individually. The first issue is the degree to which day-care teachers can be trained and motivated to use dialogic reading; the second issue is whether enough teacher time can be freed for such a program.

Low-SES Day Care in the United States Using Teachers and Parents

We addressed these issues by utilizing day care teachers as the dialogic readers to children in small groups (Whitehurst et al., 1992). We expected that a home intervention component could supplement

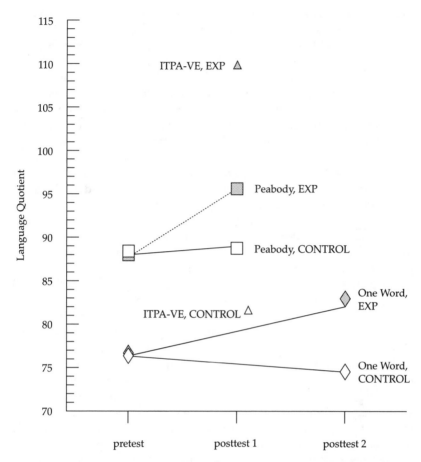

Figure 2. Mexican day care. Standardized language quotient means on language tests given at pretest, posttest, and two-month delayed posttest (posttest 2) for children in the experimental (EXP) and control groups. Results are depicted for the Expressive One Word Picture Vocabulary Test (One Word), the Illinois Test of Psycholinguistic Abilities expressive subscale (ITPA-VE), and the Peabody Picture Vocabulary Test – revised (Peabody).

the effects of a day-care intervention, so we also evaluated the effects of such a combined intervention. Most of the children were black or Hispanic. They were drawn from five government subsidized day-care centers in Suffolk County, NY. The children averaged three and a half years old, which was older than in the prior studies of dialogic reading. Their language skills, however, were actually less advanced than our original sample of two-year-olds. Their average One Word LQ score was 82, which corresponds to two years, eight months at pretest. The children were randomly assigned to one of three groups: (a) a school-only group: these children were read to using dialogic reading by their teachers; (b) a combined school + home group: these children were read to by their teachers and their parents; and (c) a control group: these children did activities like building with Lincoln Logs and Tinkertoys. We hypothesized that children who were read to by teachers in day care would show incremental improvements in language ability compared with a control group, and that children who were read to by teachers and parents would show even stronger effects, based on a greater frequency of shared reading and a synergistic interaction between shared reading experiences at home and at day care. Because dialogic reading requires frequent opportunities for a child to talk about a book with a responsive adult, we asked teachers to read to the children in small groups of three or four, in contrast to typical practices of reading to a class as a whole.

We primarily used a videotape package (described in more detail in the next section) to train readers in the principles of dialogic reading rather than the direct method provided to parents in Whitehurst et al. (1988) in order to make training less expensive and more portable. We supplemented the video training with a practice session with direct feedback. We provided day-care centers and parents with books to ensure that the reading materials would be appropriate to dialogic reading techniques and trained teachers and parents on the second assignment three weeks after the first assignment. Three weeks later the children took a posttest, resulting in a total of six weeks of intervention.

We assessed children's language skills following the six-week intervention with the three standardized measures of language skill already discussed and with the Our Word, a nonstandardized expressive vocabulary test of our devising. The Our Word was in the same format as the One Word. It consisted of black and white photocopies of 36 pictures from the books used in this study that were judged to call for novel vocabulary (e.g., a picture of a telescope). For each picture, the child was asked "What is this?" or "What is this part of the picture?" Six months later we retested the children on the standardized tests.

The reading and activity logs that the teachers completed showed substantial variability in the fidelity with which they followed the reading or activities schedule that they learned from the training. Three of the centers had relatively high rates of reading, consistent with the "once-per-day" instructions they had received, whereas at the two remaining centers, children in the reading conditions were read to much less frequently.

The results of this study are presented in figure 3. The significant differences in the effects of the program that we found across the centers were consistent with the differences in program implementation. However, even including the two noncompliant centers, we obtained significant effects of the reading intervention at posttest on the One Word and the Our Word. We found significant effects on the *Peabody* as well if only the compliant centers were considered. At the six-month follow-up overall effects of the intervention were evident on the One Word and the ITPA-VE, and again at the compliant centers for the Peabody. The gains exhibited in the intervention groups were as large as ten LQ points. Where significant differences occurred between the two reading interventions, they favored the school + home group. Specifically, the school+home group performed significantly better than the school-only group on the posttest One Word. The school+home group also outperformed the other groups on the ITPA at follow-up.

The practical implications of this day-care study are considerable because the results indicate that dialogic reading can have a large impact on the language skills of high-risk children, and that the benefits of the program can be obtained by implementing dialogic reading via day-care teachers who read to the children in small groups. The effects of the intervention were supplemented by involving the parents, although it appears that significant benefits can be obtained even when parents are not involved.

Video Training

Though we used a video presentation of the dialogic reading techniques in this study, we supplemented it with direct training in the form of the feedback sessions. Because it is not feasible to provide direct training to all families that might benefit from the program, we reasoned that a stand-alone instructional package would greatly increase the potential impact of the program. Hence we created the videotape package. Videotape training also allowed us to standardize the intervention and could allow the same techniques to be taught in different areas of the country without the cost or uncertainty involved in using other trainers. Our initial study examining the effectiveness of the videotape package as a stand-alone unit is encouraging.

Like direct training, the videotape package contained two presentations. The first segment was 20 minutes long and the second segment

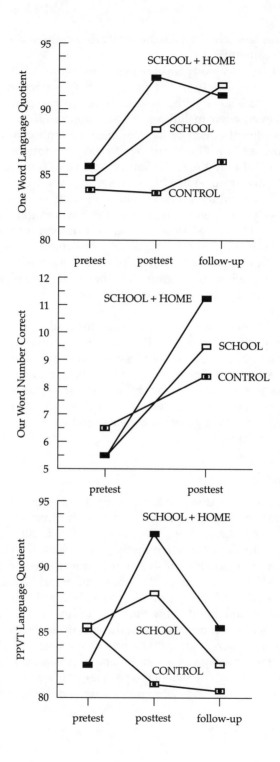

lasted 15 minutes. The didactic instruction and modeling that were included in the direct training method were also presented via videotape. The tape provided a description of each technique (e.g., open-ended questions and expansions) followed by several examples of mothers utilizing the technique with their children. Since actual mothers and children were the models, the videotape may have provided an advantage over direct training. That is, in the videotape mothers watched other mothers with their children, whereas in direct training an adult played the role of the child.

The portion of direct training that could not be duplicated via videotape was the direct feedback given parents during role-play. However, our experiences in training parents indicated that they made only a limited number of mistakes. The video package warned against these common problems. Moreover, a separate section of the video training required the viewer to identify mistakes made by other mothers reading with their children and to suggest ways of correcting them. For example, the viewer watches a clip of a mother asking "Is that a fire truck?" The voice of the narrator asks the mother what could have been done differently, and following a pause explains that the question "What is that called?" would have encouraged more speech from the child. We expected that practice in spotting and correcting common mistakes would replace feedback in helping mothers to avoid such mistakes.

The children in this study (Arnold, Lonigan, Whitehurst & Epstein, in press) were from middle- to upper-SES families, similar to those from our first study of dialogic reading. We use advantaged children when we want to explore the components or processes of dialogic reading. It is much easier to recruit these children and their parents for basic research studies than it is to recruit children from low-income backgrounds. Our interest, however, is primarily in at-risk children. Our assumption is that components or processes of dialogic reading that are shown to be important to advantaged children may be important to broader interventions with children from low-income families.

Children in the present study were divided into a direct training

---

Figure 3. Low-SES U.S. day care. Standardized language quotient means on language tests given at pretest, posttest, and six-month follow-up for children in the school+home, school, and control groups. Results are depicted for the Expressive One Word Picture Vocabulary Test (One Word), the Our Word Picture Vocabulary Test (Our Word) and the Peabody Picture Vocabulary Test – revised (Peabody). Results for the Peabody exclude one noncompliant center.

group, a video training group, and a control group. Mothers in the direct training group received the same training as in the original study of dialogic reading. The video group received no direct instruction or feedback, and the control group read to the children in their usual fashion.

Children were administered the three standardized tests of language ability already described and the grammatical closure subscale of the ITPA (ITPA-GC), a standardized test of grammatical sophistication. The ITPA-GC involves presenting the child with a sequence of pictures and verbal prompts that require the child to respond with an altered grammatical form. For example, the child is shown a picture of one dog and a picture of two dogs and given the verbal prompt, "This is a dog and these are two _____." Children in the video group exhibited significantly improved language abilities on all four outcome measures compared with the control group (see figure 4). More specifically, the video group scored 5.1 months ahead on the One Word, 3.9 months ahead on the ITPA-VE, and 4.6 months ahead on the ITPA-GC. The video group scored 3.3 months ahead of the control group on the Peabody. Effects of the intervention were also evident in the direct training group. The video training group scored significantly higher than the direct training group on the One Word and the Peabody. These results suggest that video training may produce more reliable effects than the more time-consuming and costly direct training protocol.

The video training format provides a potential vehicle for making the intervention available to a wide audience in a standardized format and at a low cost. On the other hand, the effects of the training program must be evaluated with lower-SES groups. We are cautious about assuming that the videotape alone will be effective for training the parents of high-risk children. It may be that in some groups the videotape needs to be supplemented with role playing and direct feedback.

Discussion

Story time is a common activity in most middle-class homes and preschool programs in the United States. We have shown that shared picture book reading, at least in one form, promotes language learning among two- and three-year-olds. This series of studies demonstrates that dialogic reading can affect children's language skills to an extent that is both statistically and clinically meaningful, but there are aspects of our results that suggest the need for additional work.

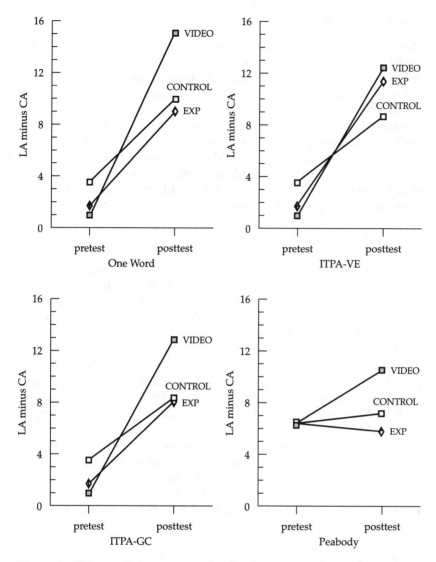

Figure 4. Video training. Means for the four tests of language for children in the experimental (EXP) and control groups. The plotted variable is corrected language age, that is, language age (LA) minus chronological age (CA). Results are depicted for the Expressive One Word Picture Vocabulary Test (One Word), the Illinois Test of Psycholinguistic Abilities expressive subscale (ITPA-VE) and grammatical closure subscale (ITPA-GC), and the Peabody Picture Vocabulary Test – revised (Peabody). Pretest scores for the first three tests are the Reynell Developmental Language Scales.

Reading at School versus Home

One issue that suggests the need for additional research involves the contributions of the school versus those of the parents to the success of the school–home condition. The U.S. day-care study indicated added value of the school–home condition compared with the school-only condition. The effects were relatively small and not present on each measure, but all significant differences between the two conditions favored that condition. However, interpretation of the effects of the school–home condition relative to the school condition is difficult because the study did not include an option in which parents alone engaged in dialogic reading with their children. Future research will have to address the independent effects of shared reading at home.

Variability

A second issue is the striking difference in the patterns of results across the various studies presented here. In the studies of high-SES children and Mexican day care, the strongest effects were obtained on the ITPA-VE. In contrast, only weak effects were obtained on the ITPA-VE in the U.S. daycare project. There is some evidence for a social-class effect concerning the use of open-ended questions and directives in a comparison of the results of a study by Valdez-Menchaca (1990), who trained lower-class Mexican mothers to use dialogic reading, and the results of Whitehurst et al. (1988), who trained upper-middle-class mothers. The lower-class Mexican women used open directives at a rate of about six percent of total utterances at the end of training, compared with a rate of about eleven percent for upper-middle-class mothers in the United States. Taken together, these findings and interpretations suggest that training procedures for parents and teachers may need to be altered with a particular emphasis on increasing the use of open-ended, conversational techniques in lower-SES adults.

Implementation Issues

The third issue suggests the need for revisions in the use of small groups of children for shared reading in the classroom. Dialogic reading calls for reading in groups of no more than four children. Teachers in the U.S. day-care study followed this design during the six weeks of the intervention, but an interview of teachers conducted at the follow-up testing indicated that no teacher had continued to read to children in groups of that size during the ensuing six months. The principles underlying dialogic reading suggest that children benefit from active responding to picture books when an adult gently guides the child through questions, expansions, and sensitivity to the child's interests and abilities. These interactions must diminish for any single child as the ratio of children to adults gets larger.

These facts suggest that within the current organization of day-care classrooms, the small group reading program we designed may not work. Why not? One reason is that the adult-to-child ratio is not what it appears to be on paper. Though there are two or more adults in each classroom, rarely do both of them engage in teaching at the same time. Instead, one adult is often preparing or putting away materials, taking care of problems with individual children, or dealing with various administrative chores, while the other adult is responsible for the group. A second reason is that dialogic reading is hard work, requiring careful attention to individual children for extended periods. A third reason is that most day care centers have a developmental rather than an instructional philosophy. They provide a supportive environment for a child's naturally unfolding interests and needs. The teaching of specific skills is often seen as the province of the school system, not of preschool programs. Such a philosophy sometimes makes it difficult to motivate staff to utilize a technique based on teaching children specific skills.

Something must change if dialogic reading procedures are to be widely disseminated and utilized. One promising direction is the use of adult volunteers as reading partners in lieu of teachers. The success of programs such as Literacy Volunteers of America points to a large reservoir of public interest in literacy writing to be channeled into volunteering. Parents and relatives of children in a day-care center are another source of readers. School-aged children (grade five through college) are another source of readers when a school or college is geographically close to a day-care center. One of the centers that participated in our day-care project later organized a successful dialogic reading program using community volunteers, recognizing that it was unable to sustain a dialogic reading program with its own staff as reading partners.

Older Children

We have begun extending and modifying our program in order to create a preliteracy program that is appropriate for four- and five-year-olds. The changes that we have made target more advanced skills that are related to emerging literacy. One of the additions in the training program for older children emphasizes the structure of a story.

We add *recall* and *distancing* questions to the *what* and *open-ended* questions employed in the program for younger children.

Recall prompts are questions about what happened in a book a child has already read. They work for nearly everything except alphabet books. For example, you might say, "Can you tell me what happened to the little blue engine in this story?" Such a recall prompt helps children understand story plot and describe sequences of events. Recall prompts can be used not only at the end of a book, but also at the beginning of a book that a child has been read before.

Distancing prompts ask children to relate the pictures or words in the book they are reading to experiences outside the book. For example, while looking at a book with a picture of animals on a farm, you might say, "Remember when we went to animal park last week? Which of these animals did we see there?" Distancing prompts help children form a bridge between books and the real world, as well as help with verbal fluency, conversational ability, and narrative skill.

Another modification for older children is to place a greater emphasis on sound structure, as with the *completion* prompt. You leave a blank at the end of a sentence for the child to fill in. Completion prompts are typically used in books with rhyme or books with repetitive phases. For example, you might say "I think I'd be a glossy cat. A little plump but not too _____," letting the child fill in the blank with the word "fat." Completion prompts provide children with information about the structure of language that is critical to later reading.

We are in the process of evaluating these and other modifications for older children in the context of designing and assessing the outcomes of a year-long emergent literacy curriculum for Head Start centers.

The Importance of Early Shared Reading: Long-Term Effects

Perhaps the most important issue that arises from the present studies concerns the long-term effects of preschool, shared picture book reading. Our society is convinced that reading to preschool children is very important. Barbara Bush (1990) has fostered family literacy programs based on the assumption that reading to children "has a tremendous impact on a young mind" (p. 67), and an ever-increasing number of books and articles inform parents of the value of reading to preschoolers. Picture book reading has the potential to teach so many things – vocabulary, rhyme, the meaning of print, the structure of stories and language, sustained attention, and so on – that many experts assume that early shared book reading affects later school performance substantially.

Our research demonstrates that during the preschool period dialogic reading enhances some language skills. Early language skills, in turn, are strongly related to later literacy. For example, kindergarteners' receptive language abilities predict reading ability at the end of the first grade (Pikulski and Tobin, 1989). Preschool expressive-language measures correlate with second grade reading ability, even after controlling for children's IQ (Scarborough, 1989). Similar results have linked early language development to school performance through the sixth grade.

Correlational and descriptive research is consistent with the conviction that early picture book reading provides an important academic foundation for young children. Wells (1985) followed the children in his study to age seven, and found that the frequency of story time from ages one to three was associated with reading comprehension later on. Other studies have found that children who learn to read early are likely to have been read to very often as young children. For instance, Durkin (1966) directly compared early readers with a control group matched for IQ and found that early readers were read to by their parents much more often as young children. Consistent with these findings, disabled readers tended to engage in few book related activities as preschoolers (e.g., Scarborough, Dobrich & Hager, 1991).

Conclusions from these studies, however, are restricted by the limitations of correlational studies. In other words, the relation between early literary experiences and later academic achievement may be due to a third variable or a child effect. Though it is easy to imagine that reading picture books at home and in day care or preschool directly prepares children for the demands of formal reading, it is also easy to imagine that shared picture book reading at home is simply a marker of parental values. Homes in which books are provided for young children and in which shared reading occurs frequently are also likely to be homes in which parents value education, read frequently themselves, use sophisticated vocabulary, and provide other forms of intellectual stimulation for children. The difficulty, if not the impossibility of prying these influences apart in naturalistic studies that use correlational methods points to the need for experimental studies of the long-term effects of early shared reading. Regrettably, few such studies exist. Karweit (1989; chapter 2) implemented a story reading program that utilized such materials as sequence cards and flannel boards with the goal of increasing children's language use. She found that children who received this intervention substantially outscored control children on a variety of language and preliteracy tests. However, because her program was conducted within the context of a larger intervention project, the results cannot necessarily be attributed to the reading program per se. The only experimental work that has directly examined the link between preschool experience with books and later school performance is that of Mason and colleagues (Mason, Sinha, Kerr & McCormick, 1991; McCormick & Mason, 1986). These researchers gave what they call "little books" (very short picture books with simple text that children can memorize and "read") to children during the summer prior to kindergarten and found enhanced print knowledge during kindergarten and first grade; they found no effects for reading comprehension or word knowledge. In addition, the "little book" intervention involves atypical materials and activities, making it difficult to generalize results to prototypical adult–child literacy activities during the preschool period. In sum, no experimental research clearly demonstrates that the frequency or form of shared picture book reading during the preschool period affects later reading achievement. In a recent review of the research on this issue, Scarborough and Dobrich (1991, p. 35) concluded that "the evidence for the efficacy of reading to preschoolers is considerably weaker than is generally believed."

On the other hand, the results from this and related research programs (e.g., Karweit, 1989; Mason et al., 1991) are sufficiently promising to warrant long-term outcome studies, research on the specific processes that underlie early literacy experiences, and clinical use of preliteracy interventions. Our general advice to those interested in improving children's preliteracy abilities is to actively engage the child. Shared reading has far more impact when it is an interactive process that captures the child's attention and involvement. Practical limitations necessitate creative solutions to finding the human resources to accomplish this end. Whether through teachers, volunteers, grandparent aides, college students, school-aged readers, or parent rotations, we must find some way to provide children with small-group reading experiences and to make the level of the shared reading sensitive to the child's ability level. Questions too hard or too easy for the child will be ineffective. Above all, shared reading should be fun. Enjoyment will occur naturally if topics are chosen and pursued according to the child's interest. More important than improving specific preliteracy skills is fostering a love of reading. Shared storybook reading is not a magic potion: Academic failure is complex and variously determined. However, with this complicated problem that cries out for any practical contribution, the study of reading interactions with children at the onset of language development seems a good place for meaningful research and social policy initiatives.

Appendix. Resources for Implementing and Evaluating Dialogic Reading

Training Videotapes

1) *Dialogic Reading: A Video Workshop* (for two- and three-year-olds)
2) *Dialogic Reading for Head Start, K, and pre-K*

For information on these videotape training packages write to: Acorn Productions, 1 Youngs Lane, Setauket, NY 11733.

Evaluation Measures

Peabody Picture Vocabulary Test-Revised. Circle Pines, MN: American Guidance Service.

Expressive One Word Picture Vocabulary Test. Novato, CA: Academic Therapy Publications.

Illinois Test of Psycholinguistic Abilities. Urbana: University of Illinois Press.

Developing Skills Checklist. Monterey, CA: McMillan/McGraw Hill.

Recommended Books

Bond, Michael, *Paddington's ABC*: New York: Viking.

Bridwell, Norman, *Clifford Takes a Trip*, New York: Scholastic.

Dubanevich, Arlene, *Pigs in Hiding*. New York: Four Winds Press.

Duke, Kate, *Guinea Pigs Far and Near*. New York: E.P. Dutton.

Duke, Kate, *What Would a Guinea Pig Do?*. New York: E.P. Dutton.

Edwards, Hazel, *Stickybeak*. Milwaukee: Gareth Stevens.

Freeman, Don, *A Pocket For Corduroy*. New York: Viking.

Gackenbach, Dick, *A Bag Full of Pups*. New York: Houghton Mifflin.

Gantos, Jack, *Rotten Ralph's Show and Tell*. Boston: Houghton Mifflin Company.

Gay, Marie-Louise, *Rainy Day Magic*. Niles, Illinois: Albert Whitman & Company.

Hill, Eric, *Spot's Baby Sister*. New York: G.P. Putnam's Sons.

Hill, Eric, *Spot's Birthday Party*. New York: G.P. Putnam's Sons.

Hood, Thomas, *Before I Go To Sleep*. New York: G.P. Putnam's Sons.

Huff, Barbara, *Once Inside the Library*. Boston: Little, Brown, Inc.

Johnson, Angela, *Do Like Kyla*. New York: Orchard, Division of Franklin Watts.

Kimmel, Eric, *I Took My Frog to the Library*. New York: Viking Penguin.

Lingren, Astrid, *I Want to Go to School Too*. New York: R & S.

Saunders, Dave & Julie, *Dibble and Dabble*. New York: Bradbury Press.

Seuss, Dr., *Hop On Pop*. Baltimore: Random House.

Slobodkina, Esphyr, *Caps for Sale*. New York: Harper Collins.

Wolff, Ashley. *Come With Me*. New York: E.P. Dutton.

Book Guides

Guides for reading the books listed above, designed for either teachers or parents, are available for a nominal charge from The Stony Brook Reading and Language Project, Department of Psychology, Stony Brook, NY 11794–2500.

An extensive set of book guides for an interactive reading technique similar to dialogic reading are available from the Center for Social Organization of Schools, The John Hopkins University, 3505 North Charles Street, Baltimore, MD 21218–2498.

References

Adams, M.J. (1990). *Beginning to read: Thinking and learning about print*. Cambridge: MIT Press.

Alexander, K.L. & Entwisle, D.R. (1988). Achievement in the first 2 years of school: Patterns and processes. *Monographs of the Society for Research in Child Development, 53* (2, Serial No. 218).

Arnold, D.S., Lonigan, C.J., Whitehurst, G.J. & Epstein, J.N. (in press). *Accelerating language development through picture book reading: Replication and extension to a videotape training format*. Journal of Educational Psychology.

Black, M.H. (1966). Characteristics of the culturally disadvantaged child. In J.L. Frost & G.R. Hawkes (Eds.), *The disadvantaged child: Issues and innovation* (pp. 45–50). Boston: Houghton Mifflin.

Bush, B. (1990). Parenting's best kept secret: Reading to your children. *Reader's Digest, 136*, 67–70.

Cornell, E.H., Senechal, M. & Broda, L.S. (1988). Recall of picture books by 3-year-old children: Testing and repetition effects in joint reading activities. *Journal of Educational Psychology, 80*, 537–42.

Durkin, D. (1966). *Children who read early*. New York: Teacher's College Press.

Elley, W.B. (1989). Vocabulary acquisition from listening to stories. *Reading Research Quarterly, 24*, 175–87.

Feitelson, D. & Goldstein, Z. (1986). Patterns of book ownership and reading to young children in Israeli school-oriented and nonschool-oriented families. *Reading Teacher, 39*, 924–30.

Gordon, A.M. (1984). Adequacy of responses given by low-income and middle-income kindergarten children in structured adult-child conversations. *Developmental Psychology, 20*, 881–98.

Karweit, N. (1989). The effects of a story-reading program on the vocabulary and story comprehension skills of disadvantaged prekindergarten and kindergarten students. *Early Education and Development, 1*, 105–14.

Lesser, G.S., Fifer, G. & Clark, D.H. (1965). Mental abilities of children from different social-class and cultural groups. *Society for Research in Child Development Monographs, 30* (4, Serial No. 102).

Leung, C.B. & Pikulski, J.J. (1990). Incidental learning of word meanings by kindergarten and first grade children through repeated read aloud events.

Yearbook of the National Reading Conference. Chicago: National Reading Conference.

Mason, J.M., Sinha, S., Kerr, B. & McCormick, C.E. (1991, June). *Emergent literacy intervention: Theory and application*. Paper presented at the national conference, New Directions in Child and Family Research: Shaping Head Start in the Nineties, Arlington, VA.

McCormick, C.E. & Mason, J.M. (1986). Intervention procedures for increasing preschool children's interest in and knowledge about reading. In W.H. Teale & E. Sulzby (Eds.), *Emergent literacy: Writing and reading* (pp. 90–115). Norwood, NJ: Ablex.

Moerk, E.L. (1985). Picture-book reading by mothers and young children and its impact upon language development. *Journal of Pragmatics, 9,* 547–66.

Moore, E.G.J. (1982). Language behavior in the test situation and the intelligence test achievement of transracially and traditionally adopted black children. In L. Feagans & D.C. Farran (Eds.), *The language of children reared in poverty* (pp. 141–62). London: Academic Press.

National Assessment of Educational Progress (1991). *The 1989–90 national assessment of reading and literature*. Denver: NAEP.

Ninio, A. (1980). Picture book reading in mother-infant dyads belonging to two subgroups in Israel. *Child Development, 51,* 587–90.

Ninio, A. & Bruner, J.S. (1978). The achievement and antecedents of labeling. *Journal of Child Language, 5,* 1–15.

Olson, S.L., Bayles, K. & Bates, J.E. (1986). Mother-child interaction and children's speech progress: A longitudinal study of the first two years. *Merrill-Palmer Quarterly, 32,* 1–20.

Pikulski, J.J. & Tobin, A.W. (1989). Factors associated with long-term reading achievement of early readers. In S. McCormick, J. Zutell, P. Scharer & P. O'Keefe (Eds.), *Cognitive and social perspectives for literacy research and instruction* (pp. 123–34). Chicago: National Reading Conference.

Raz, I.S. & Bryant, P. (1990). Social background, phonological awareness and children's reading. *British Journal of Developmental Psychology, 8,* 209–25.

Scarborough, H.S. (1989). Prediction of reading dysfunction from familial and individual differences. *Journal of Educational Psychology, 81,* 101–8.

Scarborough, H.S. & Dobrich, W. (1991). *On the efficacy of reading to preschoolers*. Manuscript submitted for publication.

Scarborough, H.S., Dobrich, W. & Hager, M. (1991). Preschool literacy experience and later reading achievement. *Journal of Learning Disabilities, 24,* 508–11.

Scherer, N.J. & Olswang, L.B. (1984). Role of mothers' expansions in stimulating children's language production. *Journal of Speech and Hearing Research, 27,* 387–96.

Share, D.L., Jorn, A.F., MacLean, R., Matthews, R. & Waterman, B. (1983). Early reading achievement, oral language ability, and a child's home background. *Australian Psychologist, 18,* 75–87.

Stevenson, H.W. & Newman, R.S. (1986). Long-term prediction of achievement and attitudes in mathematics and reading. *Child Development, 57,* 646–59.

Valdez-Menchaca, M.C. (1990). *Child effects on maternal language: Their implication for long-term maintenance of early intervention effects.* Unpublished doctoral dissertation, State University of New York, Stony Brook, NY.

Valdez-Menchaca, M.C. & Whitehurst, G.J. (in press). Accelerating language development through picture-book reading: A systematic extension to Mexican day-care. *Developmental Psychology.*

Vygotsky, L. (1978). *Mind in society.* Cambridge: Harvard.

Ward, M. (1971). *Them children: A study in language learning.* New York: Holt, Rinehart, & Winston.

Wells, G. (1985). Preschool literacy-related activities and success in school. In D.R. Olson, N. Torrence & A. Hilyard (Eds.), *Literacy, language, and learning* (pp. 229–55). New York: Cambridge University Press.

White, K. (1982). The relation between socioeconomic status and academic achievement. *Psychological Bulletin, 91,* 461–81.

Whitehurst, G.J., Arnold, D.S., Epstein, J.N., Angell, A.L., Smith, M. & Fischel, J.E. (1992). *A picture book reading intervention in daycare and home for children from low-income families.* Manuscript submitted for publication.

Whitehurst, G.J., Falco, F., Lonigan, C.J., Fischel, J.E., Valdez-Menchaca, M.C. & Caulfield, M. (1988). Accelerating language development through picture-book reading. *Developmental Psychology, 24,* 552–8.

6 Fostering Children's Early Literacy Development through Parent Involvement: A Five-Year Program

Derek Toomey and Judith Sloane

This paper reports results of the West Heidelberg Early Literacy Project (WHELP) from 1987 to 1992. The project works to help low income and working class parents develop the literacy skills of their four-year-old children by, among other things, reading regularly with them. Findings that we report include discussion of issues related to implementation of the program, such as management of home–school relations when reaching out to disadvantaged families, and effects of the project on children's literacy competence.

The Use of Reach Out Strategies

A great deal of research has shown that children's family environments are rather more predictive of their school learning than are indicators of their socioeconomic status or "social class" (Hess and Holloway, 1984; Scott-Jones, 1984; Toomey, 1989a; White, 1982). In other words at each socioeconomic level there are great differences between family environments in their influence on children's schooling. The lack of responsiveness of schools in disadvantaged localities to this variation can actually exacerbate educational disadvantage. In an earlier study (Toomey, 1986) we worked with Prep level (kindergarten) teachers to involve parents in disadvantaged localities in their children's literacy development. Typically the teachers only worked with parents who came into the school to find out how they could help their children at home; they tended to ignore those who did not come into the school. Yet our evaluation found that many of the parents reluctant to visit the school were trying to do things to help their children's literacy development at home, for example, by reading with them. We also found many of these parents were unsure of themselves and of what they should do in this quasiteaching role. Our most successful project was one based on home visits to parents of preschoolers (Toomey, Keck & Atkinson, 1986). Generally speaking the teachers preferred to work with enthusiastic parents who willingly entered the school and who were confident in their educational role. These parents tended to give very positive feedback to the teachers, who thus were encouraged to continue the program, even though it did little for the low-contact parents. Subsequent research in other low socioeconomic-status (SES) schools showed the gap between the literacy achievements of the low-contact and high-contact parents' children widened significantly over a three-year period, even when initial differences in family supportiveness and children's literacy development were taken into account (Toomey, 1989b).

WHELP was born out of this background. We decided to work with families of four-year-olds (a) because of the importance of the earlier years in fostering children's literacy development (Teale, 1985), and (b) to avoid possible problems related to negative attitudes of teachers toward disadvantaged parents. We also decided to run the project via home visits to have a genuine "reach out" strategy and from 1989 onward to work via preschools as a more cost-effective strategy.

Influences On Children's Literacy Competence

Children learn a great deal within the home in the process of general upbringing. This natural learning (Teale, 1986) results from the child's active efforts to learn rather than an adult's deliberate intention to teach. Natural learning is also tied to outcomes with real life meaning (e.g., efforts to talk, to eat, to sing), because it occurs in a context of normal everyday activities, unlike school learning situations in which the learning is often devoid of everyday meaning, for example, phonic drills and rote learning tasks.

Much learning within the family is adult-assisted, but is natural in the above sense in that it involves the adult simplifying the task for the child until the child can operate independently (e.g., holding toddlers' hands to assist them to walk, then taking away one hand, then another). This scaffolding support bolsters naturally occurring behavior such as language learning, as shown by parents' simplifications of the language they use with a young child (Snow and Ferguson, 1978). In parent–child book-reading episodes, parents are likely to supply world knowledge and word meanings to help understanding; when reading unfamiliar books or with younger children they are likely to to ask questions that require more intellectual efforts by the child (e.g., making predictions or drawing inferences from the text), if they feel the child is competent enough or the story familiar enough. That is, parents increase their demands as the child becomes more skilled or knowledgable (Goodsit, Ralton & Perlmutter, 1988). Through such supportive interactions children acquire a great of knowledge that is required for school success (Scott-Jones, 1984; Snow, Dubber & De Blauw, 1982; Snow & Goldfield, 1983).

Preschool children informally acquire a good deal of emergent literacy knowledge in the process of being read to: knowledge of concepts about print (Clay, 1979), letter recognition (Burgess, 1982; McCormick & Mason, 1986; 1989), knowledge of the written language register (Chomsky, 1972; Feitelson, Bracha & Goldstein, 1986; Purcell-Gates, 1988; Purcell-Gates & Dahl, in press; Snow and Goldfield, 1983), word knowledge (Fodor, 1966; Moerk, 1985; Swinson, 1985), understanding of the functions of print (Teale, 1984), knowledge of how books convey meaning (Cochran-Smith, 1984; Harkness & Miller, 1982; Snow & Ninio, 1986; Robinson & Sulzby, 1984), intellectual skills (Elkins & Spreadbury, 1991; Goodsit et al., 1988; Teale, 1985), understanding the difference between the meaning and the message-carrying medium (Olson, 1982), and metalinguistic knowledge (Goodman, 1986; Sulzby, 1986). In addition, systematic studies of reading to children in the classroom have shown positive effects both on children's print knowledge and on their comprehension abilities (Brown, Cromer & Weinberg, 1986; Dowhower, 1987; Feitelson et al., 1986; Morrow, 1988; Morrow, O'Connor & Smith, 1990).

A major resource helping children understand print is their command of spoken language (Rubin, 1986). But the language of typical school texts is likely to differ considerably from the language of conversations within the home that make up young children's major experience of spoken language (Chafe, 1982; Donaldson, 1984; Heath, 1983; Purcell-Gates, 1988; Rubin, 1986). Conversationalists can use a whole range of extralinguistic devices for conveying meaning, such as gesture, posture, variations in pitch, tone, emphasis, and speed of speech, and pointing to physically present objects. They share a common spatial and temporal context, and usually a great deal of common experience, all of which facilitates implicit reference (Snow, 1983). By contrast, writers usually rely on words alone to convey meaning – the reference must be deictic and the meaning decontextualized. Writers also have more time to construct the text, and as a consequence, they tend to pack it more densely with meaning, as the result of the use of more elaborate syntax (Chafe, 1982).

The central hypothesis of this research is that reading children's literature aloud to children is an important way of bridging the gap between informal conversational language and school texts, for it gives children familiarity with the language of decontextualized texts, through the medium of speech, with all its extraverbal aids to convey meaning, and without the necessity of acquiring skills of decoding written language. Not only that, it helps children to imagine nonpresent objects, events, and relationships and to think about such objects, events, and relationships in both spatial and temporal frames of reference different from their own, and it teaches them to act as the member of an anonymous audience. In short, it assists them in thinking about the world at a distance, as it is known to them via words alone. Further, in discussion of the text, children learn to perform mental operations on representations of ideas, objects, and events mediated solely by symbolic means. A great deal of school work has this character – learning about the world at a distance via language and performing mental operations on the knowledge required. Children can also gain the same benefits from experiences with decontextualized spoken language as with traditional stories in an oral tradition. But in parent–child storybook reading sessions we find a well established and validated cultural practice that offers many opportunities for natural learning and requires little by way of formal teaching of the parents concerned.

Operation of the Project

The project developed through three phases with three different methods of delivering books to families: (a) 1987–8 via home visits (Home Visit); (b) 1989 via Preschool (1), and (c) 1990–1 via Preschool (2) and Preschool (3).

The Home Visit Phase

The target population was all families with children who were to begin school in February, 1988, at two particular schools. Families were recruited via contacts with preschools, schools, and Infant Welfare Clinics. Of the 82 families initially contacted we eventually worked with 60 having the following characteristics: 51.8 percent were single-parent families, all of the males were unemployed or in semi- or unskilled occupations, 42 percent of parents left school before grade 10, 48 percent at grade 10, and 10 percent above grade 10, and all lived in public housing.

The aim was to give families relatively intensive contact (one visit per week) until they were judged to be self-operating, at which point they were phased out of the program of visits and replaced by another family. Visits continued into 1988 until the whole group had been served. On average, each family received books for a period of eight weeks. The Home Visit program was essentially exploratory, attempting to establish the feasibility of the project and working out effective strategies. Judith Sloane, an experienced teacher and researcher, conducted the home visits, and her work was crucial in developing the approach we adopted to instruct parents. The approach derived in part from our ideas in the beginning but also from what we found out later.

The main aim of the home visits was to enthuse the children and through them the parents, about books. At each home visit the children would usually greet the visitor with eagerness to see the new books. Initially the visitor would read to the children, but the aim was to encourage the parents to do so. The function of the home visits was to exchange books (five at each visit) and to give the parents advice about literacy-encouraging behaviour, including pamphlets and fliers on occasion. This advice was adjusted to the level of competence and interest of the parent, as were the literacy demands of the books left behind.

Our parent-education program had three primary goals that we attempted to achieve with a variety of strategies. The first goal was to interest the children in books and thus increase their attention span for decontextualized text by reading with expression to imitate speech and gradually increasing the amount of text parents can read continuously without discouraging children's questions and comments. The second goal was to ensure that the children understand the text by having parents intersperse it with explanations and context clues, make connections to the children's own experience, and explain unfamiliar words and ideas, using pictures when possible. The third goal was to help the children pay attention to print by encouraging parents to point out its uses in everyday life (e.g., newspapers, recipes, invitations, etc.), to run a finger under it while reading to ensure that children can see it, and to read favorite stories repeatedly, thereby freeing their attention to focus on it itself. Other strategies were to provide families with alphabet friezes, alphabet books, and information about such television programs as "Sesame Street" as well as to supply them with paper and pencils for drawing, scribbling, and writing.

Essential to our program was careful selection of books. Criteria that we used when selecting books included strong phonological attraction, including onomatopoeia, assonance, alliteration, rhymes, and rhythm; the move from picture books used for labeling to books with a strong story line and dramatic interest (e.g., traditional stories familiar to the culture such as "The Three Bears"); attractive, well-spaced print; and nonsexist language with no racist elements.

For families who did not read English we used audiotaped spoken readings of the text, in addition to the text; for ESL families we used books in the first language and children's books in English accompanied by translations in the first language (in Melbourne the Free Kindergarten Union makes these translations available). A small number of non-English reading parents were referred to an adult-literacy agency.

Evaluation of the Home Visit Program

We obtained information for evaluation purposes from written records of weekly visits that updated children's progress and other significant information, structured interviews that enabled an assessment of the initial supportiveness of the home for literacy development, an assessment of the child's interest in literacy, a battery of performance tests covering letter recognition, recognition of environmental print with and without logo, knowledge of concepts about print, and children's ability to read and write their own names. In addition, we assessed the children at the end of 1988 using the Sloane-Tuer Early Literacy Profile and obtained test data and teacher report data for a comparison group of children who in 1987 planned to attend a nearby low-SES school. The results, in the main, showed hardly any significant differences in subsequent literacy competence between the two groups. More differences favored the comparison group than the experimental, but, because membership in the experimental and comparison groups was confounded with school membership, it is impossible to tell whether results were because of an ineffective program or because of differences between schools.

Despite the failure to find evidence of significant effects on children's literacy, we did learn a great deal as a result of the Home Program (Sloane & Toomey, 1988). One important finding was that the key to involving parents was the child's enjoyment of being read to. At the initial visit the home visitor read a story to the child with the parent present, reading with much expression and dramatic involvement. Any doubts the parent had about participating usually dissolved on seeing their child's enjoyment. The children would look forward to each visit and participate actively in the choice of books. This enjoyment frequently lead the children to request reading sessions and helped to maintain the momentum of the program. The home visitors reading to the child also had the effect of showing parents how to read with expression. Some of them had already tried reading to the child, but without success, because of their reading in a monotone. Remarks were made to the home visitor such as, "I try to do it like you now and she loves it."

We also discovered the need for short books. Many of the children in the program had not been read to regularly before, or before their preschool year; consequently, their attention span for listening to a story was often limited. Also, many of the mothers were not used to reading and preferred to read short books aloud. In buying books we tried to build up a supply of short books with repetitive and predictable patterns (Bridge, 1985) and themes and language likely to appeal to this group.

Another benefit of this project was the categorization of parents' reactions to the program. This system was based on interview data and the home visitor's knowledge, which was gained as she worked to establish an open, trusting relationship with the parents. Thus the boundary between project-related issues and other issues blurred, and the conversations touched on many other matters. Issues discussed include such matters as choice of schools, school problems, problems of older children, managing of disciplinary problems, sickness, domestic relationships, money problems, and concerns with government agencies, as well as matters more directly concerned with literacy development. The visitor became well known in the locality as "the book lady," an identity which helped ease of access with families new to the project.

Drawing on her detailed notes of these home visits, the home visitor produced the following categorization after a lengthy process of analysis and discussion with both researchers. After deciding which categories to use, she placed each family in the scheme. One month later the home visitor produced a description of each case, and Toomey then made an independent classification of each family according to the categories. The level of agreement was 86 percent. Discrepant classifications were then discussed and reclassified.

Supportive-sophisticated.   One parent stood out from the rest as especially interested in her children's education and relatively confident and sophisticated about how she supported it. She strongly encouraged her children's language development, talking with them often, asking their opinions, and promoting their critical thinking. She encouraged the use of "decontextualised" language, e.g., speaking in complete sentences. She asked *how* as well as *what* questions. She also voiced firm beliefs that children have rights to make decisions for themselves. She also urged them to have their own opinions about events in the news or issues arising at school. The family environment scored high on the literacy support scale. This mother was a member of the School Council, and the preschool teacher admitted feeling intimidated by her confident and articulate manner. All told 11 or 12 percent of parents could be classified in this way, but not at such a high level of sophistication.

Supportive-unsophisticated.   Most parents, some 69 percent, fall into this group. They are extremely interested in their children's education and keen to help but, generally speaking, lack in knowledge and confidence about how to go about it. There are considerable variations within the group. Some of the parents had already been doing some of the activities we suggest (e.g., reading to the child, providing pencils and paper, teaching the alphabet). However, the frequency of reading to the children and the supply of books did not reach the desired level. Some had already read to their children but without success because of the absence of expression and had given up. Modeling by the home visitor and the use of audiotapes, however, led to a definite improvement in all these cases. One such parent, Jocelyn, remarked, "I really enjoy doing it now." Other parents had bought books on child development and preparing for school.

Overall, these parents who were already engaged in support activities were seeking confirmation and guidance. They tended to be unsure whether they were doing the "right thing." For example they would ask questions about whether to teach sounds or letter names for the alphabet or to read favorite books or encourage variety. Others had been rather less active and were more unsure about what to do, though very keen to help. Some of them read to their child with the child facing them, holding up the book for the child to see (following the kindergarten teachers' practice in reading to the group).

Supportive-independent-minded.   This small group of parents (two families) showed interest in helping with the children's education but were initially resistant to advice and critical of professionals working in schools and preschools. For example, Holly's child was due to be four and a half at the beginning of the school year, and both the preschool teacher and the home visitor advised keeping the child home for another year. Holly was unwilling to heed this advice. She thought that keeping her child back for a year would be a sign of low confidence in her child's ability. A similar reaction occurred in two or three other cases. Lisa was extremely critical of the fact that her child had three different teachers in the first weeks of beginning school. If she had had the required transport resources she would have moved the child to another school. These parents were willing to support their children's education at school (e.g., by buying them books, teaching them to write their names, and reading to them), and membership in this category was subject to change, as some parents became less critical and resistant.

Supportive-stressed. This group of parents cares about the children's education and wants to help but often is overwhelmed by more pressing survival needs (custody issues, domestic violence, sickness, supporting extended kin, financial problems, etc.). One of the schools asked the home visitor to continue with home visits to a number of families, presumably because of the child's low level of literacy development, all of which except one come from this category. Membership in this group was also fluid due to changing circumstances. When the pressure lifted most of these families advanced to the second category. At most, about 13 percent of the families fell into this group.

Noncoping. One family clearly fell into this category and a second was a borderline case. The parent who most clearly exemplified it agreed to be in the program but in effect did not participate. Appointments were repeatedly missed, books were lost, and little attempt appeared to have been made to follow the work of the program. The mother herself was not literate and had a problematic extramarital affair. She was involved with a number of welfare agencies in the area (Community Services Victoria and Adult Literacy, to name two), and she had three preschool children who at one time or another during the years were in care. This family was not placed in the supportive-stressed category because we believe that the parent had fundamental problems performing the parental role that were not simply the result of stressful circumstances. We resist the tendency to stigmatize the poor and disadvantaged from a "person blame" perspective, but recognize that not all parents may benefit from the program. In such cases we may merely succeed in raising the level of guilt and sense of pressure without helping the child.

Using these categories as a basis for making comparisons among families revealed some interesting facts. For these analyses, the *unsophisticated-supportive* category was divided into two groups on the basis of the level of family support. The significance of differences was tested using analyses of variance, with the results showing consistent advantages for the more supportive families (see table 1). Differences were significant on our measures of the child's initial interest in literacy ($p < .02$), print knowledge ($p < .05$), interest in writing ($p < .001$), reading self-concept ($p < .003$) and the teacher's rating of family support ($p < .02$), and of the child's level of literacy in 1990 ($p < .003$). Thus,

Table 1   Mean scores for families by type on various measures in the Home Visit study

Measure	Family type						
	1	2	3	4	5	6	Significance level
Family supportiveness for literacy scale	10.0	8.17	8.5	9.14	12.15	14.17	.008
Child's initial interest in literacy	8.5	7.5	7.0	8.33	10.0	11.0	.018
Child's print knowledge	0.85	0.87	0.94	1.04	1.26	1.51	.041
Socioeconomic status	1.92	2.94	3.0	2.52	2.87	3.13	.223
Teachers' rating[a] of family support	3.0	1.0	2.69	1.33	1.5	0.018	.020
Child's reading self-concept	–	2.67	3.5	3.5	4.77	5.5	.003
Concepts about print	–	1.79	1.9	1.86	1.94	1.99	.178
Child's interest in reading	–	1.89	2.0	1.85	1.97	2.0	.546
writing	–	2.67	2.0	4.44	4.83	6.0	.001
School literacy score 1990	–	5.5	9.5	6.47	7.36	13.00	.003

[a] High scores indicate low support
1 = Noncoping; 2 = Stressed; 3 = Supportive-suspicious; 4 = Unsophisticated-supportive, lower level; 5 = Unsophisticated-supportive, higher level; 6 = Sophisticated-supportive.

we found a fairly clear hierarchy of support, which tends to confirm the classification set out above. It is of some note that the measure of SES does not strongly divide these groupings, which reflect important differences between families. This observation gives a strong warning against stereotyping working-class and low-income families on the basis of crude socioeconomic indicators.

An assessment of the extent of the program's adoption during the period of home visits, based on the home visitor's informal observations and discussions with the parents as well as on a follow-up interview in mid-1988 revealed systematic differences across these groups. All parents in the supportive-sophisticated and the supportive-unsophisticated categories were judged to be reading regularly to their children. The one noncoping parent was not. Of the other two categories about half were doing so, as far as we could tell, indicating a success rate of about 86 percent.

There is little doubt in our minds that this success rate is due to the regular supply of books delivered in such a convenient way. The larger of the two schools involved would not allow children to borrow books from the library. The books sent home by the classroom teachers appeared to be from a reading series, intended for the children to read to the parent. We heard many unfavorable comments about these books from parents. Moreover, although the school provided a library of attractive books for parents to borrow and read to their children, only four of the parents in the program used this library, which they had to enter the school to use. Thus we have clear evidence of the need to reach out to parents and of the efficacy of a method of delivering books that bridges the home–school gap.

Although not a prime aim of the project, we also tried to improve the parents' confidence and competence in dealing with the school, which had some influence on parents' participation in the school. For example, at one school the induction program for parents held toward the end of 1987 was attended by twenty parents, whereas normally only about five people would have been expected to turn up. The school's vice-principal expressed the firm opinion that this increased attendance was a result of the program. The Parents Club also saw a considerable increase in attendance after the home visitor at the request of the school encouraged parents to attend. A number of parents in the project are members of the School Council and, generally speaking, the parents have shown a greater readiness to be involved in the school.

The home visitor became a well-known figure in the locality and was greeted warmly by the children. This identity made her access to the families easier, since many parents and children knew about her in advance. Her visits were usually welcome, and she often found that people asked her for advice on all manner of problems. We are in little doubt that the success of the project was due in large part to the element of personal contact.

The Preschool (1), (2), and (3) Programs

Though the Home Visit Program was quite successful in involving the target-group families, the strategy was very costly. The finding that the child's enjoyment of being read to was critical encouraged us to think of working via the preschools, where we could find a captive group of children to enjoy reading and an inexpensive distribution point for the books. The success of a similar project by McCormick and Mason (1986, 1989) gave some support to this approach.

The Preschool (1) program took place in four preschools in the locality, one of which was chosen because over 70 percent of families had non-English speaking backgrounds. The program was run entirely by project staff who visited the preschools to read with the children, attempting to excite them about reading. After having obtained the agreement of the parents to participate, they sent books home with the children for parents to read to them. They held two instruction sessions for parents and sent pamphlets and alphabet friezes home to them. The children took home three books twice a week for a six-month period from June to December (the school year ends in December).

Visits to the preschools in the Preschool (1) project were made by members of the research team, trained teachers with special competences and interest in literacy development. The books chosen were of the same kind as in the Home Visit project. The visitors read to the children in whole classes, small groups, and individually, the accent being on enjoyment. Visitors spent, on average, two hours per week in each preschool. Instruction of parents, along the lines of the Home Visit project, took place at two sessions in the preschool; many parents did not attend them. Instruction also took place individually after the interview conducted for research purposes at home.

Each of the preschools had a morning and an afternoon group. We operated the program with one of the groups and used the alternate group for comparison purposes. There were 68 in the project group, for whom we have complete data, and 32 in the comparison group.

The Preschool (2) program repeated the Preschool (1) program but was implemented by the preschool teachers using books supplied by the project. The data from the 1989 comparison group were used for comparative purposes. Also a posttest-only comparison was made with students from a nearby preschool with a similar catchment area. The Preschool (3) program was the same as the Pre-school (2) program, with the exception that the evaluation design included analysis of a comparison group with pre- and posttests.

Measures Used to Evaluate the Preschool Programs

A battery of tests was used to assess the impact of the programs on children's literacy development, Sulzby's (1985) test of emergent literacy, tests of letter recognition, of ability to read and write one's own name, of recognition of environmental print with and without logo, and of concepts about print. We also used mothers' reports of the child's ability to write his or her name, recognition of environmental print, letter recognition, alphabet knowledge, and the number of words he or she could write.

Shortly after the commencement of the project, each child's mother gave an account of the literacy environment of the home before the project commenced in a structured interview, from which various scales were developed (see Toomey and Sloane, 1991, for details):

General family support for school learning. This scale indicates the general supportiveness of the family environment for school achievement. Items tap the presence of rules, patterns of TV viewing, subscriptions, interaction during book reading.

Family literacy environment. This scale indicates the supportiveness of the family environment for the child's literacy development. Items include frequency of reading to children, family library membership, mothers' reading of books, and parents' education and occupations.

Child's interest in reading and writing. This scale assesses children's interest in books as shown through play, expression of interest in writing, and requests to parents for purchases of books.

Parental illiteracy. This scale indicates the number of parents having reading difficulties in the family (0, 1, 2), based on teachers' reports.

Ethnicity. This feature notes the child's country of birth, parents' country of birth, mother's spoken language fluency, and mother's ability to read English (based on information from preschool teachers).

Initial print knowledge/awareness. This scale includes information about the child's knowledge of the alphabet, ability to read and write, and recognition of environmental print and print concepts. It drew upon information from the performance tests as well as the mothers' reports.

For the Preschool (1) and (2) programs, we repeated the performance measures of literacy competence used in the pretest for the posttest. We then compared the children's performance on these tests and on the Sulzby posttest with the performance of children from a nearby preschool, using a posttest-only comparison ($n = 42$). We also followed up the students in the Preschool (1) program by asking their school teachers at the end of Year One (November, 1990) and in March of Year Three (1992) to make assessments of their literacy development using the Griffin Literacy Profile, a checklist of literacy competences used as part of a portfolio assessment approach (Griffin, 1989).[1] We followed up the Preschool (3) cohort in March of Year One (1992).

Results of the Preschool (1), (2), and (3) programs

Table 2 sets out correlations between the family background and child competence variables in the study. It is based largely on the pooled

Table 2 Correlations between variables in the WHELP data set, 1989–91

	1	2	3	4	5	6	7	8	9	10
1. Socioeconomic status	1.0									
2. Family literacy environment	.45**	1.0								
3. General family support for school learning	.35**	.64**	1.0							
4. Ethnicity	.17*	.49**	.41**	1.0						
5. Parental illiteracy	.30**	.46**	.49**	.60**	1.0					
6. Child's interest in print	.27**	.66**	.58**	.33**	.36**	1.0				
7. Child's initial print knowledge/awareness	.23**	.40**	.35**	.18**	.25**	.55**	1.0			
8. Sulzby pretest	.14**	.30**	.24**	.28**	.16*	.24**	.30**	1.0		
9. Sulzby posttest	.20**	.26**	.26**	.34	.31**	.25*	.35**	.40**	1.0	
10. School literacy score	.34**	.33**	.40**	.19*	.23**	.43**	.60**	.25**	.47**	1.0

For correlations involving ethnicity and parental illiteracy, the *n*s were in the range 160–76. For correlations involving School literacy the *n* was 82. For all other correlations, the *n*s were in the range 283–90.

* $p < .05$
** $p < .01$

data for the Preschool (1), (2), and (3) programs. However, in Preschool (3) some variables were left out, notably the ethnicity and parental illiteracy variables; the correlations for these are based on the Preschool (1) and (2) data alone. The correlations with school literacy (based on the Griffin Literacy Profiles) are from the Preschool (1) study.

Noteworthy is the fact that the family environment measures show stronger connections with the children's literacy competences than does SES. Correlations between SES and child measures, while significant, range between .14 and .34, whereas family measures show much stronger correlations with the child measures. The variables, family literacy environment and family support for school learning, both range from .26 to .66. It is also noteworthy that ethnicity, while highly related to parental illiteracy, showed higher correlations with child measures than did SES, though still generally lower than measures of family support for schooling and literacy.

We examined effects of the programs on children's emergent literacy by comparing the project children's growth in measured competences from start to finish of the program relative to a comparison group. Because assignment to project and comparison groups was not random, detailed information on the children's family backgrounds was acquired and taken into account in all results to be reported. Outcome measures were those described above, but the Sulzby task requires some special discussion. The approach taken in this research lays great stress on the transition from a stage in which the child's oral language competences are dominant to one in which the child begins to acquire a greater knowledge of the written language. Sulzby's (1985) test of emergent literacy development helps describe this transition. Children are asked to read a book they know; their reading is videotaped and classified in terms of the degree to which their language is less conversational and more like the written language of the book.

The effects of the Preschool projects showed a consistent pattern of beneficial effects on children's scores on Sulzby's task, with more project children shifting from oral language-style emergent reading to more written-style renditions of the story. After controlling for family background and children's prior interest in and knowledge of print and for their scores on the Sulzby task at the beginning of the project, significant gains were seen for children of Preschool (1) ($F = 31.57, p < .0001$), and Preschool (2) ($F = 7.31, p = .009$), relative to the 1989 comparison groups. A similar analysis of Preschool (3) compared with a 1991 comparison group again showed the program to raise the score on the Sulzby task ($F = 7.81, p = .007$). Unfortunately, these effects did not carry over to the school literacy score (i.e., the Griffin Literacy Profile);

no significant effects were evident on that measure for any of the intervention groups.

Discussion

The project produced clear effects on the children's performance on the Sulzby task and on their print knowledge, both when operated by the researchers and by the preschool teachers. These results cannot be explained as reflecting differences in the backgrounds of the project and comparison groups. In fact, on the average, the 1989 control group had slightly more advantageous backgrounds (Toomey and Sloane, 1991).

The lack of an effect on school literacy could not be put down to the same design fault as in the Home Visit program, because the children went on to over 40 different primary schools. One could argue that the program had an indirect effect on school literacy via its already established effect on emergent literacy and print knowledge. Each of these variables are significant predictors of school literacy (Toomey, 1992a). The small numbers involved do not justify strong conclusions, but this research does not establish an effect on school literacy and there is little quasiexperimental evidence of such an effect. McCormick and Mason (1986, 1989) provide some evidence of one, but Swinson (1985) provides negative evidence. Topping (1986) indicates that it is common for gains from early intervention programs not to be maintained in the first years of schooling. It may be that few teachers attempt to build on the literacy knowledge that children bring with them from the home, as we found in the Home Visit program.

Our studies confirm the strong influence of the informal learning processes in the home on children's literacy competence and the great value for schools in harnessing these resources for literacy learning. For the large majority of low-income and working-class parents, it is relatively easy to build on the undoubted interest of parents in their children's literacy development by the low-cost method of sending books home via preschools. We have documented a clear effect on children's print knowledge and emergent literacy competence and underlined the importance of working with the child's enjoyment, using nondidactic methods involving informal learning.

The cost effectiveness of the Preschool program was much greater than that of the Home Visit program. The Home Visit program lasted 8 weeks on average and the Preschool program six months, but the Home Visit program expended one third more time per family. The Preschool (2) and (3) programs were even more cost-effective, for, basically, only the cost of books was involved (excluding research costs). This saving provides a strong argument for using preschools in low SES localities to promote children's literacy learning via parental involvement in reading to their children at home. Also, the preschool teachers are likely to have learned much from the researchers working in their schools, so one should not conclude that it is enough to supply books to a preschool, home-reading program without some training or guidance for the teachers.

On the other hand, the Home Visit program had the great advantage of personal contact with the family, which is much more likely to be effective in recruiting families. It gives a more secure and reliable method of delivering books; choice of books and instruction can be adjusted to the individual needs of parent and child; modeling by the home visitor can take place; and parents receive a personal reminder to keep up with the program, intensified by some bonding with the visitor. In addition, it is possible to restrict the program to those in need, an option not easily available in a preschool-based program.

On reflection, the Home Visit program was probably too brief. It began as a project for families in the locality and not as a research project proper. Its aim was merely to explore the feasibility of such a project, and it certainly provided much useful information. We found that parents were interested and responded readily to their children's enjoyment; that some parents need help learning to read with expression; that the parents' attention span and interest in the books is of some importance; that nearly all parents want to help their children, though their abilities and resources for doing so vary greatly; that the element of personal contact is very effective in engaging parents; and that a regular supply of appropriate books is invaluable. The preschool-based program can provide a regular supply of books but not the element of personal contact. We were quite unsuccessful in persuading busy preschool teachers to make home visits.

Herein lies a fundamental weakness of the Preschool (1) (2) and (3) programs, their restricted ability to adapt the program to the individual needs of the family, an issue made salient by the range of differences we found among families. The rare supportive-sophisticated families are relatively easy to involve in schooling; the danger is that teachers will rely only on the easy methods of involvement that seem to work with such families (e.g., impersonal invitations) (Toomey, 1992b). Many parents of this kind may enjoy a good deal of personal development as they learn more about current educational ideas and practices, child development, and the politics of school governance. They can provide an extremely useful resource not only by reading in the school with the children who are not read to at home, but also by organizing home–school activities themselves, under the guidance of the teacher.

Similar benefits for the school and the parents can occur in the case of the supportive-unsophisticated parents, but generally speaking more effort needs to be made to reach them and to build their confidence. The element of personal contact is vital – a *personal* invitation by letter, phone call, or word of mouth can make such a difference to breaking the ice, especially when the value of the parent's contribution is emphasized. Most teachers could probably do more to involve this type of parent in their children's learning at home.

Many teachers come from noncollege-educated parents and are the first in their families to take up a professional occupation. As a result, many tend to emphasize their professional competence and identity as a source of security. In response to the challenge presented to them by the independent-minded parent, teachers are likely to define them as pushy or otherwise unsatisfactory, and they may prefer to deal only with the more compliant parents who accept the teacher's view of desirable school practice. The independent-minded need handling with openness and tolerance, and many teachers need assistance to acquire these attitudes.

The stressed families require sensitive handling and the realization that their levels of involvement will vary with circumstance. The school needs to coordinate with other agencies (see Nickse and Quezada, chapter 9) to provide support for these families and to give extra support to their children in school. Schools need to be sensitive about not making demands on the stressed and noncoping parents that raise their levels of guilt and anxiety without helping the children. Having elder siblings, grandparents, or neighbors read with children at home is one way to alleviate problems these parents face in helping their children.

It is important to note that the Preschool programs did not reach those families not using preschools (about ten percent in Victoria), a figure likely to be higher in a low-SES area. We also encountered a lot of refusals to our Home Visit program, suggesting that many families would not be reached by a preschool based program. There is then an important need for Year One programs geared toward parents of children who show early signs of encountering literacy problems. At this point parents are likely to respond to a personal invitation to become involved in order to help prevent further problems. The kind of entry-level Kindergarten program initiated by Edwards (1991) seems particularly appropriate here.

Note

1   The Griffin Literacy Profile (Griffin, 1989) is a checklist of literacy competences grouped together in a seven-part hierarchy. Children are rated as

to whether (a) they have mastered the competences in the grouping and display them as a behavior pattern (score 3), (b) this pattern of behavior is developing, some competences having been mastered, and others not (score 2), (c) the student is beginning to show the behavior pattern (score 1), and (d) the student shows none of the behavior in question (score 0). The resulting seven scores are summed to produce the total score. The groupings of behavior are based on a substantial empirical survey of the behaviors teachers report as relevant to assessing literacy competence as well as a good deal of analysis of these results and the use of standardized tests to establish validity. This form of testing is particularly appropriate in a school system that has school-based curriculum development, the widespread adoption of a whole language approach, and little use of basal reading schemes. The literacy profiles have been officially adopted by the Victorian Ministry of Education.

References

Bridge, C. (1985). Predictable books for beginning readers and writers. In M. Sampson (Ed.), *The pursuit of literacy* (pp. 74–85). Dubuque, IA: Kendall Hunt.

Brown, M.H., Cromer, P.S. & Weinberg, S.H. (1986). Shared book experiences in kindergarten: Helping children come to literacy. *Early Childhood Research Quarterly, 1,* 397–405.

Burgess, J.C. (1982). The effects of a training program for parents of pre-schoolers on the children's school readiness. *Reading Improvement, 19* (4), 313–18.

Chafe, W. (1982). Spoken and written English. In D. Tannen (Ed.), *Spoken and written language* (pp. 35–53). Norwood, NJ: Ablex.

Chomsky, C. (1972). Stages in reading development and reading exposure. *Harvard Educational Review, 42,* 1–33.

Clay, M. (1979). *The early detection of reading difficulties,* (2nd ed.). Surrey, England: Heinemann.

Cochran-Smith, M. (1984). *The making of a reader.* Norwood, NJ: Ablex.

Donaldson, M. (1984). Speech writing and modes of learning. In A. Oberg, H. Goelman & F. Smith (Eds.), *Awakening to literacy* (pp. 174–84). London: Heinemann Educational.

Dowhower, S.L. (1987). Effects of repeated reading on second grade transitional readers' fluency and comprehension. *Reading Research Quarterly, 4,* 389–406.

Edwards, P. (1991). Fostering early literacy through parent coaching. In E. Hiebert (Ed.), *Literacy for a diverse society* (pp. 45–62). New York: Teachers College Press.

Elkins, J. & Spreadbury, J. (1991, November). Family literary practices from pre-school to grade 1. Paper read to annual conference of the Australian Association for Research in Education, Surfer's Paradise, Queensland, Australia.

Feitelson, D., Bracha, K. & Goldstein, Z. (1986). Effects of listening to series stories on first graders' comprehension and use of language. *Research in the Training of English, 20* (4), 339–50.

Fodor, M. (1966). The effect of the systematic reading of stories on the language development of culturally deprived children. Unpublished doctoral dissertation, Cornell University, 1966.

Goodman, Y.M. (1986). Children coming to know literacy. In W. Teale & E. Sulzby (Eds.), *Emergent literacy* (pp. 1–14). Norwood, NJ: Ablex.

Goodsit, S., Ralton, J.G. & Perlmutter, M. (1988). Interaction between mothers and pre-school children when reading a novel and a familiar book. *International Journal of Behavioural Development, 114,* 489–508.

Griffin, P. (1989). *Literacy profile.* Melbourne: Ministry of Education.

Harkness, F. & Miller, L. (1982). A description of the interaction among mother, child and books in a bedtime reading situation. Paper presented at Seventh Annual Boston Conference on language development.

Heath, S.B. (1983). *Ways with words.* Cambridge: Cambridge University Press.

Hess, R.D. & Holloway, S.D. (1983). Family and School as educational institutions. In R.D. Parke (Ed.), *Review of child development research. Vol. 7, The Family,* Chicago: University of Chicago Press.

McCormick, C.E. & Mason, J.M. (1986). Intervention procedures for increasing pre-school children's interest in and knowledge about reading. In W. Teale & E. Sulzby (Eds.), *Emergent literacy* (pp. 90–115). Norwood, NJ: Ablex.

McCormick, C.E. & Mason, J.M. (1989). Fostering reading for Headstart children with little books. In J.B. Allen & J.M. Mason (Eds.), *Risk makers risk takers risk breakers* (pp. 90–115). Portsmouth, NH: Heinemann Educational.

Moerk, E. (1985). Picture book reading by mothers and young children and its impact upon language development. *Journal of Pragmatics, 9,* 547–66.

Morrow, L.M. (1988). Young children's responses to one-to-one readings in school settings. *Reading Research Quarterly, 13* (1), 89–107.

Morrow, L.M., O'Connor, E.M. & Smith, J.K. (1990). Effects of a story reading program on the literacy development of at-risk kindergarten children. *Journal of Reading Behaviour, 22,* 255–75.

Olson, D. (1982). What is said and what is meant in speech and writing. *Visible Language, 16* (2), 151–61.

Purcell-Gates, V. & Dahl, K.L. (in press). Low-SES children's success and failure at early literacy learning in skills-based classrooms. *Journal of Reading Behaviour.*

Robinson, F. & Sulzby, E. (1984). Parents, children and favorite books: an interview study? In J.A. Niles & L.A. Harris (Eds.), *Changing perspectives on reading and language processing instruction* (pp. 142–8). Chicago: 33rd Yearbook of the National Reading Conference.

Rubin, A. (1980). A theoretical taxonomy of the differences between oral and written language. In R.J. Spiro, B.C. Bruce & W.F. Brewer (Eds.), *Theoretical issues in reading comprehension* (pp. 411–38). Hillsdale, NJ: Erlbaum Associates.

Scott-Jones, D. (1984). Family influences on cognitive development and school achievement. In E.W. Gordon (Ed.), *Review of Research in Education, 11* (pp. 259–306). Washington, D.C.: American Educational Research Association.

Sloane, J. & Toomey, D.M. (1988). *The West Heidelberg Early Literacy Project: A work in progress report.* Melbourne: Centre for the Study of Community, Education and Social Change.

Snow, C.E. (1983). Literacy and language: Relationships during the pre-school years. *Harvard Education Review, 53,* 165–89.

Snow, C.E., Dubber, C. & De Blauw, A. (1982). Routines in mother-child interaction'. In L. Feagaans & D.C. Farran (Eds.), *The language of children reared in poverty* (pp. 53–72). New York: Academic Press.

Snow, C.E. & Ferguson, K. (1978). *Talking to children.* New York: Cambridge University Press.

Snow, C.E. & Goldfield, B. (1983). Turn the page please: Situation-specific language acquisition. *Journal of Child Language, 10,* 551–69.

Snow, C.E. & Ninio, A. (1986). The contracts of literacy. In W. Teale & E. Sulzby (Eds.), *Emergent literacy* (pp. 116–38). Norwood, NJ: Ablex.

Sulzby, E. (1985). Children's emergent reading of favourite story books: A developmental study. *Reading Research Quarterly, 20,* 458–81.

Sulzby, E. (1986). Writing and reading: Signs of oral and written language organisation in the young child. In W. Teale & E. Sulzby (Eds.), *Emergent literacy,* (pp. 50–89). Norwood, NJ: Ablex.

Swinson, J. (1985, April). A parental involvement project in a nursery school. *Educational Psychology in Practice,* 19–24.

Teale, W. (1985). The beginnings of reading and writing. In M. Sampson (Ed.), *The pursuit of literacy.* Dubuque, IA: Kendall Hunt.

Teale, W. (1986). Home background and children's literacy development. In W. Teale and E. Sulzby (Eds.), *Emergent Literacy* (pp. 173–205). Norwood, NJ: Ablex.

Toomey, D.M. (1986). Involving parents in their children's reading. *Collected Original Resources in Education, 10* (2), 1–70.

Toomey, D.M. (1989a). Linking class and gender inequality: The family and schooling. *British Journal of Sociology of Education, 10* (4), 389–402.

Toomey, D.M. (1989b). How home-school relations policies can increase educational inequality. *Australian Journal of Education, 33* (3), 284–98.

Toomey, D.M. (1992a, April). Short and medium term effects of parents reading to pre-schoolers in a disadvantaged locality. Paper read to 1992 meeting of the American Educational Research Association, San Francisco.

Toomey, D.M. (1992b). Can parental involvement in schooling increase educational inequality? In R. Merrtens (Ed.), *Ruling the margins: Problematising parent involvement.* London: University of North London Press.

Toomey, D.M., Keck, K. & Atkinson, P. (1986). Early literacy: An intervention program in a disadvantaged locality. *Australian Journal of Early Childhood, 12,* 4.

Toomey, D.M. & Sloane, J. (1991). Developing emergent literacy for children of low socio-economic status: A pre-school based program. *Australian Journal of Reading, 14* (1), 40–9.

Topping, K. (1986). *Parents as educators.* London: Croom Helm.

White, K.R. (1982). The relation between socio-economic status and academic achievement. *Psychological Bulletin, 91* (3), 461–81.

7 Family Reading – Still Got It: Adults As Learners, Literacy Resources, and Actors in the World

Ruth D. Handel and Ellen Goldsmith

Eloise Greenfield's poem "Things" serves as a point of entry into our report on Family Reading.

> Went to the corner
> Walked in the store
> Bought me some candy
> Ain't got it no more
> Ain't got it no more
>
> Went to the beach
> Played on the shore
> Built me a sandhouse
> Ain't got it no more
> Ain't got it no more
>
> Went to the kitchen
> Lay down on the floor
> Made me a poem
> Still got it
> Still got it[1]

Family Reading, like a poem, offers permanent gifts. It provides enjoyable and nourishing reading experiences for adults. It provides rich literacy experiences for children. It deepens relationships between adults and children. By regarding the family as a learning unit engaged in shared literacy experiences, Family Reading offers benefits to all members of the family.

Family Reading is part of the national effort to reach disadvantaged families with the goal of interrupting the cycle of underachievement. This vision has guided our work in the field of family literacy and the development of the Family Reading model. Our curriculum model focuses on book reading, encouraging the development of active reading strategies, and discussion about the books (Goldsmith & Handel, 1990). The objective is to provide tools that will enable adults to foster children's literacy and to develop their own as well. It is our belief that changes in how adults introduce literacy into the family come from new experiences that they have with other adults and with books. Indeed, our stance is that nourishing adults is a necessary first step in fostering family literacy.

In this chapter, we describe our Family Reading model and its theoretical matrix. We present its operation in school and college sites and discuss its effects on adults and the family system. Our focus here is on the impact of the experience on the adult participants. We view the adult participants as literacy learners, as literacy resources in the family, and as actors in the world. We intend this report on Family Reading to suggest some of the conditions that enable adult caretakers – parents and other family members – to foster children's literacy and enhance their own competencies.

Theoretical Matrix

Our goal was to create the conditions that would enable adults to develop the knowledge and disposition to enrich their home literacy environment. The workshops aimed to nourish adults as a necessary first step. Because learning within families takes place within a context of affectively charged relationships, we were mindful of the need to link cognitive and affective elements of learning and to design a workshop model that combined instruction and enjoyment.

We adopt the point of view that literacy is the exercise of competencies needed to "function in society, to achieve one's goals, and to develop one's knowledge and potential" (Kirsch & Jungeblut, 1986), in other words, the ability to use communication to meet personal and social goals. This perspective implies a view of literacy as consisting of points along a broad continuum, rather than as a discrete achievement. Literacy is regarded as occurring in a social context, in many different settings, some overtly instructional, some not, both in and out of school.

The program operationalizes cognitive theories of reading which view the reader as an active constructor of meaning and meaning-making as an interaction between reader and text in which cognitive and metacognitive strategies for generating meaning are employed (see Anderson, Hibert, Scott & Wilkinson, 1985; Freire & Macedo, 1987). Accordingly, generic strategies used by good readers are presented in Family Reading workshops with a pedagogical focus on demonstration and interaction rather than mere telling. In addition, informed by research in reciprocal teaching (Palincsar & Brown, 1984), instructional conversation (Tharp & Gallimore, 1988), and the relation of discussion to reading comprehension (Snow, Barnes, Chandler, Goodman & Hemphill, 1991), the program emphasizes discussion and social interaction.

Our conviction that teaching adults strategies to use with their children is productive in terms of the child's development is based on theories of adult mediation of children's learning following Vygotsky (1978) as well as various ethnographic studies of adult–child book reading (e.g., Cochran-Smith, 1984; Snow, 1983). Research showing reading gains for tutors as well as recipients of tutoring suggested that benefits in adult reading development would result from the parent–child interactions (Cohen, Kulik & Kulik, et al., 1982). Adults scaffold feelings as well as cognitions for their children; Family Reading aimed to link those two domains, seeing children's literature as providing a natural bridge between the two (Taylor & Strickland, 1986). More generally, because parents are influential in transmitting interests, dispositions, and values about learning to their children, we expected they would be particularly powerful sources for linking the cognitive and affective domains (Clark, 1983).

We also drew upon the perspective of adult education, which recognizes and values the rich background of life experience adults bring to a learning situation. Incorporating their parenting and related experiences, the program both builds on and respects adult strengths (Auerbach, 1989). We assume the usefulness for cognitive development and social agency – acting in the world – of making connections between family life and personal goals on one side and literacy enhancement on the other. A corollary to our focus on learner participation and strengths is that the instructor becomes facilitator and colearner rather than top-down teacher.

Finally, following theories of intrinsic motivation, the program endorses enjoyment as a condition for adult learning in the workshop, facilitating the transmission of learning experiences to children at home and sustaining these learnings over time (Csikszentmihalyi, 1990). Attentiveness to motivation was particularly important because, as with most family literacy programs, Family Reading is directed to low-income participants who are not good readers, whose early school experiences may have been problematic, and who are often under a great deal of life stress. The perennial issue of transfer was especially salient in view of Family Reading's goal of helping parents become literacy resources for their children; it was crucial for participants to develop the abilities and dispositions to help them recreate their initial learning experiences in the workshops within the context of the home. Accordingly, motivational elements were built into the workshop structure through the use of children's literature, the focus on enjoyable group interaction, and an overall welcoming, informal, and nonthreatening atmosphere.

Drawing on this multidisciplinary base, we constructed a model that uses "good reader" theory, provides interesting and engaging reading material, creates a social context for reading, builds on the strengths that participants bring to the program, and, through the linkage of instruction and enjoyment, empowers adults by giving them tools to help others as well as themselves.

One additional element that helped shape the program were our own values with regard to reading and our own personal reading histories. We found ourselves remembering books we read as children and books our own children had enjoyed; we recalled stories around the dinner table, poems chanted aloud, the warm orange tones of a favorite illustration, vivid characters, and powerful language. These were the kinds of experiences we wanted to build into Family Reading.

The Workshop Model

In terms of a family literacy typology (Nickse, 1989; chapter 9), the Family Reading model provides direct services to adults and through them to their children. The Family Reading workshop series uses children's literature to promote reading development and integrates practice of reading strategies into demonstrations and discussions of the books. All components of the Family Reading workshop model have instructional and social content. The informal sessions not only provide familiarity with a wealth of good children's books, but are often the first occasion for participants to share and discuss books in a nonjudgmental setting. Throughout the workshop experience participants are invited to construct meaning and to encourage their children to do the same.

Introductory Activities. At the first workshop, orientation activities include a brief overview of the program, book browsing, and an activity in which participants share with others their own childhood memories of storytelling, books, or reading (see table 1 for workshop overview). The aim is to reconnect adults to their childhood experiences. Some workshop participants remember going to libraries as

Table 1   Family reading workshop model

1. Introductory activities
2. Presentation of the genre and the children's book
3. Demonstration of the reading strategy
4. Practice in pairs
5. Group discussion
6. Preparation for the reading at home and book borrowing
7. Optional adult reading

children, or talk about teachers and neighbors who chose special books for them or took time to read to them. Others share folktales or favorite family anecdotes. However, some participants have only negative memories. For them, the workshops are an opportunity to provide better literacy experiences for their children and to enjoy the pleasures of children's literature themselves for the first time.

Presentation of the Genre and the Children's Book. Each workshop presents a different book representing a particular genre of children's literature, such as folktales, family stories, or informational books. Books that are multicultural, gender-fair, and of high quality are selected for their potential to stimulate rich discussion about human relationships and issues important to adults. The instructor reads aloud from the book to provide a model of skilled, fluent reading.

Working with a wide range of children's books helps participants develop schema for diverse text conventions. In addition, familiarity with the different genres leads to such specific understandings as multicultural awareness promoted by folktales, oral language developed through wordless picture books, and the creativity and word play of poetry. Nonfiction is included to promote background information and familiarity with nonnarrative conventions often neglected in early education (Chall, Jacobs & Baldwin, 1990). Participants develop knowledge of the many different types of children's books and learn to select books that are varied and of good quality (see table 2 for books used in a typical workshop series).

Demonstration of the Reading Strategy. Generic reading strategies used by good readers of all ages are central to the program. Presented as a whole-language experience with the children's book, strategies include making predictions, formulating questions (Singer, 1978), learning new information (adapted from Ogle, 1986), and relating reading to personal experience, an elaborative process that helps readers connect text with their own lives. For the sake of clarity, one reading strategy is

Table 2   Family reading workshops – representative titles and strategies

Genre	Children's book	Reading strategy	Adult selection
Folktales	*The Little Red Hen/La Gallina Roja* *Anansi the Spider*	Making predictions	"Strawberries" – a Cherokee tale "Bouki Dances the Kokioki"
Informational books	*Bread Bread Bread* *The People Shall Continue*	Learning new information	bread recipes "Letter from a Birmingham Jail"
Fantasy	*In The Attic*	Generating questions	*Black Boy* (excerpt)
Fables	*The Lion and the Mouse*	Making predictions	*The Mouse at the Seashore*
Family stories	*Stevie* *Tell Me a Story, Mama*	Relating reading to personal experience	"Discovery of a Father" "The Birth of My First Child"
Poetry	*Surprises*	Rereading	Selected poems

The Little Red Hen/La Gallina Roja, retold by L. McQueen (New York: Scholastic, 1985); "Strawberries," in J.N. Smith (Ed.), *Homespun Tales from America's Favorite Storytellers* (New York: Crown, 1988); "Bouki Dances the Kokioki," in D. Wolkstein (Ed.), *The Magic Orange Tree and Other Haitian Folktales* (New York: Schocken, 1980); *Anansi the Spider* (New York: Holt, 1972), by G. McDermott; *Bread Bread Bread* (New York: Lothrop, Lee & Shepherd, 1989), by A. Morris; *The People Shall Continue* (San Francisco: Children's Book Press, 1990), by S. Ortiz; "Letter from a Birmingham Jail," from *Why We Can't Wait* (New York: Harper & Row, 1964), by M.L. King, Jr.; *In the Attic* (New York: Holt, 1984), by H. Oram & S. Kitamura; *Black Boy* (New York: Harper & Row, 1937), by R. Wright; *The Lion and the Mouse* (Chicago: Children's Press, 1986), by M.L. Want; "The Mouse at the Seashore," in A. Lobel (Ed.), *Fables* (New York: Harper and Row, 1980); *Stevie* (New York: Harper & Row, 1986), by J. Steptoe; "Discovery of a Father," by S. Anderson, *Reader's Digest*, 1939; *Tell Me a Story, Mama* (New York: Orchard Books, 1989), by A. Johnson; "The Birth of My First Child," from *I Know Why the Caged Bird Sings* (New York: Random House, 1969), by M. Angelou; *Surprises* (New York: Harper & Row, 1984), poems selected by L.B. Hopkins.

highlighted per workshop. As the workshop series progresses, strategies from former sessions are integrated into the reading. Strategies are presented in simple steps and accessible language. For example, prediction making is presented as two short questions: "What do you think will happen next?" and "Why do you think so?" The workshop leader elicits and distinguishes text-based and reader-based explanations.

Table 3   Presentation of the strategies

Making Predictions
What do you think will happen next?
Why?

Asking Questions
What more do I want to know about this?
What interests me?

Learning New Information
What do you already know about the topic?
Read to learn more.
What did you learn that is new?

Relating Reading to Personal Experience
What does this remind you of?
What's the same?
What's different?

This direct instruction prepares participants to practice the strategy in the workshop and use it later with children. Integrating strategies with children's books makes the instruction appealing (see table 3 strategies; see Goldsmith and Handel, 1990, for details).

Practice in Pairs.   Practicing the strategy in pairs helps consolidate knowledge of the strategy, gain familiarity with the children's book, and anticipate the reading sessions at home. Participants take turns reading aloud with a partner and going through the steps of the strategy using the children's book. Much pleasurable conversation about the book takes place between partners at this time.

Group Discussion.   The discussion is structured to move through three levels: text-based inquiry, personal relevance, and generalization. For example, discussing the folktale of *The Little Red Hen*, initial comments center on whether participants think the hen's friends would help her. Why or why not? The next phase relates the story to the readers' personal experience and makes connections between their lives and the book. Do they know any people like the lazy friends? Have they ever felt like the Little Red Hen? Finally, the discussion brings together the range of experiences from the group and derives larger meanings. What are the issues that *The Little Red Hen* raises? What are the attitudes toward responsibility and sharing?

Typically, participants enjoy discussing the books and relish sharing their experiences. Often the discussions are far-ranging, involving a variety of possible interpretations. Engagement with the reading selection and the sharing of ideas is more important than the one "right" or "best" answer.

Preparation for Reading at Home and Book Borrowing. Next follows the transition to finding ways of presenting the book to children. A key point is that parent–child learning should take place within the context of an enjoyable reading relationship. The genre's appeal and the reading strategy's role in fostering communication and in promoting active reading come under review. Participants are briefed on adaptations that may be necessary in view of children's ages and personalities and are encouraged to try out the strategy and the workshop book at home. Copies of the workshop book are available for borrowing. Ideally, supplemental books of the same genre are also available so that participants can have a choice. Access to good children's books is especially important in low-income communities that lack bookstores and where library hours are often limited. Also provided is a Reading Record on which to document the home reading experience.

Optional Adult Reading. Providing adult readings in the workshops builds on the enthusiasm for the children's book and extends adult literacy by providing another opportunity to use the reading strategy. Adult selections in the Family Reading Program relate to the theme or genre of the children's book or deal with child development or school issues. When time permits, the selections are read and discussed in the workshop. In any case, provision of these selections reinforces the importance of adults as reading role models. A listing of coordinated adult readings is included in table 2.

Reporting on the Reading At Home. With the exception of the first workshop, sessions begin with participants reporting on reading to children at home. Typically eager to share their home experience, whether with the workshop book or another book of the same genre, they relate anecdotes and express pride in their child's responses. The parents' shared reports take on the aspect of a forum for raising and discussing important or puzzling aspects of the home reading. They treat such issues as preparing a child for new concepts, the reasons for rereading, and unexpected reactions to a story. This program component engenders a supportive environment as adults become resources for one another and a sense of group cohesion develops.

Family Reading in Operation

This section describes the Family Reading model at two different sites: the Parent Readers Program in an urban technical college and the Partnership for Family Reading in an urban school district. Both sites have been operating for six years. Holding five or six workshops per year, they represent minimal interventions. Workshops at both sites demonstrate engagement of the adults with the books and with one another. Participants learn from their workshop experience as well as from their experiences reading to children. They consistently describe the Family Reading workshops and the reading relationships established at home as enjoyable.

Scaffolding of cognition and feeling are important elements in both programs. In the Parent Readers Program, the workshop facilitator models and scaffolds reading strategies and modes of discussing books when leading the workshop for parents; parents in turn use similar techniques when reading to children. The Partnership for Family Reading has three levels: staff-development workshops for teachers conducted by a facilitator who models and coaches; the parent workshops conducted by teachers; and parents using the techniques when reading to children.

Two key differences between the sites are the educational levels of participants and the experience of the workshop leaders. While all participants in the Parent Readers Program have completed high school and are pursuing degrees at the college, the educational level of parents in the Partnership for Family Reading ranges widely from elementary school dropouts to the rare college graduate. Second, in the Parent Readers Program, workshops are conducted by a program developer, whereas in the Partnership the workshops are led by elementary school staff who have been trained by one of the program developers.

In both sites, interview, observational, and survey data were collected. Participants reported increased amounts of reading, increased use of reading strategies, and enhanced relationships with children. Content analysis of the data yield the following categories of program impact upon the adult participants: (a) adults as learners[2] (b) adults as literacy resources[3], and (c) adults as actors in the world.[4] These categories are interrelated, and each category includes a range of responses. Our hypothesis is that the learning experiences in the Family Reading workshop empower the adults to serve as literacy resources in the home, that a chain of additional learning is set in motion by the home reading, and that these factors stimulate relationships to a wider world.

The Parent Readers Program

The Parent Readers Program, the original program site, operates as a voluntary program in an urban technical college where the majority of students are first-generation college students.[5] Recruited from remedial reading classes, participants have a high school diploma or equivalent and can easily read the children's books but do not read up to the level of college work. Most participants are mothers, but fathers, aunts, uncles, siblings, as well as prospective parents attend.

The timing of the Program respects the busyness of participants' lives, many of whom have full-time jobs in addition to school and family responsibilities. Attended by 25–35 students, the workshops are scheduled at one- or two-week intervals during a student activity period. Three workshops, an hour and a half in length, are held each semester. To date, 300 students have participated. In many cases, they return semester after semester, expressing a feeling of membership in the Program. At the end of each semester, a Family Reading Celebration brings adults and children together at the college on a Saturday, and children choose books as gifts and adults receive certificates of participation. The Family Reading Celebration has become an important public confirmation of the reading experience (see Handel & Goldsmith, 1988, for details).

A 1987 survey of prospective participants ($n = 60$) indicated that the majority lacked the experience of having been read to as children, and while they read to their own children, at least occasionally, many did not appreciate the educational value of the reading activity. Also, half of them had never used the public library. Self-report data from participants in the 1987–8 workshops ($n = 35$) indicated increased awareness of the importance of reading aloud or using reading comprehension strategies – reading behaviors that had not been well understood or practiced previously. For fourteen participants, these behaviors were the most valuable lessons in the workshops. Self-reports from subsequent participants have been consistent in detailing efforts to use discussion and comprehension strategies when reading to children and in their own adult reading, as well as in reporting an increase in reading in the home.

Reported here is a case study of a mother who has participated for all five years of the Parent Readers Program. Margaret Gillyard is a representative participant in terms of her literacy level and educational background, but unusual in the length of her involvement with the program. The case study demonstrates the powerful impact of long-term connection with a minimal involvement program.

A Case Study: Margaret

Margaret is an African American woman with one child who came to college as an older student and was required to take remedial courses in reading, writing, and math. Having satisfied those requirements and completed the prenursing sequence, she now is about to begin a nursing program. Data about her were collected at two time periods. Margaret was interviewed in 1989, after she had attended twelve workshops over a two-year period. Her daughter was four years old (see Handel & Goldsmith, 1989, for details). Between 1989 and 1992 Margaret attended workshops less often but always brought her daughter to the Family Reading celebration and maintained informal contact with the program director. In 1992, when videotaping capabilities became available, data were collected again. Margaret was videotaped participating in a workshop, a Family Reading Celebration, and talking and reading with her seven-year-old daughter at home.

1989 – Margaret as Literacy Learner. In the 1989 interview, Margaret credited the Parent Readers Program with contributing to her literacy development, both through increased adult reading and through reading to her daughter. Regarding her adult reading, Margaret reported that though she had been reading *Parents Magazine* since her daughter's birth, she would skim headlines impatiently looking for something interesting and reading only bits and pieces. After attending the workshops, she reported a perseverance more characteristic of mature readers, saying, "Even though the title might not seem interesting, when I read like maybe one or two paragraphs, it's like boy this is really interesting. I didn't think this was going to be as interesting."

With pride, she reported that she now read the magazine cover to cover. Her increased ability to translate parental motivation into reading behavior contributes to her growth as a skilled reader through increased practice in addition to providing her with useful information as a parent. There was also a reciprocal relationship between Margaret's own reading development and her reading to her daughter. As with many Family Reading participants, Margaret indicated that reading to the child promoted adult learning: "When I'm reading to her, I'm also learning. Even if it's a simple story, I'm getting something out of it. . . . I'm building my vocabulary." Reading to her daughter has also stimulated her to read more for herself. "After I read to her," Margaret says, " I want to read something grown up."

Margaret learned about her child as a reader. She perceived that her daughter learned to "use her imagination," to have feelings for people in the story, to know that books are a source of information, and to learn something about story structure ("Stories may be sad in the beginning, but have happy endings"). Margaret's increased attentiveness to her daughter as reader and her awareness of the benefits of their reading times together contributed to her motivation to read regularly and made reading to her daughter a self-confirming experience.

1989 – Margaret as Literacy Resource. Margaret functioned as a literacy resource in several ways. As a result of participating in the Parent Readers Program, she became a home tutor. Her frequency of reading to her daughter increased from once to three or four times a week. She credited the workshops with teaching her how to select age-appropriate books ("With too many words on one page her attention span is going to drop") and stimulating her to become sensitive to the effect of her daughter's mood on her response to particular books ("Sometimes one book works, sometimes another").

Margaret also brought more books into her home. In addition to using books from Parent Readers Program workshops, she took her daughter to the library every two weeks, borrowing about seven books each time. She also carried books along whenever she took the child out visiting. In short, she established a reading routine and wove it into the fabric of family life. The child's expectations of being read to were strong. On an overnight visit alone with her grandmother the child insisted on bedtime reading, saying, "Grandma, my mommy reads to me when I go to bed. You have to read to me." So the grandmother did. This incident illustrates how the habit of reading can extend to widening circles.

Margaret recognized that she was serving as a reading role model and was very pleased when her daughter took out a book and imitated her. She expressed pride that her daughter "read" to her, explaining how the child liked to "look at the page and make up her own little stories." She especially delighted in how her daughter lined up "all her little dollies" on the bed and then read to them, "just like Mommy does to me." Margaret's descriptions of reading experiences with her daughter were characterized by pleasure; she explicitly stated that her reading relationship with her daughter brought them closer.

1989 – Margaret as Actor in World.   Margaret extended herself to other children by visiting her daughter's day-care center to read to the children on a regular basis. She reported asking the children questions "to see if they know what's going on," as she learned from the Parent Readers Program workshops. This confidence in her skills and ability to reach out to a community institution appeared to be an outgrowth of her participation in the Program.

Data from four additional case studies conducted in 1989 (Handel & Goldsmith, 1989) confirm the representativeness of Margaret's experiences as learner, literacy resource, and actor in the world. Follow-up data three years later show Margaret's increased understanding of literacy, her contributions to her daughter's school achievement, and her flexible, skilled use of reading strategies.

1992 – Margaret as Learner.   By this time Margaret was more articulate about the specific factors that promote literacy development. She showed an understanding of how strategic reading contributes to motivation and comprehension, explaining that her daughter "was getting more out of me reading to her because I was using strategies that I learned in the workshop . . . and asking more specific questions." She contrasted this with prior behavior in which she would ask names of objects. Having experienced how interest led to competency in her own reading, Margaret worked to promote her daughter's interest. She said, "By me using these strategies, I think she became more interested in reading. When she did learn to read, she became a better reader." Margaret again stated that the workshops made her become a better reader, adding that this helped her become a better student in college as well.

1992 – Margaret as Actor in the World.   Margaret became involved in her daughter's elementary school, frequently visiting and consulting with her daughter's teachers. She monitored and valued her daughter's achievements, saying:

> She made the principals' reading club. She's gotten numerous certificates. And I have to say this. This is great. During National Library Week her teacher chose 15 of the best readers to read to fifth grade classes and she was chosen. . . . And she read the book *Amazing Grace.*

Amazing Grace was one of the books that Margaret brought home from a Parent Readers Program workshop. Her daughter liked the book so much that she brought it in to her teacher to read to the class and learned to read it herself. In this, we see an example of how a bridge was formed between Margaret's workshop experience and her daughter's school experience.

1992 – Margaret as Skilled Literacy Resource. The videotape of Margaret reading to her daughter suggests that she extended her repertoire of behaviors as a reading tutor. Excerpts of conversation during the reading illustrate the range and flexibility of strategies Margaret used to promote learning and make reading enjoyable. In relation to vocabulary in the book (a story about a group of animals on a trip to the country), she uses a variety of question and explanation approaches. Sometimes she provides the meaning of words she assumes will be unfamiliar to her daughter, describing, for example, what a barge is after reading that word. In other cases when the child might be able to infer the meaning, she asks her daughter to explain what the word means. "You have any idea what hip boots are?" she asks at one point. When her daughter replies that hip boots are regular boots, Margaret does not say no or correct her immediately. Rather, she prompts her daughter to another response by saying "Hmmm" and waiting. When her daughter says she doesn't know what mosquito netting is, Margaret uses both personal experience ("It's like a net, like a hair net") and information from books to explain it ("I think we saw a picture of bees and this man had on a big net"). The flexibility and fine-tuning of Margaret's interactions resemble those of a skilled teacher.

The following brief sequence shows Margaret working in a number of important reading interactions. She asks a question, offers an opinion, requests an explanation, negotiates different cultural meanings of words, and creates interest in the story. Throughout, she reads with expression and uses gesture and facial expression to convey meaning. The obviously pleasurable nature of the interaction is seen in the smiling and attentive demeanor of both mother and daughter on the videotape.

Margaret: You still think they're going to have a bad time in the country?
Daughter: Yes.
Margaret: I think they're going to have a good time. Why you think they're going to have a bad time? And what kind of bad – bad-bad or bad-good?
Daughter: I think a bad-bad time because it's hot.
Margaret: OK. You think a bad time because it's hot. We'll see.

In the last interchange, Margaret accepts her daughter's prediction while raising the possibility of another outcome.

In another sequence, Margaret asks about characters' reactions and directs her daughter to pictures as a way to derive meaning from text.

Margaret: You think they're having a nice time on the train?
Daughter: Yes.
Margaret: Yes, I think so too. Why you think so?
Daughter: Because there's food and they can look out the window.
Margaret: But how does their expression look to tell you they're hav-
              ing a good time?
Daughter: They look happy and their faces are smiling.
Margaret: Good.

While reading, Margaret often stops, looks at the pictures and says "Wow."

It is hard not to say "Wow" about Margaret's level of functioning as a literacy resource for her daughter. What emerges from the data is Margaret's movement from global understandings to much more specialized knowledge and the ability to put this knowledge into practice in a sophisticated and flexible way. Though Margaret attributes many of her learnings and behaviors to Parent Readers Program workshops, it is important to recognize that factors such as her college work, life experiences, and daughter's ongoing development have undoubtedly contributed to her literacy skills as well. Still, Margaret's attribution of a reciprocal connection between her own reading development and her ability to promote that of her daughter suggests the benefit of fostering a view of adult and child as a learning unit. Further, Margaret's pride in her daughter, enjoyment of their time together, and appreciation of its effect on deepening their relationship have been integral to development of both mother and daughter and point to an inextricable connection between cognition and affect in effecting changes in family literacy.

The Partnership for Family Reading

A second major site for the Family Reading Program is the Partnership for Family Reading, which operates in an urban school district in New Jersey in collaboration with Montclair State College.[6] Thirty-three elementary schools now participate in providing services to families with children of preschool age through second grade. Over a five-year period, Partnership schools have held 137 workshops serving approximately 1,300 families. Families are predominantly African American or Hispanic; most are low-income and educationally disadvantaged.

Collaboration between home and school in promoting literacy is an explicit goal of the Partnership. Staff development focusing on ways to reach out to parents as well as in Family Reading methodology is provided to the elementary school staff who conduct the program. Schools hold a series of four or five workshops during the year conducted in Spanish or English. In most schools adults read to their children in the classroom at the conclusion of the workshop and borrow books for home reading. Provision of optional reading material for adults is less common. The series concludes with a recognition ceremony in the schools to honor adult caregivers for their Family Reading efforts. The college has also held Family Reading Festivals. (See also Handel, 1990, 1991, 1992).

Data documenting program operation and impact were collected through interviews with parents in four schools, parent and teacher surveys, and over fifty formal and informal observations by the project director and school district officials. Systematic data collection from all schools throughout the five years of the program could not be managed because of the project's limited resources and the competing needs of program and staff development. Best estimates are that 25 percent of participants read to their children daily at the outset of the project. Reported here are data from post-program surveys of parents administered in June 1990 (n = 21) and June 1991 (n = 12) in one school (called here Central Elementary School) and in June 1992 (n = 14) in a second (called here Benjamin School). The data are typical of survey responses and interviews with parents in other Partnership schools. The surveys asked adults to respond to open-ended questions about what they liked best about Family Reading and what they and their child had learned from the program.

Central Elementary and Benjamin Schools

Family Reading has been ongoing in Central Elementary for four years. The program is directed at families of kindergarten and first-grade children, but some parents continue when their children are in second and third grades as well. Workshop attendance ranges from twelve to thirty adults, a core of "regulars" and a fluctuating group who participate on a less predictable basis. Some fathers and grandparents as well as mothers attend. At Benjamin School, Family Reading began in 1992 with four workshops attended by twenty-four mothers of kindergarten children.

Adults as Literacy Resources. At both sites, observations and surveys show that the adults are serving as literacy resources for their children.

Observations of adult–child book reading in the schools confirm that the bookreading is a pleasurable experience – smiles are everywhere; enjoyment and interest in reading are reported in every survey. School observation shows the adults employing or attempting to employ the reading strategies taught in the workshops. Teachers believe parents have developed confidence in their book reading abilities and pride at no longer being "standbys" in their children's education.

Teachers' records indicate that all participants borrow books for home reading at the end of each workshop. Some request books at other times as well and search for books on their own. At the outset of the project at Central, over half of the families did not go to the library at all or visited it only once a year. Teachers, parents, and children now report increased use. Children's and parents' conversations with teachers also attest to the families' enthusiasm for the home reading ("As a family, reading is more exciting especially when you see the interest on your child's face"). Although there is no preprogram data to indicate parents' reading attitudes, it seems reasonable to assume that few were book-lovers and that their very enthusiasm is indicative of a change.

Participants felt that children benefited from Family Reading in very recognizable ways. As a result of their efforts, parents saw the children as more interested in books both for information value and for fun, a reaction noted by classroom teachers as well. Several parents noted that the children were learning to use such good reader strategies as asking questions and discussing what was read. One Central parent noted and approved her child's elaboration of text, saying he had learned to "make up a little story to add into the story (we) were reading." Benjamin parents, who attended smaller, more personalized workshops, were particularly explicit about their children's constructivist strategies, such as "explaining" a story or illustration in their own words, and their expectation that the adults engage them in discussion when reading. A child's enlarged concept of reading and the parent's endorsement of it are apparent in the report of one kindergarten child who now "has exciting times probing into the story to see if he is right or wrong in his mind. And when he's wrong he knows it's okay because he tells me someday he's going to write a book with his ending." Benjamin parents also reported their children learned book-handling skills appropriate for kindergarteners.

Adults as Learners.   Participants reported a strong sense of themselves as learners and of their own reading improvement. Replying to a survey question one parent said, "I am like my child. I learn each time." "My vocabulary and my reading have picked up" is another typical response. Reflecting on her own reading status, one mother said, "I need to read more." Another, alluding to a lack in her own childhood, wrote that the program "gave me a chance to read some interesting books that I missed when I was a kid." Another learned that reading was important for herself as well as for her child.

In addition to these reciprocal effects, parents reported that they had learned to help their children, citing time spent and specific reading strategies they were now able to use. Attitudes had changed as well. They reported learning the importance of reading and the value of working with their children ("It was very good for me and my children to learn and read together"). Family Reading gave them an opportunity to learn more about their children. "I learned my child is bright," one said; others noted that reading stimulated a desire in their child to learn more as well as new ideas in themselves about the educational role of parents ("I learned that I must be an active partner in my child's reading program." "I learned that working with your children helps a lot with their education"). Parents in both schools reported an awareness that their very participation in Family Reading sent a signal. They noted that the children liked to see them involved in the school and liked the books they brought home. "My child learned that when I attend the workshop we both learn things about reading together," one mother said.

Parents at Benjamin also felt they had learned from the program, but did not report details of their own reading improvement. They offered only general comments about their own increased knowledge of reading and concentrated instead on the importance of reading to children and the "many ways" they had learned to help. Those ways, which included learning "to explain" a book, learning how to teach "more than just words," and helping children "make decisions on what happens next or who the characters are," reflect the emphasis on strategic reading and discussion in the Family Reading workshops. Parents also reported learning such pragmatics of the reading relationship as the timing of the home reading, the need for patience, and how to "put a little fun and games into the idea of reading a book" so as to avoid the "frustration of trying to get a child interested."

The home–school connection is reinforced by changes on the part of teachers as well as parents. Participating teachers report greater use of children's literature in the classroom and the integration of reading strategies and discussion into their instructional repertoire. Thus, Partnership children are receiving congruent messages about reading from both school and home.

Adults as Actors in the World.   As a result of the program, parent involvement with the school has increased. Parents appreciate the welcoming atmosphere created by school staff and are forming warm bonds with schools and teachers. At Central, where parent participation had been minimal, scheduled and spontaneous meetings with teachers are occurring in addition to the well-attended Family Reading sessions. At Benjamin, where home–school relations have been strong, participating parents are more likely to stay in the school to talk with teachers. They also volunteered to help organize and decorate a new kindergarten library. At both schools, parents bring the program to older siblings and prepare their preschool children for school by including them in the book reading and discussion at home. Parents of preschoolers typically bring them to the Family Reading workshops for direct exposure as well. They often disseminate Family Reading informally to a wider circle of relatives and friends, and some have obtained jobs as school aides or are studying for high-school equivalency diplomas. Thus, parents at these Partnership schools are becoming actors in a world beyond the home and using knowledge of that world to enrich their home literacy environment.

The Affective Context.　　The Family Reading workshops and the home reading experience evoke very positive feelings. A theme that runs throughout the survey responses and conversations is that reading itself is both enjoyable and important and that the program engenders enjoyable reading relationships between the generations. All family members shared the benefits. Many participants reported that families became closer because they sat down together and read and that they had more to talk about and enjoy. "As a family, reading is more exciting, especially when you see the interest on your child's face." The affective context in which the program operates appears to stimulate learning, sustain motivation, and bring increased engagement with literacy to a population that has lacked positive experiences with books and reading.

Discussion and Implications

The impact on adults as learners, literacy resources, and actors in the world that we have found reflects outcomes experienced by other participants in the Parent Readers Program and other schools in the Partnership for Family Reading. Although the Parent Readers Program and the Partnership for Family Reading have been limited in their research agenda, available data strongly indicate replication of these outcomes over time and across the two major sites. The difficulties of obtaining comprehensive baseline data in a voluntary program of this type have meant reliance on postprogram self-report as a measure of change and on observations of parents in the workshops and, to a lesser degree, when reading to children.

One of the issues that we have treated is whether parents can apply the reading strategies taught in the workshops. We have observed lively and pertinent interaction in the workshop setting when the instructor engaged participants with the strategies; during reading in pairs, participants try out the strategies with one another. Of the four strategies, making predictions and relating reading to personal experience appear to be most accessible. As for transfer to reading with children, data from parent surveys, reports on the home reading, and observations of parent–child reading in school indicate that the majority of parents are using interactive book-reading strategies. In Partnership surveys (n = 81), parents report the use of specific interactive strategies or of a general comprehension focus when reading. Typical examples of the latter are "Now, I explain things," "I help her read and also understand," and "I try to open her mind with my questions." Teachers also observed indications of a broadened view of reading as exemplified by the comment of parents, "There is more to reading than pronouncing words."

Not surprisingly, observation shows considerable variation in parents' skill with the strategies, from the inexperienced mother, stumbling over words as she reads to her child and mechanically repeating one of the workshop questions, to such flexible and self-directed practitioners as Margaret Gillyard. Other variations on parent–child relationships have also been observed. What is common to them all are the willingness to try new comprehension-related activities, the engagement of the parent in reading with the child, and the enjoyment of the process. It is of some value to reflect on the reasons for the changed behaviors and positive attitudes. We believe that the cognitive and affective mix in the workshop experience accounts for the positive response to Family Reading and motivates participants to take new behaviors into their lives. Three aspects of the workshop model seem particularly influential.

First, participants love the children's literature. Most have never been in contact with such books before, and the stories and the illustrations are a source of new delight. Adults are eager to discuss them, borrow them, and read them at home. The children are delighted to see their parents come home with exciting new books. Clearly, the choice of program materials is important.

Second, the instructional pedagogy, focusing on constructivist reading strategies applied to the reading of children's books is important. Those participants who are able to put the strategies into practice discover that they contribute to their own reading development as well. Even for those not yet able to operate as strategic readers the strategies carry the important message that books are communication vehicles and ways of learning about self and others. Even if used inexpertly and tentatively, the reading and discussion strategies serve as means to promote communication and interaction during the reading process. Consistent with constructivist theory, we have found that the teaching role contributes an important element to adult learning. It is the experience at home that allows parents to own the strategies and to develop perceptions of themselves as home educators.

The third aspect of the workshop model that we see as responsible for the positive response to Family Reading is the quality of the workshop experience. Participants appreciate its informality and sociability, its respect for adults and the opportunity to share experiences and responses to the literature with "a community of talkers who make the text mean something" (Heath, 1985). Reading becomes a meaning-making enterprise to which all may contribute. The sharing also validates in a public forum experiences and impressions that might have been kept private before.

On a cognitive level, each workshop is sufficiently structured so that participants come away with a specific technique that they can use with their child. This immediate ability to act as a more effective literacy resource for their child creates a sense of self-efficacy and empowerment for the adults.

Besides the workshop model, another major reason for the positive response to Family Reading and the changed behavior of participants is the fact that the programs have enhanced family life. Reading relationships have been forged across generations. Family closeness was frequently cited by children as well as adults: "It creates family togetherness because we all sit down and read." "We read together as a family; we have more to talk about and enjoy." Routines centering around reading have become a source of pleasure and knowledge.

Family Reading also broadened the scope of family life; participants take advantage of such community resources as library story hours and museum programs for children. Relations with school became more proactive, and children benefited from the increased knowledge of the goals and processes of schooling that comes with parental involvement (Henderson, 1987). The workshops motivated some parents to think of resuming their own education, or to become school aides. A visit to a college campus for a Family Reading celebration set both generations thinking of the children's future. Such heightened aspirations can serve as achievement-fostering processes within the family.

Participants have extended Family Reading to a wider audience. For example, a grandmother brought Family Reading to the homes of all three grown children and her many grandchildren. A mother read to a neighbor's child. Another started a reading club in her home, still another in her church. An uncle took the program back to his native Colombia. In short, the program has spurred participants to act as agents of change and literacy resources for an extended community.

We doubt that any of the effects described would have occurred without the presence of a very powerful motivator, the enjoyment that is built into the workshops and that enables adults to transmit that enjoyment when reading to their chilcen. It is our belief that the affective and enjoyable qualities of the project – the children's literature, experiential curriculum, and peer interaction – and their articulation with the literacy values deeply felt by the participants serve to develop cognitive competencies of parents and to promote their ability to develop those of their children.

Implications for Practice

The following are key insights and provisions that we believe should inform development of family literacy programs:

1 Programs must provide adults with enriching and meaningful experiences in their own right, and they must see adults as more than the instrumental carriers of skills to their children.
2 The breadth of the intervention should be appropriate to the population served. As a voluntary and minimal intervention, Family Reading has primarily served those who are willing and ready to learn. Although a high school diploma or college enrollment does not guarantee literacy competence, most participants come with the ability to read children's books on a literal level (see St. Pierre, 1992, for discussion of program scope).
3 Although the social constructivist view of literacy is widely accepted, not all institutions and instructors are familiar with it. Views of literacy as the acquisition of skill and teaching as the transmission of knowledge still prevail in some circles, raising issues of policy and practice to be negotiated.
4 Family Reading is a labor intensive and highly personalized program. Teachers who conduct Partnership for Family Reading workshops receive twelve hours of training from Handel, plus follow-up consultation and demonstration.
5 School staff need time to work out logistics and become completely comfortable and effective with the methodology.
6 Variability in program content may occur in multi-site programs.

Family Reading workshops, designed to represent the reading process as a whole, instill participants with insight and motivation that enrich their home literacy environment. Participants develop new attitudes and aspirations and learn the pleasure of reading through children's literature. The reading strategies they learn to use with their children as home tutors make the hidden processes of cognition visible and accessible and allow them to become strategic and purposeful readers.

Family Reading is characterized by several dimensions of reciprocal relationships. On the level of home–school relationships, the learning obtained in Family Reading workshops contribute to and benefit from experiences with reading at home. Similarly, participants and instructors learn from one another as children and parents do. The adult participants serve as literacy resources to one another through peer learning in the workshop.

The enjoyment associated with these relationships establishes strong motivation in individuals whose prior reading experiences have not been satisfactory. The Family Reading model leads to the creation of mutually enriching collaborations that represent literacy in its broadest sense. Family Reading creates bridges between home and school, between adulthood and childhood, and between intention and action. As a result, adults bring children into new territories by introducing them to reading experiences that their own childhood might not have included.

Returning to the point of Eloise Greenfield's poem, it is our hope and belief that the participants served by Family Reading have created lasting gifts for themselves and their families. Memories of reading to our own children are warm and clear: *Curious George, Goodnight Moon, Tuck Everlasting.*

still got it
still got it

Notes

1   From *Honey I Love and other love poems* by Eloise Greenfield, pictures by Diane and Leo Dillon (Harper & Row, 1978). Reprinted with permission.
2   Indices of adults as learners include the acquisition of knowledge about the reading process, recognition of the importance of parents as home educators, knowledge about themselves and their children as readers, and adult reading improvement.
3   Indices of adults as literacy resources relate to the assumption of new roles. First is the role of home tutor (Epstein, 1988) which we describe as adults involving the child in literacy activities, teaching or evoking behaviors and attitudes similar to those experienced in Family Reading workshops,

and expressing sensitivity to affective factors such as the child's interest, disposition, or developmental stage that promote a good reading relationship. The adult as literacy resource also includes the provision of opportunities and materials for reading, such as providing books, visiting the library, and scheduling time for reading within the household routine. The third way in which adults function as literacy resources in the home is by serving as reading role models and demonstrating by act or word the importance of reading in their lives.

4 The concept of literacy as empowerment (Friere & Macedo, 1987) informs the third category, adults as actors in the world. Indices include proactive behavior and outreach beyond the home on behalf of themselves, their families, and others. In particular, we regard adult family members' relationship with the school as an important factor in children's school achievement (see Clark, 1983).

5 The Parent Readers Program has been funded by the Taconic, Aaron Diamond, Vincent Astor, Robert Bowne, New York City Technical College, Morgan Stanley Foundations, and New York Telephone.

6 The Partnership for Family Reading has been supported by Montclair State College, Newark NJ Public Schools, the Metropolitan Life Foundation, Citicorp, and Public Service Electric and Gas.

References

Anderson, R.C., Hiebert, E.H., Scott, J.A. & Wilkinson, I.A.C. (1985). *Becoming a nation of readers: The report of the Commission on Reading*. Champaign IL: The Center for the Study of Reading and the National Academy of Education.

Auerbach, E.R. (1989). Toward a social-contextual approach to family literacy. *Harvard Educational Review, 59*, 165–81.

Chall, J.S., Jacobs, V.A. & Baldwin, L.E. (1990). *The reading crisis: Why poor children fall behind*. Cambridge: Harvard University Press.

Clark, R. (1983). *Family life and school achievement:Why poor black children succeed or fail*. Chicago: University of Chicago Press.

Cochran-Smith, M. (1984). *The making of a reader*. Norwood NJ: Ablex.

Cohen, P., Kulik, J.A. & Kulik, C. (1982). Educational outcomes of tutoring: A meta-analysis of findings. *American Educational Research Journal, 19*, 237–48.

Csikszentmihalyi, M. (1990). Literacy and instrinsic motivation. *Daedalus, 119*, 115–40.

Epstein, J. (1988). Parent involvement. In R. Gorton, G. Schneider, J. Fisher (Eds.), *Encyclopedia of school administration and supervision*. Phoenix: Oryx Press.

Freire, P. & Macedo, D. (1987). *Literacy: Reading the word and the world*. South Hadley, MA: Bergin & Garvey.

Goldsmith, E. & Handel, R.D. (1990). *Family reading: An intergenerational approach to literacy*. Syracuse: New Readers Press.

Handel, R.D. (1990, April). *Shared visions, double vision, and changing perspectives: A college/school parent participation program*. Paper presented at the annual meeting of the American Educational Research Association, Boston (ERIC Document Reproduction Service No. ED 319 833).

Handel, R.D. (1991). *The partnership for family reading guide to replication.* Upper Montclair, NJ: Montclair State College.

Handel, R.D. (1992). The partnership for family reading: Benefits for families and schools. *The Reading Teacher, 46,* 2, 116–26.

Handel, R.D. & Goldsmith, E. (1988). Intergenerational literacy: A community college project. *Journal of Reading, 32,* 250–56.

Handel, R.D. & Goldsmith, E. (1989, March). Intergenerational reading: Affecting the literacy environment of the home. Paper presented at the annual meeting of the American Educational Research Association, San Francisco (ERIC Document Reproduction Service No. ED 321 225).

Heath, S.B. (1985). *Literacy and learning in the making of citizens.* AESA Butts Lecture, Stanford University.

Henderson, A. (1987). *The evidence continues to grow: Parent involvement improves student achievement.* Columbia, MD: National Committee for Citizens in Education.

Kirsch, I. & Jungeblut, A. (1986). *Literacy: Profiles of America's young adults.* Princeton NJ: National Assessment of Educational Progress.

Nickse, R.S. (1989). *The Noises of Literacy: An Overview of Intergenerational and Family Literacy Programs.* Washington, DC: Office of Educational Research and Improvement (ERIC Document Reproduction Service No. ED 308 415).

Ogle, D.M. (1986). K-W-L: A teaching model that develops active reading of expository text. *Reading Teacher, 39,* 564–70.

Palincsar, A.S. & Brown, A.L. (1984). Reciprocal teaching of comprehension-fostering and comprehension-monitoring activities. *Cognition and Instruction, 1,* 117–75.

Singer, H. (1978). Active comprehension. *Reading Teacher, 31,* 901–8.

Snow, C.E. (1983). Literacy and language. Relationships during the preschool years. *Harvard Educational Review, 53,* 165–89.

Snow, C.E., Barnes, W.S., Chandler, J., Goodman, I.F. & Hemphill, L. (1991). *Unfulfilled expectations: Home and school influences on literacy.* Cambridge: Harvard University Press.

St. Pierre, R.G. (1992, April). *Early findings from the national evaluation of the Even Start Family Literacy program.* Paper presented at the National Conference on Family Literacy, Chapel Hill.

Taylor, D. & Strickland, D.S. (1986). *Family storybook reading.* Portsmouth NH: Heinemann.

Tharp, R.G. & Gallimore, R. (1988). *Rousing minds to life: Teaching, learning, and schooling in social context.* New York: Cambridge University Press.

Vygotsky, L.S. (1978). *Mind in society: The development of higher psychological processes.* Cambridge: Harvard University Press.

8 Responses of Teachers and African-American Mothers to a Book-Reading Intervention Program

Patricia A. Edwards

Background and Theoretical Framework

Parents reading aloud to their children is assumed to be a prerequisite for success in school. As early as 1908, Huey revealed that "The secret of it all lies in the parents reading aloud to and with the child" (p. 32). In *Becoming a Nation of Readers*, the authors state that "parents play roles of inestimable importance in laying the foundations for learning to read" (Anderson, Hiebert, Scott & Wilkinson, 1985, p. 57). Mahoney & Wilcox (1985) concluded, "If a child comes from a reading family where books are a shared source of pleasure, he or she will have an understanding of the language of the literacy world and respond to the use of books in a classroom as a natural expansion of pleasant home experiences" (p. ix).

However, the overemphasis parent–child book reading has received in the reading research has caused concern among some researchers (Anderson & Stokes, 1984; Erickson, 1989). For example, some researchers have challenged the validity of the claim that the failure of African-American children, especially low-income African-American children, in learning to read may be related to the fact that many of these children come from homes where their parents have never read a book to them (Auerbach, 1989; Anderson & Stokes, 1984; Erickson, 1989; Heath, 1982, 1983). Some researchers have even challenged the notion that the "education" of parents for a specific kind of literacy interaction (the one-on-one middle-class dyadic interaction) should be encouraged and in some cases coerced (Anderson & Stokes, 1984; Auerbach, 1989; Erickson, 1989; Hearron, 1992; Taylor & Dorsey-Gaines, 1989). Based on these concerns, some researchers have raised two serious issues, one, the "blaming the victim" syndrome and the other, the claim that the homes of poor, minority, and immigrant children are "lacking in literacy."

Generally speaking, some researchers do not disagree that one-on-one parent–child interactions are correlated with success in literacy learning but fear that agreeing that one-on-one parent-child interactions are "the way" to encourage literacy might stigmatize those who do not readily adapt to this way of interacting (Anderson & Stokes, 1984; Erickson, 1989). For example, Erickson (1989) argues that one should not "assume that being read aloud to at home is a necessary condition for learning to read and write in school. To believe that is to allow us yet another opportunity to blame low-income parents for their children's school failure. Treating that belief as authoritative truth can be seen as a well-intentioned means of inadvertently putting those children and parents at risk in acquiring literacy" (p. xv).

Similarly, Anderson and Stokes (1984) argue that book reading is not the only way of becoming literate and that nonmainstream children participate in literacy experiences that are unrelated to books. Despite these arguments, Erickson admits that his position may be too extreme and perhaps he should "think twice before condemning all early childhood interventions as coercive and misguided" (p. xv). Anderson and Stokes admit that experiences with books are strongly considered in evaluating children's readiness for school and that nonmainstream children's lack of experience with books could be a contributing source to poor school performance.

Some researchers also get nervous when the homes of poor, minority, and, immigrant children are depicted as "lacking in literacy." As a way of debunking these claims, a growing number of researchers have been able to demonstrate that the homes of poor, minority, and immigrant families are not lacking in literacy (Auerbach, 1989; Chall & Snow, 1982; Delgado-Gaitan, 1987; Diaz, Moll & Mehan, 1986; Goldenberg, 1984). For example, Auerbach and her colleagues at the UMass/Boston English Literacy Project reported that they did not go into their students' homes or communities to examine literacy uses and practices or to collect data, but they listened, read, and talked to students about literacy in their lives. From these interactions with their students, they were able to conclude that their students' homes did not lack literacy.

The Harvard Families and Literacy Study (Chall & Snow, 1982; Snow, 1987) investigated the home literacy practices of successful and unsuccessful low-income elementary students and found a range of literacy practices and materials in the homes of working-class, minority, and ESL students. Snow (1987) stated that

Perhaps the most surprising finding was the generally high level of literacy skill and literacy use among the parents of the children. For example, only twenty percent of the parents said they did not like to read and never read books. Thirty percent read factual books . . . and could name at least one favorite author. Fifty percent read a major newspaper on a regular basis and thirty percent could remember books from their childhoods. These low-income children also demonstrated considerable familiarity with literacy. The vast majority owned some books of their own and half owned more than 20 books (p. 127).

In a study of the functions and meaning of literacy for Mexican immigrants, Delgado-Gaitan (1987) also found that each of the four families she investigated used a range of text types in a variety of ways that went beyond school-related reading. For example, she found that:

> Some parents assisted their children in school work by sitting with them to do homework and working out the problem, showing them examples for solving their problems, encouraging them to do their homework before playing, reading to them, taking them to the community library and providing them with a space at the kitchen table to do their homework (p. 28).

Anderson and Stokes (1984) uncovered a range of reading and writing experiences that young children from poor families participated in or witnessed. Sources of experiences in literacy, in addition to typical school or "literacy-for-literacy's sake" activities, included literacy events for daily living needs (e.g., paying bills or obtaining welfare assistance), entertainment (e.g., solving a crossword puzzle or reading a television guide), and religion (e.g., Bible-reading sessions with children). Similarly, Taylor and Dorsey-Gaines's (1988) in-depth account of the families and lives of black, urban six-year-olds who were successful in learning to read and write revealed that their parents provided a rich literate environment.

Based on the evidence presented in the studies cited above, few can successfully argue that the homes of poor, minority, and immigrant children lack literacy. However, it should be noted that in all of these studies the parents recognized the importance of literacy, and especially the importance of reading to their children. To reiterate this point, Anderson and Stokes (1984) describe the situation of a mother who could not read well enough to read storybooks aloud to her child but who recognized the importance of literacy, was being tutored to learn how to write, and passed on what she was learning to her child. Taylor and Dorsey-Gaines (1988) highlighted Tanya, who had been a mother of two children since the end of eleventh grade and lived in an abandoned apartment building, but still considered reading aloud to her children an important means to helping them learn how to read and write.

Should They or Shouldn't They?

As an African-American researcher, I am amazed that there has been such a heated debate over the issue of whether parents, and especially low-income, African-American parents should receive assistance in how to participate in one-on-one interactions with their children. Researchers agree that parents are their children's first teachers, especially with respect to reading (Taylor & Strickland, 1986), that book reading is the parent-involvement activity most frequently requested by teachers (Vukelich, 1984), that parents need to understand that storybook reading is the cornerstone of reading instruction in the early grades (Edwards & Garcia, 1991; Taylor & Strickland, 1986), and that "parents, [especially low-income African-American parents] have the right to know that sharing books with their children may be the most powerful and significant predictor of school achievement. Not only do they have the right to know, they have the right to receive assistance in how to participate in book reading interactions with their young children" (Edwards, 1991, p. 211). This message is echoed by Darling (1988) when she says that "Parents must be assisted in literacy development, and they must be provided with targeted services that help them support the development of their children" (p. 3).

Due to the fact that there is overwhelming evidence that one-on-one parent–child interactions are correlated with school success for middle-class children, we should assist low-income, African-American parents and children in how to participate in successful one-on-one book-reading interactions. Researchers who are uncomfortable with the idea of one-on-one parent–child interactions as "the way" to encourage literacy should both recognize and respect the fact that some minority researchers are just as nervous and upset when other researchers insist on neither informing nor assisting low-income African-American parents in how to participate in one-on-one interactions with their children. Further, the present-day achievement gap between black and white children that places black children educationally at risk dictates that something must be done to assure improved educational outcomes for black children (Hale-Benson, 1990).

Darling (1988) notes that "parents act as role models for the literacy behaviors of their children, and the children of those parents who are poor models find that each year they slip farther behind in school. For them school is not the key to opportunity but to failure" (p. 3). Shannon (1989) points out that "the promise of reading instruction was broken for women, minorities, and the poor, who for one reason or another were excluded from formal education" (pp. vii–viii). He further notes that "this promise is still broken today, even though laws require compulsory school attendance" (pp. vii–viii). Shannon's views have been strongly echoed by Catherine Snow and her colleagues (Snow, Barnes, Chandler, Goodman & Hemphill, 1991).

We learned from researchers (for example, Anderson & Stokes, 1984; Auerbach, 1989; Delgado-Gaitan, 1987; Snow, 1987; Taylor & Dorsey-Gaines, 1989) that literacy is not lacking in the homes of poor, minority, and immigrant families, but we did not learn how to help teachers build upon the multiple literacy environments from which these students come. Edwards and Garcia (1991) point out that

> Ideally, schools should recognize and incorporate the different interaction patterns and literacy events that characterize nonmainstream and mainstream communities. For this to happen, however, we need considerably more research – documenting the different types of interaction patterns and literacy events common in nonmainstream communities – and more teacher training (p. 183).

Is the Concern over One-on-One Parent–Child Interactions Justified?

The argument posed by some researchers who question the premise that one-on-one parent–child interactions may be the most powerful and significant predictors of school success reminds me of what James Moffett calls "agnosis: not wanting to know, the fear of knowing." Moffett argues that

> Agnosis functions on all levels on behalf of hegemonic interests – in government, in the media, on school boards, and, not least of all, in our own minds. It is not wanting to know that sustains our sense of who we are by protecting us from the knowledge both of who we are not – of who the other is – and of what we may, with more courage, become. It is the fear of knowing that leads us to embrace simplistic solutions to complex literacy problems (as cited by Lundsford, Moglen & Sleven, 1990, p. 5).

The complex problem is that poor, minority, and immigrant children are not doing well in school and their parents want to help them, but in many instances they are unaware of how to help their children understand school-based literacy practices. Clark (1988) offers some insight into the problem by stating that

> Very often, parents don't know to which standards, methods, and content their school-age child should be exposed. Their sense of uncertainty, anxiety, and fear increases because they begin to perceive themselves as inadequate. They feel they should know how to respond to their child's out-of-school linguistic and social capital needs, and they feel increasingly frustrated at having failed due to their incomplete knowledge about how best to help their children learn increasingly complex school lessons. When schools fail to provide these parents with factual, empowering information and strategies for supporting their child's learning, the parents are even more likely to feel ambivalence as educators (p. 95).

Poor, minority and immigrant parents want to give their children linguistic, social, and cultural capital to deal in the "marketplace" of schools. Their wanting to know represents the social construction of a new identity. The process could be seen as one of redefinition (Gallimore, Weisner, Kaufman & Bernhiemier, 1989; Super & Harkness, 1986). Yet, the simplistic solution of some researchers to the complex literacy problem of poor, minority, and immigrant children is to continue saying that literacy exists in their homes without informing classroom teachers of how to build upon the literacy environments from which these children come.

The importance of parents in promoting literacy learning has been emphasized by a number of researchers (Leichter, 1984; Potter, 1989; Schickedanz, 1986). Potter (1989) notes that "Children will have many teachers in their lives, but only one family. It must be the family who helps maintain the continuity of the child's education. The parents were the child's first teacher and will remain the most important throughout the child's life" (p. 28).

Schickedanz (1986) argues that "Although schools may have capable and dedicated teachers, schools are by their nature isolated from the larger world. Children learn from everything they see and do – at home, at school, and everywhere else" (p. 128).

Leichter (1984) wrote that "It may be that children can learn to become literate on their own without formal instruction, but when experiences with literacy take in family environments, the emotional reactions of the parents can affect the child's progress significantly" (p. 46).

As an African-American researcher, I was determined to acquaint African-American parents with the most frequently requested parent-involvement activity, namely, "read to your child." My decision was based on the fact that millions of parents with poor reading skills cannot engage in book-reading interactions with their children because of their own reading deficiencies, and millions of others have neither the knowledge of its importance nor the skills to do it (Chall, Heron & Hilferty, 1987; Nickse, Speicher & Bucheck, 1988). Sharon Darling (1988) states that "America is awakening to the tragedy and threat of illiteracy, the fact that tens of millions of its adults lack the essential literacy skills needed to survive and prosper in our increasingly complex society (p. 1)." She goes on to say that "parents who lack basic literacy skills cannot know the joy of reading a story to their children, and these children cannot reap the documented educational benefits of being read to" (p. 2).

My decision was also based on the belief that African-American parents could learn to share books with their children, that they could become active partners in their children's literacy development, and that past researchers have criticized African-American parents' book-reading practices but failed to go on to describe strategies for improvement (Heath & Thomas, 1984; Ninio, 1980). Consequently, during the 1985–86 school year I volunteered to be parent-consultant at a local Head Start Center in a rural community located in northern Louisiana. I met with families once each month for 90-minute sessions over a period of nine months, focusing on how parents could become better prepared to support their children's education at the Head Start Center and later in the public-school setting. As I became more familiar with the families, I proposed a book-reading project and solicited volunteers. Five low-income, African-American mothers were randomly selected from a total of eighteen who volunteered to participate in an eight-week book-reading program designed to examine low-income, African-American mothers' understanding of how to share books with their preschool children. The results revealed that four out of the five low-income, African-American mothers who participated were unable to successfully share books with their children and needed assistance with their own personal literacy skills (see Edwards, 1989). The results of the 1985–6 study led to the development of the Parents as Partners in Reading Program in 1987 in Donaldsonville, LA (see Edwards, 1990a, 1991, 1992 for descriptions of earlier work).

In this chapter I focus on the response of parents to the parent-training materials used in a book-reading program and their suggestions for improving the training materials. I address three important questions: (a) What is the impact of parent-training materials on non-mainstream parents' ability to share books with their children? (b) How can these materials be improved? and (c) Are these materials useful by themselves, or must they be monitored by a reading professional?

The Invitation to Donaldsonville

During the Spring of 1987, the SPUR (Special Plan Upgrading Reading) technical assistant for Ascension Parish Schools contacted me after reading a chapter that I was preparing for a book (see Edwards, 1989). She arranged a meeting with the principal and assistant principal of Donaldsonville Elementary School (DES). The technical assistant's interest in my research stemmed from the fact that the principal, the assistant principal, and the teachers at DES had asked her to help them look for ways to increase the amount of parental involvement at DES.

The technical assistant described the racial tensions in the school, tensions between the predominately white faculty and the predominately black parent and student population. The staff, sensing that the teaching profession was slowly turning white and the student population rapidly turning nonwhite, were extremely interested in opening lines of communication with the parents of the children they were serving. The Technical Assistant, a white female, felt that I could bridge the gap among parents, teachers, and administrators.

What really convinced me to conduct the book-reading project at DES, however, was the commitment of the principal and assistant principal to the project, expressed by the principal when I first met with her. In our conversation she explained that she had been an educator in Donaldsville for 37 years, including being a home economics teacher, which gave her a good understanding of child growth and development. She went on to say, "I am now encountering third generation students – that is, I taught the grandparent, the parent, and now grandchildren." She further explained that the area had changed greatly from the farming community of the 1950s to the chemical plants of today, resulting in job loss and unemployment. "Now, Donaldsonville," she said, "has two federally subsidized housing projects, and several apartment complexes that are federally subsidized." Added to the economic problems was the fact that there was a high teen pregnancy rate and many parents were illiterate or semiliterate. She said they had tried to make a difference, but a more structured approach was needed.

> I know the feeling of longing for the better things life has to offer. As a depression baby of unemployed parents I can relate to being hungry, being cold, and being rejected by peers from affluent circumstances. I have walked a mile to the grocery store because we did not have a car. I know that to rise from unfortunate circumstances one must possess an education. No matter how hard one has to struggle and sacrifice the price is small compared with the benefits of having that education.

Table 1   Role of university leader, teacher, and parents in the development of the training materials

University leader	Primary teachers	Parents
Taught a course in parent involvement/family literacy	Took course on parent involvement/family literacy	Did not participate in development of training materials
Collaborated with teachers on the development of training materials	Selected book reading strategies to model for parents	
With two graduate students critiqued two rounds of teacher tapes	Reviewed and critiqued tapes that they made	

She stated emphatically that she knew the parents wanted their children to succeed in school and that they themselves were key to their children's success. She felt that her effort to unite home, school, and neighborhood would benefit considerably from my reading program. She concluded:

> Please agree to help us. The teachers feel that because many of our parents are illiterate they cannot help their children. The book reading program you have described is exactly what we need.

I accepted the principal and assistant principal's offer to implement the book-reading program at Donaldsonville Elementary School. I did not feel that I was being intrusive but that I was being solicited to provide advice and guidance. Because I was strongly recruited to work at DES, my suggestions for change were adhered to by parents, teachers, and administrators. Table 1 outlines the roles of the university leader (the way I refer to myself in the remainder of the chapter for clarity) and the teachers. As noted in table 1, parents did not participate in the development of the materials.

University Leader

Teaching a Course.   In this course the university leader wanted to increase teacher knowledge and understanding of multiple literacy environments and African-American children's learning styles. As a way to accomplish this goal, she included readings to help teachers begin to think more critically and reflectively about multiple literacy environments and African-American children's learning styles (see Appendix A for complete listing).

Soliciting Teacher Participation in the Development of Training Materials. To solicit the teachers' participation in the development of the training materials, the university leader told the teachers that "simply to inform parents about the importance of reading to their children" is not sufficient. Classroom teachers must go beyond "telling" lower-socioeconomic-status (SES) parents to help their children with reading. They must show them how to participate in parent–child book reading and support their efforts to do so. Teachers must help them become confident readers simultaneously. They must also not assume that lower-SES parents cannot acquire the necessary skills to engage in successful book-reading interactions with their children. She told them that they were going to show parents how to read with children using a series of videotapes in which they would model beneficial strategies.

The university leader observed that the teachers appeared nervous when she said that she wanted them to model effective book-reading strategies for parents. The teachers also seemed puzzled about what the university leader meant by effective book-reading strategies. She then asked them to explain what they felt "reading to your child meant." The teachers encountered difficulty in explaining the concepts to the university leader, indicating that they would probably have a more difficult time explaining the concepts to low-income parents. Though the teachers recognized the importance of showing parents how to share books with their children, the university leader could tell from their smiles and body language that they did not believe that there would be any significant changes in the parents' ability to share books with their children because the parents they served were poor and minority. The university leader's response to this nonverbal behavior was, "When teachers see a class of all black or low-income white children, they often think that they have a group of losers. I want you to recommend all of your losers." The teachers laughed. The leader then said, "We are going to make those losers winners this year." Even though the teachers felt uncomfortable participating in the development of the training materials, they agreed to participate.

Collaborating with Teachers on the Development of the Training Materials. The university leader, five kindergarten, and five first-grade teachers collaborated on the development of the parent-training materials, which were four videotapes on two sets of book-reading strategies. One set was derived from the mother–child observational checklist of Resnick,

Roth, Aaron, Scott, Wolking, Laren, and Packer (1987) that includes body management (e.g., sitting opposite child), management of book (e.g., encouraging child to hold the book and turn the pages, and varying one's voice), language interactions (e.g., labeling and describing pictures), and affect (e.g., pausing for child's responses and making approving gestures). The checklist also gives parents a general progression of steps to follow with a story: attention-getting, questioning, labeling, and providing feedback (Ninio & Bruner, 1978). Teachers became familiar with both sets of strategies and selected dimensions to highlight in the videotapes (see figure 1).

The university leader asked teachers to select book-reading strategies they felt most comfortable modeling and encouraged them to explain what the strategies meant so that a parent who lacked training could understand. The teachers were not given any specific coaching or training on how to do the videotaped demonstration. Instead, they were encouraged to come up with their own creative ways to demonstrate the book reading strategies. Taping sessions were in late August and early September. Prior to the sessions, the university leader asked the teachers if they had any questions about the strategy or strategies they were going to model and/or demonstrate. In many instances, they did. Teachers would ask: "How long should I model the strategy?" "Would you explain a little more about what you want?" They would often say "If I mess up can we do it over?" or "Let me know if I'm doing ok." These interchanges served to calm the teachers' nerves. At the end of the taping session, the teachers and the university leader reviewed the tape. Only in a few instances did the university leader actually retape the teacher modeling the strategy.

Teachers

Enrolled in a Course. The teachers enrolled in a course on parent involvement/family literacy taught by the university leader. They also collaborated with the university leader on the development of the training materials for the book reading intervention. The course was designed to increase teacher knowledge and understanding of multiple literacy environments and African-American children's learning styles.

Collaborating with University Leader on the Training Materials and Selected Book-Reading Strategies to Model for Parents. The primary teachers collaborated with the university leader on the development of the training materials for the book-reading intervention as described earlier. In a typical tape the teacher announces what skill she is going to

1. MOTHER'S BODY MANAGEMENT

—— Sits opposite child.
—— Places child on lap.
—— Partially encircles child.
—— Completely encircles child.
—— Lies alongside child.
—— Sits adjacent to child.
—— Maintains physical contact.

2. MOTHER'S MANAGEMENT OF BOOK

—— Previews book.
—— Allows child to hold book.
—— Allows child to turn pages.
—— Permits child to explore book.
—— Guides child's attention to book.
—— Points to pictures / words.
—— Asks child questions.
—— Links items in text to child's life.
—— Varies voice.
—— Emphasizes syllables.
—— Acts [makes noises, motions].
—— Comments on book's content.
—— Refers to reading as joint enterprise.
—— Ends reading episode when child loses interest.
—— Continues to read after child loses interest.
—— Resists child turning pages.
—— Becomes absorbed by book and ignores child.

3. MOTHER'S LANGUAGE PROFICIENCY

—— Uses multiple word sentences.
—— Uses multiple grammatical modes.
—— Labels pictures.
—— Describes pictures.
—— Repeat's child's vocalization.
—— Corrects child's vocalization.
—— Elaborates child's vocalization.
—— Gives words to child's vocalization.

4. MOTHER'S ATTENTION TO AFFECT

—— Pauses for child's response.
—— Inspects child's face.
—— Praises child.
—— Comments positively about child's participation.
—— Gives spoken affirmation.
—— Makes approving gesture.
—— Reprimands child.
—— Commands negatively about child's participation.

Figure 1. Checklist used to guide preparation of videotaped book-reading demonstrations. This modified observation tool is based on the work of Michael B. Resnick et al. (1987). "Mothers reading to infants: A new observational tool." *The Reading Teacher, 40* (9), 888–95.

model, she gives a description of the skill(s) to be modeled, and then she models the skill(s) using a children's book.

Mrs. Dykes, a first grade teacher, demonstrates this format using Harriet Ziefart's (1985) *Baby Ben Gets Dressed*, a picture book with labeled illustrations. As she says in the introduction to her tape, "If children see a word often enough, they will remember it and that's why labeling and describing pictures is important when you read to your child. When attempting to practice the skill I'm modeling at home with your child, try to select a book that lends itself easily to the skill you would like to emphasize. Wordless picture books and picture storybooks are excellent books to use for labeling and describing pictures." Mrs. Dykes then modeled the skill for the parents.

Mrs. Dykes:	The name of this book is *Baby Ben Gets Dressed*. Teddy thinks he will get dressed all by himself. Do you think he can?
Felicia:	Yes.
Mrs. Dykes:	You do? Let's see. Look at Baby Ben. What is he wearing?
Felicia:	A shirt.
Mrs. Dykes:	Let's point to the word *shirt* (directing child's attention toward *shirt*). Now, look at Baby Ben. What is he wearing?
Felicia:	A shirt.
Mrs. Dykes:	Where is the word *shirt*, Felicia? That's right (confirming the child's pointing to the correct word). He's wearing socks and sneakers too. Let's find the word *sneakers*. " 'You look funny, Teddy,' said Baby Ben" (she reads). Do you know what's funny about Teddy's socks, Felicia?
Felicia:	They're different colors. One is hot pink, and the other is green.
Mrs. Dykes:	Now, Baby Ben is wearing a *shirt, socks* (pointing to each word), *sneakers*, and *overalls*.

Mrs. Dykes modeled the skill of labeling and describing pictures. She pointed to the pictures for Felicia, a first-grade student, and prompted her to tell what the pictures were about, and then she turned the book toward the camera for the parents to see what she was talking about and reexplained what she just did.

Critique of the Teacher Tapes

Two rounds of taping were required. The university leader and two graduate students critiqued the initial teacher tapes and made many

Table 2 Suggestions for producing high-quality training videotapes

Suggestions for enhancing quality of tapes	Suggestions for improving content of tapes
Model no more than two strategies per tape	Teachers should provide overviews of the book, then describe the strategies they will be modeling
If sentence strips are used to announce strategies, allow time for camera focusing and audience reading; display strips on a chart instead of holding them by hand	Discuss the content in the book in a manner that explains to nonreaders ways they can share books with their children
Focus on the title and author of the book and give time for writing the title and author	Attempt to describe in detail the strategies they modeled; avoid simply labeling the strategy
Remove all distractors from the teacher tapes, e.g., bells, announcements over the public announcement system	Discuss why the particular strategy they are modeling is important in a bookreading interaction
While teachers are modeling the strategies, parents and children should participate	Inform the audience why they are using certain hand gestures; beware of overuse of distracting gestures
Teachers should not appear nervous	Teachers should pause long enough after each of the strategies to allow parents time to respond

suggestions about enhancing production quality of the tapes and improving their content, which can be found in table 2. The second taping session went better than the first, but some of the teachers still needed help on the strategies they were demonstrating. Also, the comments parents made concerning the second taping session reveal that they, too, felt that some of the teachers could have benefited from additional coaching (see table 2).

While the teachers appeared to be satisfied with their involvement in the tapes, some of them began to sense some of the frustration that parents have when they try to implement teachers' requests to read to their children at home, because of their difficulty modeling effective book-reading strategies.

The teachers only modeled a limited number of the strategies suggested by the university leader. They concentrated on body management (completely encircling the child), language-interactions, and predominantly management of book (e.g., previewing book, allowing the child to hold book, pointing to pictures / words, and varying voice). Teachers only modeled two strategies from the language-interactions category (labeling and describing pictures). Teachers stated that it was hard to model "multiple-word sentences and multiple grammatical modes." From the university leader's perspective, the parents had a hard time incorporating into their reading style strategies like "giving words to and correcting child's vocalization, and asking probing / challenging questions."

Role of the University Leader, Primary Teachers, and Parents in the Three Phases of the Book-Reading Intervention

The participants in the book-reading program were 25 lower-socioeconomic-status mothers (18 African-American, 7 white) and their children. Mothers had been recommended by kindergarten and first-grade teachers on the basis of their children's performance in kindergarten and grade 1. The book-reading intervention fell into three phases: coaching, peer modeling, and parent–child interaction. Each phase was approximately the same length (6 or 7 weeks). Sessions were held weekly beginning in October 1987 and ending in May 1988, and each session lasted for two hours. There were 23 book-reading sessions, although not all mothers attended every session. Table 3 outlines the roles played by the university leader, teachers, and parents in the coaching phase of the book-reading intervention. See figure 2 for a pictorial description of what happened in a typical book-reading session in the coaching phase.

Phase One – Coaching

The first phase, coaching, consisted of the university leader modeling book reading behaviors and introducing the videotapes of teachers modeling specific book-reading strategies. This approach was also used to guide the teacher–child interaction on the videotape and was intended for parents to emulate in their interactions with children. That is, when there was a breakdown in parents' understanding or use of a strategy, the leader would prompt and support their use of difficult strategies. Overall, the parents felt the training materials alone would not be sufficient to help them learn to share books with their children. Without the assistance of the university leader, they felt that they

Table 3   Role of the university leader, primary teachers, and parents
in the coaching phase

University Leader	Primary Teachers	Parents
Outlined skills to enhance	Modeled for parents on videotape effective reading strategies	Discussed the strategies introduced by the university leader
Modeled effective strategies		Imitated strategies modeled by the university leader
Introduced training tapes		Viewed teacher tapes
Discussed beneficial effects of sharing books with children		Participated in rap sessions about their feelings about the program
Praised and supported parents' attempts		Completed a parent's response sheet and learning log

would not have known how to make sense out of what they saw in the teacher tapes.

Each strategy had its own videotape in which a teacher explained it and then demonstrated it with one of the target children. After parents viewed the videotape, the university leader guided them in a discussion on the application of the strategy. This discussion sought to promote parents' ability to talk about content and strategies of book reading and to make text-to-life and life-to-text connections. During the coaching phase, the university leader acquainted the parents with all of the book-reading strategies derived from the Resnick et al. checklist (1987).

By the end of the coaching phase, the parents had begun to view book reading as a routine, ordered language event between themselves and their children. They also had begun to adjust their language to their child's level of understanding and were developing an interest and sophistication in book reading. For example, they were able to label and describe pictures, vary their voices, and make motions while interacting with the texts. More important, parents seemed to be acquiring an internal understanding of what it meant to share books with children.

Phase One – Coaching

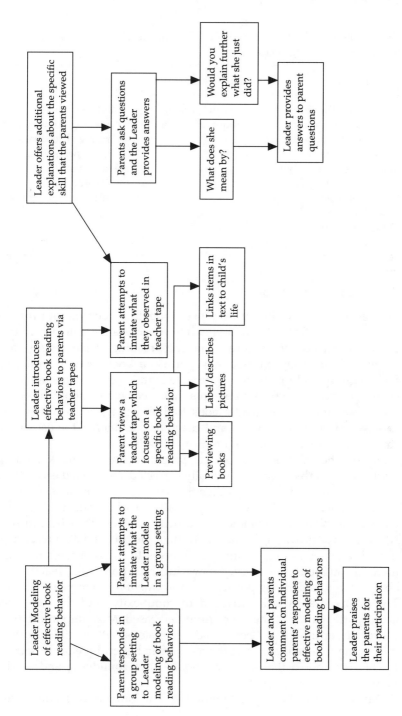

Figure 2. Description of the coaching phase.

Table 4   Role of the University leader, primary teachers, and parents
in the peer-modeling phase

University Leader	Primary Teacher	Parents
Guided parents' book reading interactions with each other and provided praise Modeled effective book reading strategies for parents when needed Conducted rap sessions	Reacted to parents critique of teacher tapes	Modeled a book reading strategy and received feedback from peers Attempted to incorporate suggestions offered by peers

Phase Two – Peer Modeling

The second phase of instruction, peer modeling, focused on promoting parents' control of the book-reading sessions and strategies. In this phase parents began to direct the book-reading strategies sessions themselves, focusing on modeling particular book-reading strategies for the group and practicing the targeted strategies with one another. More specifically, one or two parents each week would show the entire group how they would read a book to their child, and the other parents would provide feedback and coach one another in the use of the strategies (see table 4 and figure 3 for details).

During the six week period the parents shared in book reading sessions and verbally and nonverbally corrected and guided each other, and they provided for each other the same instructional scaffolding the university leader had provided for them earlier. The mothers displayed the type of adult interactive behavior described by Morrow (1988), such as providing information about the book, relating responses to real-life experiences, inviting their peers to ask questions or comment throughout the story, answering questions and reacting to observations, and giving positive reinforcement for their peers' effects. The mothers' story-talk increased in complexity, and their shyness about participating in the peer group decreased. Most important, they learned to approach the book-reading sessions with confidence. It is interesting to note that one of the mothers in her critique of the second teacher-tape noted that teachers should have confidence and not be nervous.

During Phase Two, peer modeling, the university leader often

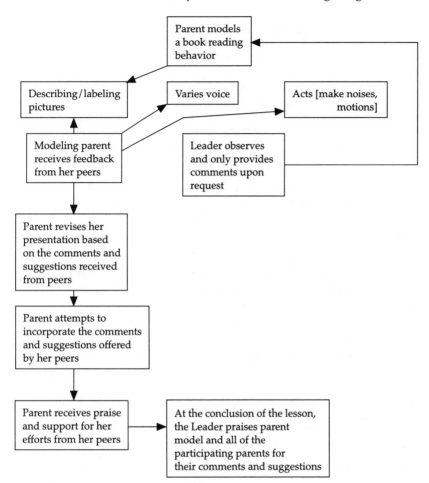

Figure 3. Description of the modeling phase.

conducted 15- to 20-minute parent rap sessions prior to the book-reading sessions, designed to give parents the opportunity to express their feelings about the book-reading program. The November 30th rap session focused on what the parents had learned about book reading thus far. A transcript of their comments can be found in figure 4.

The last rap session during Phase Two was held on February 1. Several new mothers and experienced mothers attended. Because so many new mothers came, the university leader decided to use this session to show both the new and experienced mothers the second set of teacher tapes in its entirety and seek their reactions. The second set was better than the initial one. Even though the experienced mothers

Transcript of the First Rap Session
What Have We Learned About Book Reading
November 30, 1987

Jeannette: I learned to introduce the title, author, and to preview the
              book with my child. I no longer read to get through the
              book, but instead I have learned to explain the concepts in
              the book and to carry on a conversation about the vocabulary
              and events in the book. I now understand that I may have to
              go over the words, ideas, or concepts until my daughter
              understands them. The repeated reading of a book has
              helped Erica and me.

Jackie: I learned to explain concepts, such as inside and outside, to
              my child. I also learned that just because the parent
              understands doesn't mean that the children do.

Charlene: Before, Kyle asked me questions and asked for definitions,
              I never realized that I should play an active role in book
              reading interactions. I now take a more active role when
              reading to him. I talk about the pictures and vocabulary as
              well as the action or ideas in the story.

Tessie: I spent a great deal of time talking to Keith. I now realize
              that reading has a purpose.

Jeannette: Some people just read but don't comprehend and that is just
              word calling. There must be understanding for it to count as
              reading. I want to make sure my child understands what's in
              the book.

All Parents: That's right (nodding their heads in agreement).

Figure 4. November 30th rap session.

had viewed the second set of teacher tapes, they had not viewed them
alone. The university leader was always there to explain step-by-step
what the teachers were doing. An enlightening transcript of all the
attending the mothers' reactions to the second set of teacher tapes can
be found in Appendix B.

With that, the rap session, or critique, of the second teacher tapes
ended. All of the mothers had some genuine concerns with this set,
especially the new mothers who felt they could not learn from it. They
felt that the teachers were not explicit enough in their comments about
the strategy or strategies they were modeling. In some cases, the parents pointed out that the teachers' explanations were unclear and that
the teachers stressed too many strategies. They felt that the teachers
should have used charts rather than sentence strips to highlight the
strategies they modeled. The sentence strips made the videotape demonstration look too busy, which made the teachers appear nervous
and disorganized. Some of the mothers who had already received 12

weeks of training felt that what they had learned from the university leader in the book-reading sessions could be used to help the university leader and the teachers develop better training tapes.

After school on February 1, the university leader met with kindergarten and first-grade teachers to share the parents' reactions to the second teacher tape with them. The teachers were shocked at the parents' reactions to the tape. Some commented, "What do they know?" The university leader quickly reminded the teachers that several of the parents had received 12 weeks of intensive training in how to participate in effective book-reading interactions with their children. She also pointed out that it was important for them to listen to what the parents were saying, especially to the new participants' reactions to the second set of teacher tapes.

At the close of the meeting, the university leader informed the teachers that the parents would begin reading to their own children February 8 on a one-on-one basis in the classrooms and that these parent–child book-reading interactions would be taped. The university leader offered the teachers the opportunity to view tapes of the parents reading to their children. The teachers appeared interested in viewing these tapes. When the university leader met on March 7th with the core group of mothers, she caught them by surprise when she said that she was going to let the teachers view the tapes of them reading with their children. The leader said, "You had your chance to react to the teachers' tape and now I'm going to give the teachers a chance to react to yours." The mothers laughed and said, "Let them see it. We know we did good."

Two weeks later (March 21), the kindergarten and first-grade teachers did view tapes of the parents reading to their children. Teachers made comments indicating surprise at the parents' reading skills (e.g., "I can't believe my eyes"). They seemed especially impressed with the potency of modeling effective strategies for parents, with one teacher saying, "You said we should shift from telling parents to showing them how to read to their children. Showing them how has worked."

Despite the fact that the parents were not all reading accurately and fluently to their children, the teachers were both excited and encouraged by the parents' efforts to share books with children.

Phase Three – Parent-Child Interaction

During the final phase, parent–child interaction, the university leader ceded total control to the parents and functioned as a supportive and sympathetic audience: offering suggestions to the mothers as to what books to use in reading interactions with their children, evaluating the

Table 5   Role of the university leader, teachers, and parents in the
parent–child interaction phase

University Leader	Primary Teachers	Parents
Acted as a supportive and sympathetic audience	Viewed tapes of parent–child book-reading interactions	Selected a book-reading strategy to share with child
Offered suggestions of what book to read	Critiqued parent–child book reading interactions	Selected a book appropriate for the selected strategy
Evaluated parent–child book reading		Read book to child
Encouraged parents to review teacher tapes		Reviewed teacher tapes on occasion
Modeled strategies when needed		

parent–child book-reading interactions, encouraging them to review
teacher tapes, and providing feedback or modeling. In this final phase
parents brought their own children to the sessions. See table 5 for the
roles played by the university leader, primary teachers, and parents
during this phase. For a pictorial description of what happened in a
typical book-reading session during parent-child interaction see figure
5. From these interactions the parents learned the importance of
involving their children in book reading and recognized that the
"parents hold the key to unlocking the meaning represented by the
text" (Chapman, 1986, p. 12). For a fuller description of the program
see Edwards (1990a, 1990b, 1991) and Edwards and Garcia, (1991).

Impact of the Three Phases

The fact that all three phases of the book-reading sessions were
videotaped facilitated the parents' understanding of how to share a
book with their children. Videotaping the first phase of the program
(coaching) gave parents and the university leader the opportunity to
review specific sessions and to determine whether parents understood
specific strategies. It also allowed her to listen more closely to the
questions parents asked, to examine her responses to the parents'
questions, and to determine whether her responses were understood.
More important, it provided the opportunity for parents who were
unable to attend a particular session to see what they had missed.

Phase Three – Parent-Child Interaction

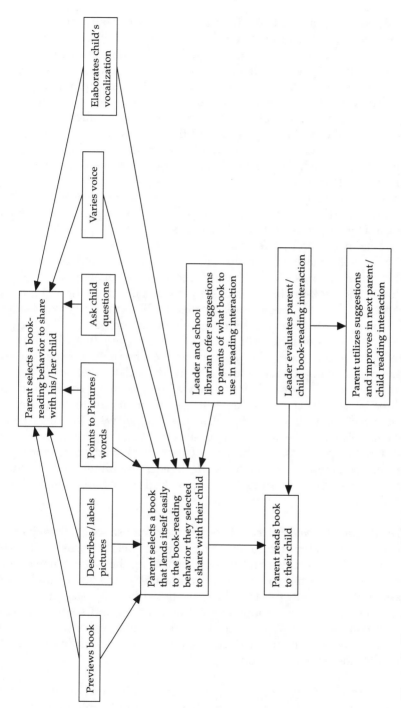

Figure 5. Typical parent–child interaction during workshop.

By videotaping sessions during the second phase (peer modeling) parents were able to evaluate their own interactions better because they could actually see some possibilities for improvement. Having the opportunity to watch their videotaped interactions with other parents encouraged them to try harder and to learn from their peers. It also allowed the university leader to monitor the parents' progress.

Videotaping during phase three (parent–child interaction) was essential. Without it, both parents and the university leader would not have been able to monitor the parents' progress or see where improvement was needed. Tapes provided instant video replay, enabling identification of specific parent problems or stages of progress. The use of videotaped sessions was a wonderful teaching and learning device, but it should be noted that the university leader prepared the parents for it. Her eagerness to tape the sessions did not take precedence over parents' needs and preferences.

Yet, another factor that contributed to the parents' understanding of how to share books with their children was the collaborative evaluation of the book-reading sessions. Evaluation occurred throughout all three phases of the book-reading program. Both the university leader and the parents continuously observed and made notes about the effectiveness of the sessions. Even though the university leader did not redo the teacher tapes, she was cognizant of the problems the parents had with them. As a result, she worked hard to facilitate parents' understanding of what they had viewed on the tapes. Throughout all three phases the parents demonstrated their ability to understand, interpret, relate, discuss, and implement what they were learning. While the university leader was teaching, she observed the parents' behavior and noted progress. At the end of each book-reading session, she asked the parents to evaluate its effectiveness by filling out a parent's response sheet and completing a parent's learning log, which were read each week by the university leader.

The Parent's Response Sheet.   The parent's response sheet allowed each parent to reflect on the session as it came to a close, focus on its key points, and select one point to work on during the week. Some of the parents were unable to write their comments, so the university leader asked other parents to assist them or offered her own assistance. Parents also worked in groups of twos and threes, and some recorded their comments on a tape recorder. The parent's response sheet was valuable because it summarized what each parent considered important to implement or retain.

The Parent's Learning Log.   The university leader felt that it was important for parents to reflect on what they were learning and how it applied to their experiences reading to their children. She further believed that it was important for parents to record their progress on daily or weekly log sheets and to keep them in a binder. Problems recording responses were handled in the same manner as for the response sheets.

The leader asked parents to bring their logs to each session and put their handouts in the binder. She read the parents' logs before she met with them to discuss their progress. The log sheets listed six possible response stems to complete: In this week's session I learned_____; At home I will work on_____; I am reading better because_____; I need to improve on_____; My child listens to the story better because _____; I still don't understand_____.

One of the most important results of this study was that with the university leader's assistance these nonmainstream parents came to understand the teacher directive that they "read to their children." Not only did they understand what it meant, they were able to critique classroom teachers' modeling of effective book-reading strategies. Unfortunately, one of the problems with involving teachers in the development of the tapes is that it often causes them anxiety and evokes subtle resistance. On a good note, the anxiety and frustration teachers experienced made them examine the requests they made of parents more closely and develop a greater sensitivity to the fact that some parents might be unable to implement their request "to read to their children."

Consequently, the work described in this chapter serves as a powerful example that, if nonmainstream parents are shown how to share books with their children, they can guide their children's participation in book-reading interactions. It also sends a powerful message to classroom teachers that they should listen closely to what parents have to say even if the parents are not highly educated. Nonmainstream parents can effectively critique and offer in-depth and insightful information to classroom teachers about ways to improve materials designed to help parents share books with their children. Based on the parents' comments and suggestions, the training materials were, in fact, revised and a set of book-reading materials for parents developed later (see Edwards, 1990a, 1990b).

Appendix A.   The Primary Teachers' Readings in the Course

Arnold, R.D. & Westphal, R.C. (1979, November). *Reading skills of good, average and poor readers in three ethnic groups.* Paper presented at the 2d annual meeting of the Pacific Reading Research Symposium, Tucson, AZ.

200   Patricia A. Edwards

Baratz, J.C. & Shuy, R. (Eds.). (1969). *Teaching black children to read*. Washington, DC: Center for Applied Linguistics.

Clark, R.M. (1983). *Family life and school achievement: Why poor black children succeed or fail*. Chicago: University of Chicago Press.

Cohen, S.A. (1969). *Teach them all to read*. New York: Random House, Inc.

Cureton, G.D. (1978). Using a black learning style. *The Reading Teacher, 31*, 751–6.

DeStefano, J.S. (1972). Social variation in language implications for teaching reading to black children. In J.A. Figurel (Ed.), *Better reading in urban schools*. Newark, DE: International Reading Association.

Durkin, D. (1982). *A study of poor black children who are successful readers* (Reading Education Report No. 33). Champaign, IL: University of Illinois, Center for the Study of Reading.

Hale, J.E. (1982). *Black children: Their roots, culture and learning styles*. Provo, UT: Brigham Young University Press.

Heath, S.B. (1982a). What no bedtime story means: Narrative skills at home and school. *Language in Society, 11*, 49–76.

Heath, S.B. (1982b). Questioning at home and at school: A comparative study. In G. Spindler (Ed.), *Doing ethnography: Educational anthropology in action* (pp. 96–101). New York: Holt, Rinehart & Winston.

Heath, S.B. (1983). *Ways with words: Language, life, and work in communities and classrooms*. London: Cambridge University Press.

Heath, S.B. (1984). The achievement of preschool literacy for mother and child. In H. Goelman, A. Oberg & F. Smith (Eds.), *Awakening to literacy* (pp. 51–72). Exeter, NH: Heinemann.

Hollins, E.R. (1982). The Marva Collins story revisited: Implications for regular classroom. *Journal of Teacher Education, 33*, 37–40.

Hollins, E.R. (1983). *An instructional design theory relating black cultural practices and values to instruction*. Unpublished doctoral dissertation, The University of Texas, Austin, TX.

Hoover, M.R. (1978). Characteristics of black schools at grade level: A description. *The Reading Teacher, 31*, 757–62.

Leichter, H.J. (1984). Families as environments for literacy. In H. Goelman, A. Oberg & F. Smith (Eds.), *Awakening to literacy* (pp. 38–50). Exeter, NH: Heinemann.

Ninio, A. & Bruner, J. (1978). The achievement and antecedents of labelling. *Journal of Child Language, 5*, 1–15.

Norman-Jackson, J. (1982). Family interactions, language development and primary reading achievement of Black children in families of low income. *Child Development, 53*, 349–58.

Schieffelin, B. & Cochran-Smith, M. (1984). Learning to read culturally: Literacy before schooling. In H. Goelman, A. Oberg & F. Smith (Eds.), *Awakening to literacy* (pp. 3–23). Exeter, NH: Heinemann.

Shade, B.J. (1982). Afro-American cognitive style: A variable in school success? *Review of Educational Research, 52*, 219–44.

Sims, R. (1985, May). *Meaning-centered/literature approach to teach reading to black children*. Paper presented at the 30th annual meeting of the International Reading Association, New Orleans, LA.

Ward, M.C. (1971). *Them children: A study in language learning.* New York: Holt, Rinehart, & Winston, Inc. (Reissued by Waveland Press, Inc.: Prospect Heights, IL, 1986)

Appendix B. New and Experienced Participants' Reaction to the Second Set of Teacher Tapes, February 1, 1988

New participant:	The first teacher really made good points. Second not making good points. The child wasn't interested in the book. She needs to come [on] stronger, get that child interested; she wasn't doin' nothing for the child.
Leader:	If teachers are going to demonstrate this to mothers, they need to be clear about what they're doing, make it clear to parents what to do with the child.
New participant:	Yes, that's right.
Leader:	Was that not clear to you as a mother? I think that's a very critical point.
Experienced participant:	It was like she said, first teacher did a good job; she talked about the pictures as they read, and asked the little child questions. Second teacher said what she was gonna do, and she started reading the pictures, but she didn't ask the child any questions. She didn't ask if the child was enjoying the book or anything; she just went on and read the book, so if a parent saw this, a parent wouldn't really get a clear idea of what this teacher was doing.
Experienced participant:	I know one of the teachers read for the first time on video, but if she had gone through the cards [i.e., sentence strips] and she was gonna tell the parents what to do, she got her cards mixed up – it kinda threw it off because a parent's going to sit and look at this and say this teacher's not organized. How can she teach me something if she's not organized to deliver what she's trying to teach? And I think this is important.
Leader:	Are there other comments?
Experienced participant:	About previewing a book first?
Leader:	Uh Uh.
Experienced participant:	That's a good idea. Like we said, you have to get a book that's gonna help relate somethin' from a child's environment or somethin' in his

surrounding to bring the child into the book, you know, for him to get somethin' out and you're supposed to relate somethin' with the child out of the book and into real life itself. That really helps the child 'cause you know there's somethin' in the book that we might not see around here but you can ask them where do they see things in the book. You know, the circus, or the zoos or wherever.

Leader: Basically what you're talking about is relating text to life and life to text.

All Mothers: Right, heads nodding, general words of agreement such as uh uh, yes. (general agreement)

Leader: Ok, pretend you are seeing this video for the first time with no training in how to share a book with your child. Could you go home and read effectively to your child after having watched the tape?

New participant: No, not really because in the first place, if you didn't get your child interested in the book, just by going through it, how can you teach them if they wasn't interested in the first place? Maybe we didn't put in anything into the book. You know, describing it, lettin 'em look through the book. How can we teach this to them, if we didn't get anything out of it [video] in the first place? While she was talking [Teacher 6], she was using hand gestures towards herself, outwardly, placing her hands on the books in front of her, and repeated these gestures as she became more and more excited about what she was talking about. I don't know why she was doing this? It looked stupid to me.

Leader: So, in other words, these teacher tapes for new parents would be weak video tapes?

All: Yes, right, uh uh.

All: Except the first teacher.

New participant: Teacher two was a good video. She did good. She stressed exactly what she had, and she delivered that to the child, and that through the child, it was a new choice, also I think that was good.

All: Yeah.

Leader: So, in other words, just making general statements like "read to your child" means absolutely nothing to a mother who doesn't know how to do it?

All:	Yeah, less effective if we don't know what the teacher means. They are always telling us to read and some of us don't know what they want us to do or how they want us to do it.
New participant:	Some of us don't read that well, anyway!
Leader:	So, she needs to not only tell you, but show you in a very specific way?
All:	Yeah.
Experienced participant:	Right. That's what it's all about. You should know that always it's a good idea to ask questions or let [your child] ask you questions about the book themselves. Did they get anything out of it? It would help let you know that they were interested in the book.
Leader:	Let me tell you that something interesting can be learned from this. These teachers are all kindergarten and first-grade teachers. They are the ones who always told you as parents to read to your child. Now don't you see how difficult it is for them to do this?
All:	Right.
New participant:	And they're teaching our children?
Leader:	But, I'm saying, face it. When I did this project, they [the teachers] really didn't know what these strategies were. They had in their heads what they thought you ought to be doing, but it was hard to explain it to you. So what you are seeing is their attempt to put into words what they've been asking you to do as parents. You can see that it isn't easy. I appreciate your comments. Now we can get them to modify the tapes and get them to explain more clearly what they mean, because I won't be able to come out here all the time [meaning come to Donaldsonville Elementary School] and work with you personally. How would you tell the teachers to modify the tapes?
Experienced participant:	Confidence first, don't be nervous. Get across exactly what you're trying to teach, so we wouldn't have to guess. Use the sentence strips, but put them somewhere else. Too much in too little space with the child, book, and strips. Maybe a chart for the strips.
New participant:	Stop after demonstrating every skill. Teachers one and five should give child/viewer a chance to find out what she [the teacher] just [said]. Give us a feel for what she is saying. For

	instance, varying voice, let her [mother] see what varying your voice is all about.
Experienced participant:	One of the teachers did do that. If they would all read this story this way. So that was good.
New participant:	And let him [the child] try to do it also.
Experienced participant:	This should be pointed out to parents.
Leader:	What other things would you point out to the teacher?
All:	Get their attention, get the child's attention.
Leader:	But this is a videotape! How would you suggest they could talk to you as a part of a videotape so you could implement these strategies at home? Remember, these are teachers who have in their minds how it is supposed to be done. They read to their own children, and of course they are effective in doing this. However, the teachers are modeling for an audience who doesn't know how to share books with their children. Are you saying that they should make their comments more explicit?
Experienced participant:	Make sure the child goes through the title, even if you do it several times, because this is what you're reading about.
Leader:	Should they [teachers] have a conversation with parents?
Experienced participant:	I think so.
Leader:	So we should get it on the general tape, the teachers having a conversation with the book.
All:	Show us exactly how it needs to be done.
Leader:	Not really focus on reading the complete book.
New participant:	Get the child interested in the book. What the book is really about. Video, we [said] before is useless, it's no good, [to] me personally; I didn't get anything from it.
Leader:	Should parents be in this video, so teachers would know when their points are getting across?
All:	Yes.
Leader:	I think I might be able to arrange for that type of interaction on tape.
Two experienced participants:	[Speaking together and alternatively, filling in each other's sentences.] We felt bad! Lord, we were nervous. We were shy. We wanted Dr. Edwards to talk; we didn't want to raise our voices.
Experienced participant:	I think you have confidence because you all are speaking out. [Talking to the new mothers]. We didn't know what to say at first.

Leader:	Would other parents have the same reaction to these teacher tapes? Would they be scared to speak up when teachers don't get the point or message across to them?
All:	Right.
Leader:	Maybe the secret is to use your suggestions, and the purpose is to get the parents back to view the other tapes.
Experienced participant:	Have teachers make tapes and parents say what . . . give positive . . . there's always a negative and a positive. We can see the negative and point it out to her [the teacher] and maybe she can do better the next time. I know from coming every Monday, 'cause I really do get something out it. This is benefitin' me as well as my child. 'Cause when they said read to your child, I *thought* I was reading! All I was doin' was worryin' about finishin' the book, now I learned better. Last time I didn't finish the book, I felt Erica was gettin' bored with the colors. As soon as Erica learned her colors, she doesn't want to do the colors. She wants to get to somethin' else. That's why I like to get a variety of books. Even if I have to read the words and let her tell me the pictures.
Experienced participant:	I've always been a person who loved to read. I've always loved to read, but I didn't read as effectively to my child as I should have. But now I know it; now I'm always reading a child's book, and I'm enjoying it because of what I've learned.
Experienced participant:	I now feel more comfortable with a child's book. I don't ever read nothing else, I always feel more comfortable with Walter's books.
Experienced participant:	Right, I see the enjoyment of a book, now I'm teaching 'im.
Experienced participant:	We take the paper, and when she [the child] sees me reading the paper, she goes and gets her book, and she be sitting down there reading. She reads the pictures. That's the first thing I learned in the book-reading session, didn't know what them words was, but I'd read the pictures.
Leader:	They [children] learn that reading is done in our home. Reading is a literacy event and a book is a literacy artifact.
Experienced participant:	If it can help teachers to help our kids, it's good. Help the kids better themselves.
New participant:	My son tells me one teacher said "I got my

	education, now you need to get yours." I tell him, "Son, let the others do what they want; you need to do your school work."
Experienced participant:	That's right, that's what you're sending him to school for.

References

Anderson, R.C., Hiebert, E., Scott, J.A. & Wilkinson, I.A.G. (1985). *Becoming a nation of readers: The report of the commission of reading.* Washington, DC: The National Institute of Education.

Anderson, A.B. & Stokes, S.J. (1984). Social and institutional influences on the development and practice of literacy. In H. Goelman, A. Oberg & F. Smith (Eds.), *Awakening to literacy* (pp. 24–37). Exeter, NH: Heinemann.

Auerbach, E.R. (1989). Toward a social-contextual approach to family literacy. *Harvard Educational Review, 59* (2), 165–81.

Chall, J.S., Heron, E. & Hilferty, A. (1987). Adult literacy: New and enduring problems. *Phi Delta Kappan, 69,* 190–6.

Chall, J.S. & Snow, C. (1982). *Families and literacy: The contributions of out of school experiences to children's acquisition of literacy.* A final report to the National Institute of Education. Cambridge, MA: Harvard Graduate School of Education.

Chapman, D.L. (1986). Let's read another one. In D.R. Tovey & J.E. Kerber (Eds.), *Roles in literacy learning: A new perspective* (pp. 10–25). Newark, DE: International Reading Association.

Clark, R.M. (1988). Parents as providers of linguistic and social capital. *Educational Horizons, 66* (2), 93–5.

Darling, S. (1988). *Family literacy education: Replacing the cycle of failure with the legacy of success.* Washington, DC: Office of Educational Research and Improvement (ERIC Document Reproduction Service No. ED 332 749).

Delgado-Gaitan, C. (1987). Mexican adult literacy: New directions for immigrants. In S.R. Goldman & K. Trueba (Eds.), *Becoming literate in English as a second language* (pp. 9–32). Norwood, NJ: Ablex.

Diaz, S., Moll, L. & Mehan, K. (1986). Socio-cultural resources in instruction: A context-specific approach. In *Beyond language: Social and cultural factors in schooling language minority children* (pp. 87–229). Los Angeles: California State Department of Education and California State University.

Edwards, P.A. (1989). Supporting lower SES mothers' attempts to provide scaffolding for bookreading. In J. Allen & J. Mason (Eds.), *Risk makers, risk takers, risk breakers: Reducing the risks for young literacy learners* (pp. 222–50). Portsmouth, NH: Heinemann.

Edwards, P.A. (1990a). *Parents as partners in reading: A family literacy training program.* Chicago: Childrens Press.

Edwards, P.A. (1990b). *Talking your way to literacy: A program to help nonreading parents prepare their children for reading.* Chicago: Childrens Press.

Edwards, P.A. (1991). Fostering early literacy through parent coaching. In

E. Hiebert (Ed.), *Literacy for a diverse society: Perspectives, programs, and policies* (pp. 199–213). New York: Teachers College Press.

Edwards, P.A. (1992, Autumn). Involving parents in building reading instruction for African-American children. *Theory Into Practice, 31* (4), 350–9.

Edwards, P.A. & Garcia, G.E. (1991). Parental involvement in mainstream schools. In M. Foster (Ed.), *Readings on equal education: Qualitative investigations into schools and schooling* (pp. 167–87). New York: AMA Press, Inc.

Erickson, F. (1989). Forward: Literacy risks for students, parents, and teachers. In J. Allen & J. Mason (Eds.), *Risk makers, risk takers, risk breakers: Reducing the risks for young literacy learners* (pp. xiii–xvi). Portsmouth, NH: Heinemann.

Gallimore, R., Weisner, R., Kaufman, S. & Bernheimer, L.P. (1989). The social construction of ecocultural niches: Family accommodation of developmentally delayed children. *American Journal of Mental Retardation, 94* (3), 216–30.

Goldenberg, C.N. (1984, October 10–13). *Low-income parents' contributions to the reading achievement of their first-grade children.* Paper presented at the meeting of the Evaluation Network/Evaluation Research Society, San Francisco.

Hale-Benson, J. (1990). Achieving equal educational outcomes for black children. In A. Barona & E.E. Garcia (Eds.), *Children at risk: Poverty, minority status, and other issues in educational equity* (pp. 201–15). Washington, DC: National Association of School Psychologists.

Hearron, P.F. (1992). *Kindergarten homework in non-mainstream families: The school-family interface in the ecology of emergent literacy.* Unpublished doctoral dissertation, Michigan State University, East Lansing, MI.

Heath, S.B. (1982). What no bedtime story means: Narrative skills at home and school. *Language in Society, 11,* 49–76.

Heath, S.B. (1983). *Ways with words: Language, life, and work in communities and classrooms.* New York: Cambridge University Press.

Heath, S.B. & Thomas, C. (1984). The achievement of preschool literacy for mother and child. In H. Goelman, A. Oberg & F. Smith (Eds.), *Awakening to literacy* (pp. 51–72). London: Heinemann.

Huey, E.B. (1908). *The psychology and pedagogy of reading.* New York: MacMillan.

Leichter, H.J. (1984). Families as environments for literacy. In H. Goelman, A. Oberg & F. Smith (Eds.), *Awakening to literacy* (pp. 38–50). Exeter, NH: Heinemann.

Lundsford, A.A., Moglen, H. & Slevin, J. (1990). Introduction. In A.A. Lunsford, H. Moglen & J. Slevin (Eds.), *The right to literacy* (pp. 1–6). New York: The Modern Language Association of America.

Mahoney, E. & Wilcox, L. (1985). *Ready, set, read: Best books to prepare preschoolers.* Metuchen, NJ: Scarecrow Press.

Morrow, L.M. (1988). Young children's responses to one-to-one story readings in school settings. *Reading Research Quarterly, 23,* 89–107.

Nickse, R., Speicher, A.M. & Bucheck, P. (1988, April). *An intergenerational adult literacy project: A family intervention/prevention model.* Paper presented at the annual meeting of the American Educational Research Association, New Orleans, LA.

208   *Patricia A. Edwards*

Ninio, A. (1980). Picturebook reading in mother-infant dyads belonging to two subgroups in Israel. *Child Development, 51,* 587–90.

Ninio, A. & Bruner, J. (1978). The achievement and antecedents of labelling. *Journal of child Language, 5,* 1–15.

Potter, G. (1989). Parent participation in language arts programs. *Language Arts, 66* (1), 29–43.

Resnick, M.B., Roth, J., Aaron, P.M., Scott, J., Wolking, W.D., Laren, J.J. & Packer, A.B. (1987). Mothers reading to infants: A new observational tool. *The Reading Teacher, 40,* 888–95.

Schickedanz, J. (1986). *More than ABCs: The early stages of reading and writing.* Washington, DC: National Association for the Education of Young Children.

Shannon, (1989). *Broken promises: Reading instruction in 20th Century America.* Granby, MA: Bergin & Garvey.

Snow, C. (1987). Factors influencing vocabulary and reading achievement in low come children. In R. Apple (Ed.), *Toegepaste yTaalwentenschap in Artikelen,* Special 2, (pp. 124–8). Amsterdam: ANELA.

Snow, C., Barnes, W.S., Chandler, J., Goodman, I.F. & Hemphill, L. (1991). *Unfulfilled expectations: Home and school influences on literacy.* Cambridge: Harvard University.

Super, C. & Harkness, S. (1986). The developmental niche: A conceptualization at the interface of child and culture. *International Journal of Behaviour Development, 9,* 1–25.

Taylor, D. & Dorsey-Gaines, C. (1989). *Growing up literate: Learning from inner-city families.* Portsmouth, NH: Heinemann.

Taylor, D. & Strickland, D. (1986). *Family storybook reading.* Portsmouth, NH: Heinemann.

Vukelich, C. (1984). Parents' role in the reading process. A review of practical suggestions to communicate with parents. *The Reading Teacher, 37,* 472–77.

Ziefert, H. (1985). *Baby Ben gets dressed.* New York: Random House.

Part 4

Evaluating Complex Family Literacy Programs

9 Collaborations: A Key to Success in Family Literacy Programs

Ruth S. Nickse and Shelley Quezada

Family Literacy Approaches

Family and intergenerational literacy practice is a new approach which attempts to work on solutions to the ubiquitous problem of low literacy among a large proportion of adults and children in the United States. Family and intergenerational literacy programs, innovations in adult basic-education service delivery, view the parent and child as a learning unit and design special activities to improve the literacy of both. Projects use home- and center-based sites usually staffed by multidisciplinary teams. Faith in two-generational practice rests on evidence from research in several disparate areas. Each discipline contributes data that supports the need for positive interactions between parents and children for their optimal development in cognitive, emotional, physical, and social spheres.

Particularly important to these programs is the parents' role in literacy development. Studies in emergent literacy indicate that home and community values shape literacy habits, that children who are read to in a positive way on a regular basis start school with more early success in learning to read, and that parents' education, particularly mothers', has an effect on children's school achievement (see chapters 1, 3, and 5). Unfortunately, another finding is that parents with limited literacy skills are often, for a variety of reasons, unable to provide the kinds of positive support needed for optimal literacy development. These may include a lack of facility with reading itself, unfamiliarity with the idea of family reading and its benefits to children from lack of experience, and, in many poor households, a lack of children's books or much attractive reading material. Literacy improvement is only one goal in the lives of families in need of assistance in a myriad of other areas. Literacy practice does not thrive in a vacuum, or in families beset with social, emotional, and economic problems. Increasingly, developers of literacy programs are becoming aware that literacy improvement cannot be separated from the constellation of other factors that impinge on families' well being, such as poverty and its effects, quality of parenting, and communication with schools.

Literacy is not an end in itself, rather it is a means to a better life for families. Programs are being developed with the realization that literacy is a slender thread that binds many issues together. Family literacy programs place an emphasis on the enjoyment of literacy as well as such functional aspects as its importance to children's school achievement and adults' success in finding work in a worsening job market. This larger focus on the enabling of literacy development reflects a broader definition of the term and is a departure from the more mechanical and skills-oriented focus of many current adult basic-education (ABE) programs. Further, the focus on family reading and the incorporation of the young children of adult learners in programs signals a fundamental change in practice. To understand this profound change, some background information on the generic structure is now offered as a context for a further discussion of significant common features of these programs, and of the collaboration required for the delivery of services.

Models of Family Literacy

Though the concept of family literacy has gained power in recent years, there is considerable variety in its practice. The proliferation of many approaches has lead to difficulty in documenting effectiveness. One problem has been the lack of a descriptive framework. In an effort to help remedy this problem, Nickse (1990; 1991) developed a typology of generic models of family literacy practice, which is presented in table 1. It helps identify characteristics of programs that serve adults and children and is useful in program planning and evaluation.

Each model has different beneficiaries and purposes. Goals range from complex, joint instructional programs with direct teaching of parents and children to less formal programs that supplement formal school instruction for children. Models vary in duration, intensity, and program features. Nationally, the Even Start Family Literacy program, described in detail in a later section, is a good example of the Type I model, and another is the Kenan Family Trust program, both of which have projects in many states. These programs directly instruct parents and children in reading as well as in other family-oriented activities, including parenting. Type 2 programs are often found in libraries where

Table 1 Four generic types of family and intergenerational literacy programs

Type	Examples of features	Examples of concerns and issues
Type 1 Parent/child	Goal is positive, long term family intervention parent/child; parent; child; activities intense, frequent participation highly structured; formal instruction direct instruction; dual curriculum ECE/ABE staff team monitored attendance dedicated site; collaborations long term intervention	long term program high time commitment necessary retention in program is a problem facilities for ECE/ABE together transportation for families child care for infants, toddlers high degree of collaboration needed substantial costs to initiate and maintain; funding an issue
Type 2 Adult/child	Goal is supplementary, for skill building and enjoyment nonrelated adults and children; parents and children lower level of intensity, participation less structured; more informal weekends, after school programs collaborations (none to many) adapted sites short term intervention	little or no formal, sustained literacy instruction for adult/child less intensive participation lacks full time ECE/ABE staff less parent/child interaction parttime staffing short term programs costs to initiate and maintain; funding an issue

Table 1 Four generic types of family and intergenerational literacy programs

Type		Examples of features	Examples of concerns and issues
Type 3	Adult alone	Goal is parent education parents/adults alone – children present infrequently or not at all workshop formats; low intensity peer instruction and practice "portable" curriculum parent networking short term intervention	short term program no supervised parent/child interaction parttime staffing; consultants parent reports of programs' success developmentally inappropriate activities may be used by parents costs to initiate and maintain; funding an issue
Type 4	Child alone	Goal is supplementary school related literacy improvement for children school-based children; at-home parents school linked program teacher supervised take-home materials for children short term intervention	short term program parents receive no literacy instruction for themselves parent may not provide support at home for child parent may not participate in workshops, rallies low cost

Source: © R. Nickse (1993). A typology of family and intergenerational literacy programs: Implications for evaluation (ERIC ED 333 166)

volunteers and/or senior citizens read to neighborhood children. They differ from Type 1 programs because they are often of shorter duration and may focus less on formal instruction and more on the enjoyment of reading. Type 3 programs serve parents, reaching their children indirectly by enhancing the parents' abilities to select books and read to their children. The Family Reading Program described in chapter 7 is representative. Reading Is Fundamental is a good example of a Type 4 program in which children are the primary beneficiaries of a supplemental reading program, and the participation of parents is supportive of children's efforts (though the parents are not involved in literacy improvement themselves). Each of the generic models is useful in specific contexts, but because structures are different, expectations, outcomes, and prefered evaluation strategies are also.

Regardless of generic variations or specific program differences, one common features of model types is their attention to literacy development as a social activity and their support for family reading. Another is their reliance on collaborations of one type or another to organize and deliver literacy services. None of the model types can be administered successfully without some degree of collaboration.

The Need for Collaborations

Family literacy programs attempt to assist families in a more holistic manner than do traditional adult education programs, the fragmentation of which results in frequent failures to serve families adequately. The current system of social welfare and education divides the problems of families into rigid categories (e.g., adult basic education and early childhood education), failing to deal with their interrelated causes and solutions as well as with their intergenerational nature. Programs are under way in human services and education that involve structuring interagency partnerships in order to connect children and their parents in more comprehensive and better coordinated services (Habana-Hafner & Reed, 1990; Himmelman, 1990; Kagan, 1991; Quezada & Nickse, 1992; Smith, 1991a; 1991b). An example of the problem is the "three turkeys" scenario, in which families receive bountiful provisions on a holiday from three separate agencies and are largely forgotten the rest of the year. More important services are overlooked or drop through the cracks on a regular basis when human services are poorly coordinated and work in isolation. It is hoped that collaborations can reduce costly duplication of programs and can initiate better organized services (Bruner, 1991).

The Collaborative Process

The administration of family literacy programs depends on collaborations, yet human service workers may not understand the process and mechanisms involved in any sophisticated way. Though the notion of collaborations may be a new concept to them, literature on the topic does exist, mainly in the fields of economics, business, and organizational psychology, as reported by Kagan (1991b). She treats collaborations from a perspective drawn from these three fields but does not directly address issues specific to the family literacy context, focusing instead on the less complex issue of child care. Despite this narrower focus, Kagan's book contains much that is pertinent to family literacy projects interested in fostering collaboration.

Driven by the desire to improve the quality and distribution of service, the need for cost-effective and family-centered services, and the growing number of low-income families, collaborations for children's care and education are accelerating. However, ambiguity surrounds their outcomes, processes, rationales, and history. In the arena of early childhood education, confusion about collaborations rests on several failures: lack of systematic investigation of collaborations as social constructs; lack of analysis of their evolution; and lack of distillation of the many frameworks developed for understanding them (Kagan, 1991). These shortcomings are also present in the family literacy movement, even though collaborations are a key component in many of them. Understanding the collaborative process and the mediating variables that hasten or halt a collaboration is important to any human services delivery. Goal setting, sharing of resources, power, and authority, and flexibility in the collaborative structure are four important features of smooth and effective operations. In offering her own definition, Kagan distinguishes collaboration as the apex capping two other constructs, namely, cooperation and coordination: "Collaboration entails organizational and interorganizational structures where resources, power and authority are shared and where people are brought together to achieve common goals that could not be accomplished by a single individual or organization independently" (Kagan, 1991, p. 3).

Theoretically, this interaction between different structures may seem easy to accomplish with its assumptions about egalitarian leadership and sharing, good will and mutually acceptable goals, and a dependable pool of resources. The neatness of the definition and these unspoken values, however, belie the true processes that go on in actual practice. The building and maintaining of collaborations often proceed erratically and idiosyncratically. Barriers do appear, and whether collaborations survive them and invoke appropriate solutions to achieve their common goals is key to their success.

An Example of a Collaborative Family Literacy Program

One of the pioneering programs in family literacy, which predated Even Start and was cited as a precedent, was deliberately titled Collaborations for Literacy (CFL, 1984–9). Illustrative of Kagan's quotation, it was initially planned as a collaborative project in recognition of the complex nature of literacy improvement in families. It was developed and administered as a public/private venture in both implementation and funding and included: (a) literacy tutors provided by Boston University through its College Work-Study program and release time for a faculty member to direct the project; (b) a community school that provided recruitment access to an adult basic education population with children; (c) a branch of the Boston Public Library, which offered tutoring space and its book collections; and (d) the state affiliate of Literacy Volunteers of America, which trained the original tutors. Later, a complete computer center for use by families was added to the activities under the supervision of Playing To Win, Inc. Funding over the years came from a variety of sources including Boston University, the Massachusetts State Department of Education, a local foundation, and a national foundation (Nickse and Englander, 1985).

In the CFL example, a basic Type 3 family literacy program was established and was modified over a period of five years. The project provided an initiation for its members into collaborative practice in a local program. An advisory board with key representatives made decisions for the Collaboration, and formal memoranda outlined responsibilities. While power and authority remained stable, members changed, and resources waxed and waned. Over the duration of the project, hundreds of adults and children received services related to the improvement of literacy. The project overcame many obstacles as it metamorphosed. Through the dedication of the group and the belief in a common goal, a full-time neighborhood Family Learning Center was opened and served 85 families in a short eight-month period before its funding was cut. This experience proved the viability of a family reading project (helped in part by the use of the Reading Rainbow television programs and accompanying children's literature) and shaped the investigators' interests in the collaborative process, resulting in a second project, Community Collaborations for Family Literacy (CCFL), which is described later in this chapter.

Public, private, federal, state, and local agencies in great variety are now attempting to alleviate the schisms in service delivery. Collaborations at both the macro- and microlevel are burgeoning among human services, health, and education departments. The success in understanding collaborations as social constructs lies in delineating some of their key elements – their origin, membership, salient characteristics, and structures. These affect the way collaborations work, the pool of resources available to them, and the types of facilitating activities they undertake.

To illustrate, the origins of a collaboration influence its structure. Legislative mandate is one way to start a collaboration; indeed it is the mechanism used to ensure cooperative projects in the Even Start Family Literacy programs mentioned earlier. The voluntary collaboration, in which diverse groups draw together to plan family literacy projects, is another way. Both the original CFL project and its successor, CCFL, are examples of voluntary collaboratives. Whether mandated or voluntary, delivery of services in a collaborative framework is a new experience for most human-service workers and educators. Too little attention has been paid to the *process* of being part of collaborations, a process that can be organized rather easily in theory but is difficult to maintain in practice. A missing topic in discussions of collaborations is the notion that the collaborative process can be taught and learned. An example of a project that addressed this learning process directly is described in the next section.

Building Collaborations for Family Literacy

An example of an attempt to facilitate collaboration comes from the project Community Collaborations for Family Literacy (CCFL). The Massachusetts Board of Library Commissioners, which is the State Library Agency in the Commonwealth of Massachusetts, received federal funds in 1989–90 under the Library Services and Construction Act (LSCA), Title VI, to implement a statewide planning process for family literacy. The project targeted six diverse geographic communities in the state (urban, suburban, and rural). Its mission was to initiate and implement voluntary collaborations which would then plan local family literacy projects during 1990–1. If the collaborations were successful in preparing promising preproposal applications, they would be invited to apply for seed grants during 1992–3 to begin their projects, an incentive that the financially strapped communities greeted with pleasure. Furthermore, those who prepared proposals revealed that this project was a first for them – an experiment in nourishing community planning.

Each local library coordinated a team of representatives from adult basic education, Chapter I programs, and family support services. Local teams had little or no prior experience in collaborative planning for community service delivery. The six teams (which varied in size and composition) held a series of planning meetings during a nine-month period. Technical assistance was provided by the authors through (a) information sharing about collaborations and their organization; (b) participation in a special, invitational, statewide family literacy conference; (c) site visits by staff members to each community; (d) provision of new books, articles, and research materials on family literacy for the libraries; and (e) ongoing technical assistance through personal contact, telephone, or mail. Methods of data collection included site visits, a review of site notebooks that documented the process of each collaboration as it formed, evaluations of conferences and workshops, and in-depth interviews with participants about their experiences.

The projects resulted in the establishment of local collaboratives in six communities; five groups jointly wrote and submitted preproposal applications to the lead agency. Teams cited the project as a unique and positive experience in community planning and process. Participants agreed that it created an unusual opportunity for local networking and changed their perception of literacy service from a matter of individuals to a matter of families.

Features of the Collaborative Process

Kagan (1991) notes that there have been sustained pleas for co-ordination, consolidation, and collaboration in human services, with similar calls resounding through early child care and education. She also notes that the practice is accelerating and calls for research to investigate the evolution of collaborations, and for efforts to distill the many frameworks developed in other fields that might be germane to early child care. Unfortunately, Kagan's book was not available when this project was designed. So, while the present work is not the robust examination Kagan calls for, it does lend insight into the collaborative process.

The conceptualization of the key elements of collaborations emerged (table 2) as a result of the study. It sorts out the members, their roles and responsibilities, and the structures, resources, and events necessary to promote the development of family literacy practice. This working model describes the Massachusetts project and thus is selective rather than comprehensive; we hope that readers can apply it to similar situations.

From two successive experiences, the investigators have learned that agencies and organizations at three different levels of action must be

Table 2 Key elements of collaboration in support of family literacy

Level	Members	Characteristics	Structure	Resources committed	Facilitative activities
Level 3 *State and/or corporate*	State Directors of Adult Education; Chapter I; Head Start; Even Start State librarian Corporate director of public relations Other appropriate designees	Systems orientation Mandates or encourages local collaborations Initiates/implements state policies State and Federal political considerations Networks with multiple agencies Formal written agreements Formal leadership Quarterly meetings (or less frequently) Mandated or voluntary origin	Agencies maintain separate identities and missions Targets overlapping client groups Delegates representative as decision maker Requires written agreements Maintains line relationships with Level 2	Supports technical assistance consultant Dedicates state monies and federal set asides Provides incentives for participation Sponsors shared training events Provides resources and collections on family literacy	Initiates interagency collaborative policy agenda Issues joint plans for RFP format, process Initiates joint program evaluation Arranges joint funding and funding cycle Conducts Informational and Bidders' Conference Disseminates information Arranges for training Communicates with Level 2

Level 2 Local community					
Local Directors of Adult basic/ESL education; Chapter I; Head Start Local library Community agencies Other appropriate designees	Service area orientation Initiates or responds to mandate to collaborate Initiates/implements local community policies State and local political considerations Networks with local agencies Formal written agreements Collegial leadership Monthly meetings (or more frequently) Mandated or voluntary origin	Gain of new group identity and focus on shared mission Targets overlapping client groups Individual decision-makers from various agencies Requires written agreements Maintains line relationships with Levels 1 and 3	Supports representative to collaborative Dedicates a portion of funds and resources Responds to incentives for participation Publicizes activities of collaboration and focus on family literacy Arranges for joint training Supports joint referrals Distributes resource materials	Develops, administers, maintains collaboration Develops shared mission for joint planning Conducts joint training; needs assessment Writes funding proposal Disseminates information Develops job criteria for staff Communicates with Levels 1 and 3	

Table 2 Key elements of collaboration in support of family literacy

Level	Members	Characteristics	Structure	Resources committed	Facilitative activities
Level 1 *Program site*	Teachers of Adult basic/ESL education; Chapter I; Head Start Adult services/ Children's librarians Volunteer tutors Home Visitors Parents and children	Participant families orientation Implements new or combined program Implements, revises, suggests site policies Local and site political considerations Implements collaborative instructional practices Formal or informal agreements Team-based case management Weekly or day-to-day contact	Identification as team members with shared mission Serves diverse client group Team based decision making Informal agreements within written framework Maintains line relationships with Level 2	Supports team-based staff Provides program space Provides incentives to client families Publicizes joint activities Attends joint training Uses joint referrals	Conducts team-based case management program Implements shared mission Conducts joint training; curriculum design; joint instruction Implements center and home-based program special events Involves parent participation Communicates infrequently with other Levels

Source: © S. Quezada and R. Nickse (1993). *Community collaborations for family literacy.* NY: Neal Schuman Publishers, Inc.

involved in interagency relationships in order to successfully propel collaborations. Both the CFL and the CCFL projects found that relationships between partners in the hierarchy impact on the success (or perhaps the failure) of the collaborations – collaborations are "nested" within each other much like children's Russian dolls. For the sake of convenience, these hierarchical elements can be categorized in three levels and arrayed by five categories, as shown in table 2.

Key Elements of Collaborations in Support of Family Literacy

Level 1

The most tangible evidence of collaborative family literacy activities in table 2 is at Level 1. On-site collaboration involves local program practice and implementation of a new family literacy program under the aegis of the community collaboration. Its orientation is to provide direct program service to participant families within a new team-based administrative framework. At this level, the shared mission is implemented, and policies for the program practice are revised and maintained. The essence of collaboration is joining the skills of teachers possessing different expertise in early childhood and adult basic education and melding them into a new, integrated team to conduct a family literacy program. Level 1 teachers, home workers, and volunteers identify themselves as team members and operate by team-based decision making to ensure the smooth functioning of the program. Whether the agreements about practice are formal or informal, local site and community political considerations prevail. Facilitating activities such as joint training take place to establish the curricula and delineate responsibilities among members. The participation of parents is extremely important to the operation of Level I collaboration and mechanisms for their input integral to staff training. Level 1 communication flows from daily or weekly personal contacts of multidisciplinary staff and families. The original Collaborations for Literacy project is an example of a Level 1 collaboration with Level 2 supervision and partial funding from a Level 3 agency.

Level 2

The community collaboration level (Level 2) has a broad service-area responsibility and orientation. The initiation and administrative aspects of this type of collaboration may begin with Level 2. Through the collaboration members gain identification and focus by designing a new cooperative project for a target population in which they have a vested interest. Members must develop shared goals to benefit the participant group. Directors or managers are challenged to maintain the integrity of their own city or county agencies or organizations while allowing for the necessary negotiation with other agencies. This may entail an individual agency giving up some power or authority in order to develop a successful project. A balance has to be struck between implementing local community policies and practices and being responsive to those with concerns in the hierarchy above. Collegial leadership helps even out power disparities caused by unequal resources. A key factor in successful communication here is the ability of the agency representative (if that person is not the director) to accurately report the actions or activities of the collaboration so that informed decisions can be made by the agency director.

Level 2 local directors were the participants targeted to begin the collaborations in the CCFL project. Key individuals represented local libraries, programs such as Adult Basic Education, Chapter I, Head Start, and designees from a great variety of other organizations and agencies. The mix included a total of 26 different types of agencies and organizations. Though educational agencies were common, more unusual teams had representatives from such groups as employment and training organizations, the Girl Scouts, service clubs, the criminal justice system, and local cable television companies. Over time, the successful teams learned to share power, authority, and resources to achieve the common goal (i.e., developing a working collaborative that could design a Level 1 project in each community). Although joined to meet common local needs, successful collaborations structured themselves differently to complete important facilitating activities. For instance, some groups met more frequently than others, more than twice as much as their commitment entailed. Some groups were large, with more than 15 organizations involved; others were smaller, with five or six agencies represented. Regardless of size, all committed resources of funds, time, and materials, and publicized the activities of their local collaboration. Each successful team conducted some type of needs assessment and agreed on a target population to be served. As they moved toward a working collaboration, they progressed developmentally, but differently.

One community had already developed a small family literacy program and needed to expand its collaborative umbrella to obtain more resources. This group moved more quickly into the collaborative process at Level 2 because it had an existing Level 1 model developed internally within the local school department. It needed external agency partners to stabilize its work. Other communities, new to the collaborative process, found themselves sharing many common concerns about community literacy development and were thus able to develop working relationships and structures on that basis. Diminishing resources were a shared problem – each community depended on local or state funding that became more scarce and mired in budget crises during the project year. One community lacked a crucial Level 2 participant organization (an Adult Basic Education program) and decided to collaborate with a neighboring community, which slowed the process of team building and changed the nature of the local collaboration.

Level 3

Level 3 has a systems orientation and includes a number of state educational and human-service agencies. It is represented by directors or their designees who speak for their agencies to a broad range of others, both internally and externally. State (or corporate) directors or designees have critical power and authority and are a connection to resources that cannot be accessed directly by Level 2 (or Level 1) collaborators. They can initiate broad policy agendas and set family literacy priorities across and within bureaucratic organizations. Structurally, Level 3 agencies maintain separate identities and missions, and target a large and overlapping client group. While Level 3 groups may meet less regularly, their range of resources and initiatives are singular. They have the power to mandate or encourage volunteer agency collaborations at Level 2, and they control the incentives for participation that attract community action. The challenge at this Level is to maintain the integrity of the agency while allowing some leeway for negotiations with other agencies, a dilemma similar to that confronting Level 2 collaborations.

The present economy stifles the opportunities for visionary realignment of working relationships at Level 3 in Massachusetts because of slow response time of bureaucracies, budget cuts, and concerns about turf and accountability. Ideally, the success of Level 3 collaborations might include the issuance of a collaborative "Request for Proposal" process, the development of joint evaluation plans, the use of the same funding cycle, and possibly the establishment of a liaison at the state level to provide technical assistance to agencies.

The implementation of the CCFL project occurred at Level 3, with the state level agency, the Massachusetts Board of Library Commissioners, as the initiator. The idea of the project began in dialogues with other Level 3 agencies (especially Adult Basic Education in the

State Department of Education). The lead agency administered the grant and undertook facilitating activities. It committed resources of several kinds: incentives to the participant communities with the promise of project seed money, technical assistance, and sponsorship of workshops and a state conference.

The current case illustrates the need for an integration of the hierarchy of support for the development of family literacy projects. The earlier CFL project was designed as a Level 2 project, and received partial funding from the State Department of Education (Level 3) for several years as a special project but little help for the development of the original idea and early research into program effects. While the pioneering CFL project published research reports and administrative manuals on family literacy practice that circulated throughout adult basic education programs, the project itself had little influence on State practice. The CCFL project was designed at Level 3 with a larger role, and it established, within its own agency, a state priority for family literacy development. In both examples, Level 3 support was vital for success. However, CCFL had a broader impact on the family literacy agenda in the State partly because of the wise handling of power and authority by the lead agency, and partly because of timing; the climate for family literacy was more favorable for the CCFL project. In fact, as a direct result of CCFL, the concept of family literacy was supported in a new, statewide plan for educational reform, that, if passed, would broaden support for the idea at Level 3.

Results of the CCFL Project.   Kagan (1991) speaks of two goals in collaborations, to produce direct services and to foster or create system changes. The order of these goals is important. The intent of the CCFL project was to reverse the order of the two goals (i.e., first to create systems changes at Level 2 and then to produce new direct services at Level 1). By this standard, CCFL was a success. There were systems changes in the behaviors and attitudes about and in preparations for joint projects. According to the data collected, Level 2 community teams gained:

- New tools for interagency planning
- Better ways to serve the same target population
- Reduced isolation in agencies
- A local network of service providers
- New materials and resources in communities through the libraries
- Establishment of libraries as a traditional support for family literacy

- New outreach strategies to attract different target populations
- The exchange of information to aid problem solving and goal setting for educationally disadvantaged families
- Encouragement of state policy makers to make a public commitment to family literacy
- Five preproposals for future family literacy projects

Barriers to Collaborations.   We found Kagan's depiction of collaborations as "microstrategies subjected to macroevents" to be true. While participants identified many insights into the processes of successful collaborations (see table 2), they often confronted barriers to collaboration and the planning process. Using the table 2 framework as a post-hoc guide for analysis, we can attribute most of the interruptions to Level 2 problems, the level of the project teams. They included

- Lack of sufficient authority on the part of a few team members to commit their agencies to the final project development
- Fluctuations in the compositions of the teams that created an inability to focus and complete the mission
- Lack of representation on the teams by key agencies
- Time constraints of members who still had to do their "real jobs"
- Turf issues that could not be solved
- Lack of resources for such simple tasks as photocopying and mailing
- "Force majeure" – state and local budget cuts that forced agencies to fight for survival
- Obstacles to facilitating activities in Level 3 agencies

That the barriers to the collaborative process experienced in the CCFL project were not unusual is the topic of the next section, which discusses Even Start, a nationwide project in family literacy. Because Even Start projects are involved in a national evaluation, and because collaboration is a mandated component, they are an excellent source of information about the use of collaborations to promote the family literacy agenda.

Collaborations in Even Start

The CFL and CCFL projects were relatively small-scale inexpensive interventions in Massachusetts. Are the insights from these projects, although limited in scope, helpful in discussing the potential benefits, problems, and challenges in a national effort like Even Start?

Background

The Even Start Family Literacy program began as a federal program in 1989 and became a state-administered program in 1992. The theory behind the Even Start Act is that literacy develops in contexts, that it is a social process fostered in the relationships between parents and children. Even Start programs are examples of generic Type 1 programs and are innovative efforts to deliver services to educationally and economically disadvantaged families. The Act requires that projects be "family focused" (rather than parent- or child-focused), and must provide an integrated program of "core services" including adult basic-education skills, parenting, and early childhood education. It is thought that these components are interrelated and that addressing them simultaneously in one intervention may be necessary to effect the lasting changes in families that will ultimately improve children's chances for school success. Programs also supply "support services" (e.g., transportation and child care) so that families can participate. Eligibility for the program pertains to families in which an adult qualifies for adult basic education, has a child eight years old or younger, and lives in a Chapter I attendance area. The goals of the demonstration projects are to: (a) help parents become full partners in the education of their children, (b) assist children in reaching their full potential as learners, and (c) provide literacy training for the parents.

Examples of parent–child activities include working on readiness skills, playing together using arts and crafts, and reading storybooks. Parenting education may cover topics such as child development, techniques for discipline, building self-esteem, life-skills instruction, and health and nutrition education. Adult education activities include preparation for earning a high school diploma, basic literacy skills, and English as a Second Language (ESL). Early childhood education programs include curricula to foster healthy social and emotional development as well as to prepare children for school success. This inclusion of the early childhood curricula may strike readers as similar to the more familiar Head Start, and to Parent Support programs conducted in some states. One key difference is Even Start's emphasis on the educational needs of the *parents* of at-risk children and *family* literacy.[1]

Depending on local collaborations, families may be enrolled in both Head Start and Even Start for different services; they serve a similar population. Demographic information provides some selected characteristics of Even Start families. Early results reported in 1992 (the most recent data) indicate that about 4,777 families participated in Even Start in fiscal year 1990–1. Though the most common family structure is in the form of couples (49%), single parents account for 39 percent of those served. Seventy-three percent of the adults are in the age range from 22 to 39 years. Their primary language is English, but 81 percent of those who read English evaluate their skills as marginal. The annual income of Even Start families is low: Seventy percent of families have an annual income under $10,000. Of all adults participating 70 percent are unemployed. The education level of the adults varies: Twenty-four percent have a high school diploma or a GED, 53 percent have some high school experience and 23 percent have no high school experience. Forty percent of the children are white, 30 percent are black, 16 percent are Hispanic, and 14 percent are of other racial backgrounds (Even Start National Evaluation, 1992; St. Pierre, 1992; St. Pierre et al., 1991).

The National Even Start Act, passed in 1989 and revised in 1991, requires "cooperative projects" – a description that, in practice, is taken to mean collaborations. In part, the text reads that "the program shall be implemented through cooperative projects that build on existing community resources to create a new range of services" (Elementary and Secondary Education Act, Part B, Chapter I, Title I, Public Law 100–297).

Given the broad charge to improve literacy in this manner and the major expectations of the Even Start Law, how do the local projects deliver their services? Does Even Start, which mandates cooperative projects, have anything to learn from the voluntary collaborations established in the CFL/CCFL projects?

Even Start Collaborations

The mechanisms Even Start programs use to deliver their core and support services are collaborations that operate broadly like those in the CFL/CCFL projects. They are administered through cooperative arrangements and are provided by a range of local agencies. Typically, the cooperating agencies provide support services so that families can participate in the core services. Theoretically, collaboration enables Even Start programs to take advantage of local resources without replicating them, thus reducing costly redundancies in services. Mechanisms for decision making are handled primarily through informal communications and agreements, with formal written agreements less common. Interestingly, according to early data, joint advisory boards for making decisions are rare.

The membership agencies in Even Start resemble those in the CFL/CCFL projects with one exception. The lead support for Even Start is provided by Chapter I, which is administered through public schools. It is not surprising to find that its major collaborators are other departments and programs within the public schools within the same administrative structure. External partners include local county, state, and tribal agencies; postsecondary institutions; Head Start/Home Start; and other religious, fraternal, or volunteer groups in communities. The services they provide to families include transportation, personal and nutrition counseling, health and child care, meals, employment referrals, family advocacy, help for battered women, help with drug abuse, and handicap care. Even Start projects were involved in 1,059 cooperative arrangements during the 1990–1 program year. Both in core and support services, then, Even Start projects depend heavily on collaboration with a variety of local agencies for diverse services. In many instances, if not most, these represent new alliances and new ways of delivering educational interventions in support of literacy.

In the absence of the completed national evaluation,[2] using the lens provided by the CLF/CCFL experiences, we can speculate on some of the possibilities, problems, and challenges which may affect program success.

Potential Benefits

If the CFL/CCFL findings summarized in table 2 can be generalized, the collaborations in Even Start should benefit key elements (structure, resources, and facilitating activities) within communities in support of family literacy. Ideally, success for Even Start projects develops from a combination of efforts, that is, vertical collaborations between the three Levels (state, community, and local program sites) listed in table 2. Power, authority, shared resources, and the synergy created by a unidirectional flow of communications and activities should create an unusual and effective new literacy intervention. At Level 1, shared goals, multidisciplinary, team-based staffs, team-based decision making, access to dedicated resources and the facilitating activities needed to push the agenda are possible and in many instances in place. In other programs such resources can become available through collaborations and advisory boards at Level 2. Administration of the Even Start program at Level 3 in states allows for wider control of the programs and should trigger local community acceptance and support. The success of Level 1 programs rests on their flexibility and responsiveness, and in their ability to develop and maintain their local program collaborations. Yet, there are indications of some barriers to success.

Barriers

Membership.   Even Start projects may confront several problems in systems and service implementation experienced by the CFL/CCFL projects, which may take the form of fluctuations in the memberships that inhibit the joint mission. A lack of representation by key agencies (such as adult basic education), for example, may tilt the curricula toward a strong early childhood program and a weak ABE/ESL program, with the result being a loss of balance and integration.

Constraints. Time or resource constraints (i.e., lack of funding) may cramp purchase of necessary external services – there may be no money to buy a dedicated van to pick up families who have odd schedules or live far away. Unresolvable turf issues can virtually shut down or skew the collaboration membership. Obstacles in Level 2 or Level 3 agencies may also frustrate the smooth operation of collaborations. Indeed, among the implementation problems reported by at least one-third of the Even Start projects, many were related to "coordination and communication with cooperating agencies." Several of these scenarios were typical problems faced by the CFL/CCFL projects. In these cases, more personal contact was often, but not always, a useful solution.

The CFL project had a strong advisory board (Level 2) to conduct it; yet according to early data, few Even Start programs have such boards. This finding is perplexing, and may indicate a structural weakness. Advisory boards with representative agencies supply facilities and resources, and have vested ownership in program success: They expand the circle of responsibility. They also increase personal contact and improve communication. In the CCFL project, strong leadership by the lead agency (Level 3) helped negotiate most, not all, barriers to the collaborations.

Service. Several other systems and service problems in Even Start collaborations are foreshadowed by the CFL/CCFL research. For example, there may be a lack of integration in Even Start across the local program curricula, which could be a result of poor communication between the Even Start projects and, say, the local Adult Basic Education (ABE) program. Though the aims of the two programs are similar in that each hopes to increase the literacy development of parents and though context is undoubtedly important in literacy learning, each of these programs may approach literacy development with a different philosophy or instructional purpose. If poor communication occurs at Level 1, or if the Even Start program staff does not attempt to understand the instructional mission of ABE and the early childhood services with which it collaborates (or vice versa), there may be a failure of curriculum integration that results in a fragmented literacy program from the parents' perspective. Jointly funded staff members specifically assigned to plan for curricula integration could alleviate this source of problems – and some projects have added such staff.

Another service delivery problem could occur with scheduling. The work or home schedules of Even Start parents may not jibe with the availability of local services. This common problem is difficult to solve, and may cause Even Start projects to plan their own ABE programs thereby risking redundancy.

The likelihood that Even Start conducts its own ABE or early child-hood program increases with the lack of local services. In some com-munities, for example, ABE classes may be offered by part-time programs with overenrolled classes (particularly in ESL programs). A shortage of staff and money may limit ABE/ESL services to "regular" students as well as fail to meet the needs of Even Start parents. Early childhood services, including Head Start, may be limited in slot capac-ity. The need of Even Start families for special dispensations or slots so that they can participate in early childhood services as they are expected to may strain local resources, put more demand on services than the staff, site, or budget can accommodate, and curtail services for those populations not in the Even Start program. Is it fair to dis-criminate in favor of Even Start parents, whose participation in adult education is mandated? This question may arise when collaborations are legislated.

Travel distance to collaborative services may prevent or inhibit their use, as might occur when GED testing takes place infrequently or at a distance from the local Even Start program. Lack of transportation and child care to enable Even Start parents to attend classes is a problem faced by many projects as they implement programs. Collaborations for these important support services are not always available, and they may result in costly expenses.

Finally, lack of experience in collaboration may burden projects with uneasy moments. If some services must, by law, be collaborative, and for some reason collaborations are difficult to initiate or maintain, the basic structure and premises of the Even Start Act may be threatened. The CCFL project was designed to address this problem directly; it allowed time for members to *learn* to work together, a most valuable objective.

Despite these obstacles, are the Even Start projects the models for collaborations they appear to be? What is the nature of their collabor-ations and how smoothly do they proceed? What were the problems faced and how were they solved over time? What have Even Start projects learned through this experience that has value for others? Questions like these may be answered by the national evaluation and are of interest to researchers and to practitioners. Other questions, about the initiation and maintenance of collaborations, are proper subjects for research as well.

Systems

With overall responsibility for program administration now at the state level, opportunities for cooperation become a new challenge. Will states (Level 3) mirror locally designed programs and develop interagency partnerships for policy development and coordinated administration of Even Start programs? Movement in this direction would be a refreshing practice that new family literacy programs in local communities could copy. If effective, state level coordination would complement the evolution of Even Start in its spirit as well as its practice.

Recommendations for Future Collaborations

The CFL and CCFL projects were action-oriented research into the processes needed to initiate and maintain a complex intervention, family literacy. Their history and early information from Even Start programs point to several recommendations that policy makers, legislators, educators, and other supporters of the family and community literacy concept should take as a call for action. Many other models of family literacy services tailored to a variety of at-risk families may also find these suggestions valuable but difficult to implement, because the systems are not advanced enough yet.

Individuals who are preparing for work in education, health, and human service areas (particularly in adult literacy, early childhood education, library science, health, and social work) need content preparation in human development and life-span education. Multicultural orientations and a broad multidisciplinary background are advantages. A new group of professionals trained for intergenerational and family literacy work are necessary to staff the complex programs which will increase in the next decade. Sadly, only a handful of relevant courses exist in colleges and universities.

Further, universities and colleges that prepare professionals for these fields must also teach the *process* of working in collaborative teams. The skills of joint planning, negotiation, conflict resolution, and communication can be practiced under supervision in small-scale projects, at both the undergraduate and graduate level. The future of literacy development lies in this direction.

The authors also believe that the key collaborations framework (table 2) could be extended to a fourth level to identify members, structures, and facilitating activities for regional collaborations in support of family literacy. As practice expands, local programs need ongoing access to a regional network of professionals for help with training and technical assistance. (Most Even Start projects, typical of many family literacy efforts, have received very little technical assistance in the implementation of new and complex services.)

We have proposed a New England Family Literacy Collaborative, open to any agencies interested in family literacy practice, that would serve these six states in much the same way that regional offices for technical assistance in Head Start operate across the nation. Family literacy programs in several states in New England have formed an informal group which meets annually. The field of family literacy moves quickly, and bureaucratic agencies and funders have had trouble keeping up. Practice is exploding, and program quality is an issue.

There is much that is visionary in family literacy practice. It includes a diverse collection of approaches and should continue to do so. No one model can be expected to meet multiple, family-literacy needs. With success, they will change systems, service delivery, and professional preparation in adult basic and early childhood education. At long last, there will be holistic approaches to family-based literacy services. But without attention to the process of collaboration, expectations for their achievements will have to be cautious.

Notes

1   Recently (1992), Head Start itself has addressed this issue by developing demonstration models that focus in part on parents' own improvement in reading.
2   The final Report is to be delivered to Congress in fall, 1993.

References

Bruner, C. (1991). *Thinking collaboratively: Ten question and answers to help makes improve children's services.* Washington, D.C.: Education and Human Services Consortium.

Even Start National Evaluation (1992). Evaluation Conference. Cambridge, MA: Abt Associates.

Habana-Hafner, S. & Reed, H. (1990). *Partnerships for community development: Resources for practitioners and trainers.* Amherst: University of Massachusetts, Center for Organizational Development.

Himmelman, A. (1990). *Literacy kit: Communities working collaboratively for a change.* Alexandria, VA: United Way of America.

Kagan, S. (1991). *United we stand.* New York: Teachers College Press.

Nickse, R. (1990). Family and intergenerational literacy programs: An update of "The Noises of Literacy." Monograph (ERIC Document Reproduction Service No. ED 342).

Nickse, R. (1993, March). A typology of family and intergenerational literacy programs: Implications for evaluation. *Viewpoints,* Family Literacy, *15,* 34–40. London: Adult Literacy and Basic Skills Unit. In the United States, ERIC Document Reproduction Service No. ED 333 166.

Nickse, R. & Englander, N. (1985). At-risk parents: Collaborations for literacy. *Equity and Choice 1* (3), 11–18 (ERIC Document Reproduction Service No. EJ 319 377).

Quezada, S. & Nickse, R. (1992). *Community collaborations for family literacy handbook.* Boston: Massachusetts Board of Library Commissioners.

Quezada, S. & Nickse, R. (1993). *Community collaborations for family literacy.* New York: Neal Schuman Publishers, Inc.

Smith, R. (1991a). *Let's do it our way: Working together for educational excellence (A Handbook for school community collaboration).* Chapel Hill, NC. MDC, Inc.

Smith, R. (1991b). *What it takes: Structuring interagency partnerships to connect children and families with comprehensive services.* Washington, D.C.: Education and Human Services Consortium.

St. Pierre. (1992). Early findings from The National Evaluation of the Even Start Family Literacy Program, Cambridge, MA: Abt Associates.

St. Pierre, R., Swartz, J., Gamse, B., Nickse, R., Abt Associates. Murray, S., Langhorst, B., RMC Research Corporation. (1991). National Even Start Evaluation First Year Report, Washington, D.C.: U.S. Department of Education.

10 Evaluating Family Literacy Programs: Tales from the Field

Katherine E. Ryan, Barbara Geissler, and Suzanne Knell

Introduction

> We have a 20 kids in prekindergarten downstairs whose parents do not have a high school diploma. I have a GED program upstairs with three participants. . . . I want to know why the parents from downstairs aren't upstairs in class.

> Our primary focus . . . has been GED/pre-GED/ABE/skills review. We have had a very difficult time recruiting, but have been successful twice this year in recruiting a class. These results, showing clearly the interest of the parents, suggest that we should adjust our focus. . . . we should emphasize parenting and parent support, computers and office technology, aerobic exercise, and parent–child play groups.

These kinds of tales from field interviews with Family Literacy program providers mandate a broadening of the notion of literacy and what counts as a legitimate effort to become literate. They highlight the need for providers and students to share their assumptions about literacy. The concept of "multiple literacies" – literacy practices that "differ from group to group within a society as well as from society to society" (Lytle, p. 8) – is supported by the work of Lytle (1990), Taylor and Dorsey-Gaines (1989), Street (1984), and Heath (1983), among others.

The notion of multiple literacies and what is authentic progress toward meeting the goal of becoming literate have a direct bearing on how we conduct evaluations of family literacy programs. Evaluation activities and assessment stategies that take into account the literacy context of the individual can provide a rich source of information about the "process of becoming literate," the notion of literacy in relationship to the individual and family, the differences in parents' and teachers' perspectives about the involvement of parents in the development of their children's literacy, and the integration of family literacy programs with existing services.

The John D. and Catherine T. MacArthur Foundation commissioned the Illinois Literacy Resource Development Center (ILRDC) to conduct a series of studies to examine these programs in the state (see *The mechanics of success for families*, Report No. 1 and No. 2, 1990; *Fine tuning the mechanics of success for families*; Report No. 3 and No. 4, 1992). This chapter reports a framework for evaluating family literacy programs and presents case studies of how the framework was implemented in family literacy programs (n = 6), and discusses the implications of these evaluation findings for practice in family literacy.

Jacobs (1988) has developed what she calls the five-tiered approach to family program evaluation. Her model specifies five levels of evaluation activities, theoretically requiring increasing sophistication in data collection and organization as well as specificity of program definition. We conceptualized this approach as developmental and implemented an adaptation for the evaluation of family literacy programs (*Mechanics of success for families*, Report No. 2, 1990).

Table 1 outlines this evaluation framework in relation to a family literacy program. The programmatic components of a family literacy program – adult-only, child-only, adult-child, family support services, and economic self-sufficiency – are represented on the horizontal axis. The program components are an elaboration of Weiss (1988) and findings from a previous investigation of family literacy programs in Illinois (*The mechanics of success for families*, Report No. 1 and No. 2, 1990). The program components for a family literacy program are outlined as follows:

Child-only. This program component targets the child. Educational services are provided to a child or children from birth to sixteen. In a majority of programs, the goal is to enhance children's preliteracy or literacy skills; however, goals in other areas of development have been observed. Educational services usually include programs or activities specific to birth-to-toddler, prekindergarten or elementary, or secondary populations.

Adult-only. The adult (aged 16 and above) is the focus of this component. Goals for adults often include developing literacy skills and improving self-esteem. Services are generally Adult Basic Education (ABE), high school equivalency (GED), English as a Second Language (ESL), and parenting classes.

Adult and Child. This component is a distinguishing feature in family literacy programs. Goals include improving the child's, the adult's,

Table 1   Evaluation framework for family literacy programs

Evaluation	Child	Adult	Adult–child	Family support services	Economic self-sufficiency
Level 1 Needs assessment (preimplementation)					
Level 2 Accountability (program documentation)					
Level 3 Formative evaluation (program clarification)					
Level 4 Program progress (progress toward objectives)					
Level 5 Program impact					

or the child's and adult's educational skills and abilities. It is assumed either explicitly or implicitly that the skills the adult and child learn or practice produce an intergenerational transfer and/or reciprocal transfer of skills and abilities. The adult is usually the same adult in the adult-only component and must be a significant other included within the definition of the family.[1]

Family Support Services. This component targets the family's utilization of community resources and development of social networks. Community resource goals might include learning to use medical resources, day care, counseling, and other related services. Development of social networks is part of this component and includes strengthening interfamilial relations and friendships in an effort to support family concerns.

Economic Self-Sufficiency. Family economic self-sufficiency is the focus of this component. Facilitating adaptation to the job market and mainstream economic environment are the goals. Activities range along a continuum from job-readiness assistance to job-skill enhancement.

The vertical axis in Table 1 represents five levels of evaluation: needs assessment, accountability, formative evaluation, program progress, and program impact (*The mechanics of success for families*, Report No. 2, 1990). This two-dimensional structure embeds evaluation into family literacy program design.

With Weiss (1988) we recognize the evolutionary nature of this field, and suggest the likelihood that a single program has goals in one or two of the areas and be moving toward incorporating the other two or three program components. However, the conceptual framework specified herein provides direction for program development and evaluation while capturing the dynamic nature of this process. A distinct advantage with this approach is that programs can be engaged in different levels of evaluation within different program components at the same time. For instance, a program may be at the formative evaluation level for the child-only component. However, if it does not have an adult–child component, it may implement level one as a first step in the development of that component.

Methods

Sample.   To examine the implementation of the evaluation framework 19 programs were invited to submit proposals if they were interested in receiving assistance with evaluation. Six sites were selected and provided with an evaluation grant ($2,000). The six sites represented all geographical locations in Illinois. Five of them will be profiled in this chapter. A brief description of each program is provided in table 2.

Design and Procedures.   A multilevel design was used to examine the implementation of the evaluation framework. Using the evaluation framework as a guide, each individual project conducted its own internal evaluation that addressed individual project questions. The case study method also was used. The findings from all sites were synthesized (Denzin, 1989a; 1989b).

The training process was conceptualized as a dialogue among the program providers, the ILRDC staff, and the evaluation specialist. The program providers conducted the evaluation, the ILRDC staff

Table 2   Program descriptions

Program	Description
West	The West site is situated in a semi-rural community in Western Illinois. The family literacy program at this site grew out of a strong prekindergarten program, one that emphasized parental involvement. With the help of the local community college and a volunteer literacy organization, GED and Pre-Ged classes were organized at the preschool site. Parents ride the bus with their children and once a week parents and children have lunch and an activity together. The adults also receive other support services such as a weekly "rap" session and health referrals.
East	Based in Central Illinois, the East serves women and children living in an emergency shelter. Services for the adults are highly individualized, tailored specifically to the client's interests as expressed during an initial meeting with the services coordinator. Aside from individual tutoring, the women also receive advice and referrals. Services for the children include group sessions and tutoring done by volunteers. The women and their children have the option of participating in a reading program that provides books and motivation for shared reading experiences. Staff and funding are severely limited.
North	The North site is a school-based program that operates in several of the most economically disadvantaged suburbs of Chicago. Cooperation between the school district and the community college is one of the cornerstones of this program. Family literacy services have been made available to any interested families within the school district. Adults are encouraged to attend any of a variety of adult education classes offered by the community college and held at the school. Adults can take GED, ABE, ESL, Spanish GED, exercise, keyboarding or computer classes. Special adult–child workshops are held frequently. Support services such as transportation and referrals are offered. A parent-council meets regularly to discuss and make suggestions about the program.
South	Families in four rural counties are the primary recipients of the South site's services. This networking program identifies families through cooperating agencies and provides these families with three sessions that focus on reading together. The family literacy trainer models reading strategies, discusses book selection, and provides encouragement for adults to read with their children. The trainer also provides information on available adult education services and introduces each family to the library.

Table 2 (Cont.)

Program	Description
Metro	This small program operates in an upper-class neighborhood in a major city. Of the six, it is the only center-based model, providing all services directly through the program. Adults and children spend the day at the program site. Adults receive tutoring from trained volunteers while the children receive age-appropriate instruction from the nursery coordinator. There are planned activities for the parents and children to do together each day. In addition, adults attend a weekly discussion group. The small size of the program allows staff and volunteers to meet together regularly to do program planning and curriculum development, often incorporating the themes from the parent discussion group. Staff and funding are limited.

provided technical assistance, and the evaluation specialist served as a consultant.

Each site received an initial site visit/training. At this session, ILRDC staff described the framework, potential applications, and model instruments. Site staff then portrayed their program and outlined the goals they had in mind for the evaluation project. ILRDC subsequently summarized this conversatin as a plan of action, which they shared with the staff at each site. Site staff had an opportunity to comment on their individual plans and change them to more accurately reflect the interests and needs. Plans were also reviewed and commented upon by the ILRDC evaluation specialist. Table 3 presents a summary of the evaluation questions proposed by the individual programs and the level of the evaluation activity for the first four tiers.

As the plans were being finalized, ILRDC staff disseminated materials to the sites based on the interests expressed by site staff. Instruments such as questionnaires and data collection forms collected from earlier investigations (see The mechanics of success for families, Report No. 1 and No. 2, 1990) were shared and discussed with the providers at the six sites. To encourage local control over the individual evaluation strategy, ILRDC staff stressed their consultative role. Correspondence, conversations, and site visits were documented and shared with staff at the individual sites for comments and corrections. ILRDC staff helped to define the "next step" at each stage of the process, and then responded to the concerns of site staff. Plans were revised and finalized based on site and ILRDC staff collaboration.

Table 3 Summary of guiding questions of programs, by level

Level	West	East	North	South	Metro
1			What family literacy services are needed in the North School community?	Are there accessible affordable education services available for children and are parents with low literacy skills willing to come to tutoring at the same times that their children receive free tutoring?	Who are we serving?
			In what ways are North parents already involved in their education and the education of their children?	What educational interests do adults in the community have?	
			What types of family literacy services would be most attractive to families in the North community?	What barriers might keep adults from attending?	
2	What services are available to families enrolled at West?			How many participants attend each session and how many are referred?	

3	What would assist the parents of the preschoolers to pursue adult education?	Are clients satisfied?	Are clients satisfied?	How can we do a better job of serving Metro participants?
	How might West better serve the needs of the preschool families – including provision of adult ed. services.			
4	Are shelter clients setting and meeting their goals?	Are parents reading more to their children and/or using the library more after participating in the program?		
	After a client identifies a goal, what steps does she take to work towards that goal?			

Once their plans were complete, individual site staffs began the process of putting them in place. Most sites had identified two or more goals to accomplish over the period. To achieve their goals, site staffs adopted or adapted new instruments, designed interviews, compiled data, took field notes, and conducted surveys. Each site analyzed data and prepared a final report.[2]

Results for Level One: Preimplementation Tier

This phase is more commonly known as a needs assessment. The guiding question here is "What is the problem?" The purpose is to document the need of a specific population within the community for particular services. The audience includes but is not limited to funding agencies, citizens in the community, and the potential participants.

Case 1: North

The North site was asked by the Illinois State Board of Education to consider developing a family literacy program in an accelerated school. North site staff chose to conduct a needs assessment. The process of program implementation was simultaneous to that of the needs assessment. On account of the nature of their program (see table 1 for program description), North site staff considered this assessment across the adult, adult–child, and economic self-sufficiency components. Their guiding question was "What family literacy services are needed in the local school community?" Subcomponents of that question were: "In what ways are local parents already involved in their own education and the education of their children?" and "What types of family literacy services would be most attractive to families in the local community?"

While the primary goal of the project was to answer the guiding questions, the North site staff also had two indirect goals. First, the staff hoped to empower community members through the process of involving them in the design, development, and implementation of the needs-assessment process. Second, site staff hoped to raise awareness of the program in the Local school community and possibly recruit participants.

Strategies, Tasks, and Process. Three data collection strategies were agreed upon. To determine the population characteristics of the community, the North site coordinator, Paul, gathered census information. Information on number of community residents, their cultural identities, poverty rates, and educational levels were deemed important for determining the need for educational services. Although only preliminary 1990 data were available, Paul was able to determine the number of adults and children in the school community and their cultural identities. He garnered educational levels and the rate of teen parenting from 1980 data.

A teachers' survey for kindergarten through sixth grade teachers was drafted to determine the existing level of parental involvement at the school and to investigate what teachers perceived as the needs of the adults in the community. During an all-teachers meeting, Paul discussed the needs assessment and the forthcoming survey. Following this meeting, Paul met with four teachers to draft the instrument engaging teachers in the process. The principal made an announcement requesting that all teachers complete and return the survey. Seventy percent ($n = 17$) of the teacher surveys were returned.

Paul drafted a community survey with assistance from an ILRDC consultant. This survey was reviewed and critiqued by a parent and a staff member familiar with the community to ensure credibility and relevance of the language and questions to community members. A spaced sample[3] of families was chosen to participate, selected from the 1990–91 school roster of 385 children, with a goal of interviewing 30–40 local families.

The consultant and two parents who were trained administered the survey orally in the school and in the homes of respondents. Many of the initially identified families were difficult to reach and thus unavailable to complete the survey. In order to achieve the goal set, other local families were asked to participate. These interviewees were selected by going door to door and by surveying adults who came to the school to register their children. In all, 33 adults (32 females, 1 male) representing 33 different families completed the survey.

Data Analysis. The demographic information confirmed general observations that Paul had made about the community. The census information revealed the following:

• 97 percent ($n = 3,388$) of the community is African American
• 40 percent of the population is under 18 years of age
• 33 percent of the babies are born to teen mothers
• 50 percent of adults do not have a high school diploma

These factors indicate that there is a large number of families in the local school area who might benefit from family literacy programs.
The compiled teachers survey indicated that many parents

participated in school activities. The most participation (78%, 217 parents out of 279 total children in class) was recorded for parent–teacher conferences. However, this figure does not indicate how often parents attended such conferences. Other participation occurred in these situations:

- 20 percent for field trips and special events
- 10 percent for parent meetings and disciplinary meetings
- 8 percent for parent–child workshops, observing a class, and volunteering in the classroom
- 3 percent attending adult-education classes

When teachers were asked the importance of participation in such activities, they ranked parent–teacher conferences highest. Other highly rated activities were: parent-child workshops, adult-education classes, parent meetings, and disciplinary meetings. Of less importance were field trips, classroom observations, volunteering in the classroom, and special events.

Teachers also had the opportunity to list what they perceived as the most needed activities for the parents of the children in their classes. The teachers responding indicated that "parenting" activities were needed. The teacher rankings are listed in percentages as follows:

Parenting	100
Family story time	92
Self-esteem	92
GED/Pre-GED	83
Play groups	74
Skills review	74
Vocational evaluation	42
Office technology	42
Computer workshops	42
Vocational training	33
Aerobic exercise	21
ESL	9

Teachers also identified specific student needs that a parent program could help address. Two teachers listed building self-esteem. Other comments included: communicate better verbally, improve reading skills, get along with peers, and learn discipline.

In summary, the teachers perceived that adults in the community were in need of activities that stressed parenting skills, adult–child learning (family story time, play groups), self-esteem, and adult education (GED/Pre-GED, skills review). They were less inclined to feel that adults in the community needed vocational activities (vocational evaluation, office-skills classes, computer workshops, etc.) or aerobic exercise. Not surprisingly, the teachers were very concerned with activities that had a direct relationship to the education and well-being of the children.

Although the two surveys were not designed to match exactly, the adult community survey did purposefully include some of the same questions that were on the teacher survey in the hopes of painting the broadest picture of services needed possible and in an effort to find common ground between parents and teachers. The survey revealed some similarities between teachers' and parents' views as well as some interesting divergences.

In terms of present participation at the school, 61 percent of parents agreed that their primary activity was parent–teacher conferences (n = 33). Forty-eight percent said they visited the school for parent meetings, 42 percent to observe their children's class, 39 percent to attend special events, and 36 percent to volunteer in the classroom. Parents said they were less likely to visit the school for field trips (21 percent), parent–child workshops (15 percent), GED/ABE (6 percent), or disciplinary meetings (6 percent). Paul made these observations:

> In over half the areas on the survey, parents disagreed significantly with the teacher estimates. This may be due in part to the small size of the parent sample or parent overestimation of their participation, but I also think it genuinely reflects some difference in perception. Parents said they observed classes and attended meetings four times as often as teachers said they did. Three times as many parents said they volunteered in class, and nearly double the number of parents say they have attended special events. Interestingly, fewer parents recalled attending disciplinary meetings or parent–teacher conferences.

When asked about the importance of the activities, parents were in agreement with the teachers that parent–teacher conferences and parent meetings were very important. Most parents (78%) rated "observing child's class" as very important. Teachers, on the other hand, had a mixed reaction, with only 50 percent ranking this activity as very important for parents.

In terms of activities parents felt would most help them help their child, parents ranked parent-support groups as number one. Almost half (48%) indicated that this type of activity would help their family. Although parenting and parent support are quite different, this finding indicates a convergence of teachers and parents around issues pertaining to being a parent. The other activities which parents responded to are listed by percentage in order of preference (self-esteem and play groups were not incuded as possible options):

Parent support group	48
Computer workshops	42
Aerobic exercise	36
Office technology	36
Family story time	33
Vocational training	24
GED/Pre-GED	15
ESL	15
Vocational evaluation	12
Skills review	6

Aside from parent support, the parents replied that skills classes (computer workshops, office technology, and vocational training) were important for themselves and their families. The parents also gave high priority to aerobic exercise and family story time. The vocational emphasis indicates the parents surveyed (unlike the teachers) considered activities leading to economic self-sufficiency to be almost as important as parent support.

All the parents interviewed responded that parents ought to be involved in their child's education, and they responded favorably to the list of possible ways to assist their children. The majority (91%) answered that visiting the school and helping with homework would assist their children with school. Other activities that parents felt would help their children in school were: reading clubs (82%), math clubs (73%), and after-school projects (48%). For themselves, the adults wanted to learn word processing/typing/computers (10), get their GED (6), and help their children with homework (3).

The results of the parent survey brought into question the perceived need of the adult community members for adult education services. Rather, parents indicated high interest in parenting support, vocational training, and aerobic exercise. Factoring in the demographic data and the teacher information, Paul concluded:

> Our primary focus . . . has been GED/pre-GED/ABE/skills review. We have had a very difficult time recruiting but have been successful twice this year in recruiting a class. These results, showing clearly the interest of the parents, suggest that we should adjust our focus. While continuing to offer the Adult Basic Education classes that are needed as indicated by the demographic data (and the perceptions of the teachers), we should emphasize parenting and parent support, computers and office technology, aerobic exercise, and parent–child play groups.

Resulting Program Changes

Based on findings and discussions with staff before, during, and after the evaluation, the program design will undergo modifications. One certain change will be the incorporation of ongoing community assessment into the overall North site. Paul outlined the following "next steps."

> The next steps would be to survey men (only one of the 33 parents was a man), survey Spanish speakers in the area, survey cooperating programs, and perhaps do some pilot surveys in other communities, such as Ford Heights. Prior to using the survey again, we should speak with parents, teachers, and surveyors to check for changes that we should make to the instrument. The teachers' survey [should also] be reviewed and given to teachers of the other [cooperating] programs.

Results for Level Two: Accountability Tier

This level has traditionally been known as program utilization. At this stage, the answer to "Who are we serving and what services are we providing?" is addressed. Again, funding agencies are the audience, but program providers and participants can also be considered.

Case 2: Metro

In an effort to obtain a better understanding of the lives of the present and incoming participants, Metro staff agreed on the need for intake forms. The guiding question for this component of their investigation was "What are the interests, goals, and strengths of the families that enroll in Metro's program?" Subcomponents of this question were "What are the particular interests of the adults?" and "What interests and behaviors can be expected from the children?" Information collected was to be the first step in the development of an evaluation portfolio for each family. The adult-only, child-only and adult–child components were the areas of investigation.

Strategies, Tasks, and Process. A primary desire of the staff at Metro was to create an evaluation form that was both participatory and non-intrusive. According to Dale, Executive Director,

> Metro's staff and volunteers [wanted] intake questions that provided information about adult students' positive relationships with their children, the young children attending the nursery, the family's strengths,

and the adult's important life experiences. This form [would] contrast with instruments that ask adult education students basic and frequently embarrassing questions about their prior school experiences. Metro's staff and volunteers also wanted the intake process to provide the adult students with an opportunity to ask questions about all the components of Metro's family literacy program.

Metro staff and volunteers examined several examples of intake forms and after review and discussion selected appropriate questions from these forms. The Metro site team also brainstormed and agreed upon a variety of other interesting questions, from which they generated a Child Information Form and a Parent Information Form.

The Parent Information Form was piloted with all nine adult participants of Metro, a group that included students who had been with the program from several weeks up to two years. Dale administered the questionnaire orally and also recorded the responses. Administration took place at the Metro site.

Data Analysis.   Dale conducted a content analysis of the pilot group responses.

> The information generated by the intake forms piloted during the evaluation project provided Metro staff with a deeper understanding of the adult students' lives, their personal goals, their hopes and dreams for their children, and the importance of Metro's program in their lives. The interviews yielded several especially interesting pieces of information.

> Though all of the students said that they came to Metro to improve their literacy skills, four of those interviewed said that their primary reason for continuing their education was to help their children. One student said that she wanted to be able to "bring her children up right." Another student stated that when she first came to Metro her son told her "if you don't learn, I won't learn." This kind of firsthand information confirms the importance of helping adults improve their literacy skills and how the parent's improved literacy skills are a step toward helping children succeed and stay in school.

Several other insights resulted from analysis of the responses. Most important, Dale found that "this group sees themselves as important teachers in all aspects of their children's lives."

Resulting Program Changes.   An important aspect of the adult intake form is gathering information on students' lives beyond Metro. Not only does this information influence curriculum development, but it also helps Metro students make a meaningful connection between reading and writing and their own interests. According to their report, Metro staff will continue to use information on student interest in their weekly Parent Discussion Groups. At one such session, students were asked to talk about the things they collected as a hobby because this question had led to interesting discussions before. The topic helped the students find and establish a connection between something meaningful in their own lives and reading and writing. In the future, intake questions of this nature will help Metro's staff understand and appreciate the interests of new students as they enter the program.

Results for Level Three: Program Clarification Tier

This stage, in which data are collected from the staff and participants, is more commonly recognized as formative or process evaluation. The guiding question during this phase is "How can we do a better job serving our participants?" (Jacobs, 1988, p. 57). The audience are staff members, and program participants, and sometimes funding agencies. Program structure and focus are critically examined.

Case 3: West site

Staff at the West site were concerned about the relatively limited involvement of parents in the adult-education classes at the preschool site. They felt the classes to be both supportive and convenient, but the low turnout indicated a need to determine what program staff could do "to support adults in an effort to move toward further adult education." The guiding question for this evaluation activity was "How can we better serve the families at West?" A primary subcomponent of this question was "What can West do to assist the undereducated parents of the preschoolers to pursue adult education?"

Strategies, Tasks, and Process. Because West site is primarily a prekindergarten project, involved in family literacy as part of the variety of services they offer, staff wanted to design an evaluation to assess the entire program, including but not limited to, the adult education offerings. Thus, they designed a questionnaire to be used with the parents of West site preschoolers and administered it orally to three groups of parents: a representative selection of parents from all West families eligible for services ($n = 13$), parents who were the target of the adult education classes ($n = 8$), and parents currently enrolled in the education program ($n = 3$), for a total of 24 parents (or families).

Twenty-one (21) completed the questionnaire, which was administered at a mutually agreed upon site, either at the home or in the school.

Data Analysis.   The questionnaire revealed several activities in which parents had "no interest," among them the Saturday workshops and the program's Family Relation (parenting) classes. According to the staff report only one family out of 21 had attended a Saturday workshop, primarily because weekends are very busy times. Also, over one third of the parents did not like the Family Relation classes.

> Parents seemed to enjoy the opportunity to discuss issues with other parents; so they felt that everyone should be encouraged to participate – not just a few. Other parents said that they were not interested in basic child-care information. They wanted concrete answers and suggestions to problems brought forward.

Among the suggestions parents made for improving the program were:

- Encourage fathers to participate more frequently
- Eliminate scheduling conflicts with other school events
- Add more structure to the curriculum, with such activities as learning the alphabet, numbers, name writing, etc.

Parents without a high school diploma or the equivalent ($n = 8$) were asked what problems had kept them from attending the GED class offered on site. According to the staff report, they gave such diverse answers as the unimportance of a diploma to get a job; health reasons, such as pregnancy; not enough encouragement; and not enough time.

For the most part parents were pleased with the services offered to their children. When asked if they would recommend the program to friends, all but one parent said yes, and many had already done so.

Resulting Program Changes.   Based on the findings, Maury, the Principal, made the following recommendations for program improvement, specifically improvement of the adult education component.

> [We need to] review regularly the adult education offering in the family literacy component of the program and in the community. Provide the information to all staff members so they can support parental efforts.
>
> Find resources to support the use of a staff member to work with parents at the beginning of the school year to get the adult-learner process begun. In the past we have expected the teachers to inform the parents and to assist in any way. It appears that greater time and effort is required than the teachers have available.

At the screening of the preschoolers, be sure that the intake form section, which asks about parental education is fully completed. A thorough review of all the currently enrolled children found numerous forms that were not fully completed. It may be that the form is too complicated and parents who are not print-comfortable avoid some of the sections. Our intake person at the screening for the preschool will have to be sensitive and complete the forms with people when information has not been supplied.

Results for Level Four: Progress-toward-Objectives Tier

At this stage, short-term, program-effectiveness objectives are specified and reviewed to see whether they have been achieved. The guiding question is "Are the participants making progress?" Progress includes but is not limited to behaviors, attitudes, knowledge, etc. The audience for this information are funding agencies, program participants, community members, program providers, and perhaps an external review committee. Programs which have been operating for an extended period of time with substantial financial resources would implement this phase of the evaluation process.

In contrast to that of the accountability tier, the concern here is participant progress, not whether the program is being provided, and it is characterized by three distinct elements: the objective measure of program goals; the program's responsibility for participant progress; and its resources to involve staff in instrument development, to administer standardized instruments, to collect data effectively, and to interpret the results. Professional evaluators are often engaged to design this phase of the evaluation and help staff implement it.

Case 4: South

At this stage, South site staff sought to answer the guiding question: "Are parents reading more to their children and/or using the library more after participating in the program?" Staff also wanted to compare the findings at South's three different sites. This evaluation activity focused on the adult–child component of the South site program.

Strategies, Tasks, and Process. Initial and follow-up forms that had previously been used with South site workshops were adapted for use. The forms were revised so that an analysis of responses to the pretest and posttest questionnaires could be conducted.

Pre-questionnaires were administered to individual participants attending the first session at each South site. Participants at each site who completed all sessions were administered the post-questionnaire. Staff then compared the pre- and post-questionnaires and recorded the results for each family and then aggregated the information by site.

Site 1 had 95 participants complete the pre- and post-questionnaires, Site 2 had 121, and Site 3, 54. On-site administration of the questionnaires was done by the Family Literacy Trainer. Respondents were asked to read and fill out the form and then return it the trainer.

Data Analysis.   Results from this data collection were mixed. At all three sites, 25 percent or more of the adults indicated that they read more to their children after the program. However, a similar percentage at each site reported that they read less to their children after the program. The most significant gains were in the number of books parents purchased since the program and the number of books families had after participation in the program. Sixty-four percent of Site 1 parents reported that they had bought more books since participating in South's program. Ninety-seven percent of Site 1 parents indicated they now had more books, and 63 percent were borrowing books from the library after the program. At Site 2, 55 percent of the parents had purchased books since the South program, 66 percent had more books, and 58 percent were borrowing books from the library. At Site 3, 63 percent of the parents reported buying books since the program, 67 percent indicated they had more books, and 37 percent were borrowing books from the library.

The Staff report made these observations:

> On the average, 25–31 percent of adults were reading more [to their children] after the Reading Program. This reflects the fact that due to the part-time status of South's teachers, only six hours of training were provided to [participating] parents. One fact that is shown by these statistics: over 60 percent of parents in each county bought books for their children [after the program]. An average of 60 percent of parents in the program had used the library at Sites 1 and 2, where the library is within walking distance for most parents. At Site 3, the percentage [of parents using the library after the program] was lower, but the location is not as accessible.

Resulting Program Changes.   South site staff continues to discuss this information and its potential impact on the program and to seek additional funding to expand the parent training. At the same time, South's staff members are considering other ways to increase the intensity and duration of the parent training, and South trainers are scheduling more parent training sessions at sites that are easily accessible, such as community centers. In this rural community, transportation remains a major obstacle to service delivery.

Implications for Practice

An analysis of the information collected at the model sites reveals some interesting insights about family literacy programs including what kind of activities are appealing to participants, what kinds of literacy activities are meaningful to them, how to engage parents in the education of their children, and how to demonstrate student progress.

Level 1

The needs assessment conducted by North and other programs suggests a sizable "perception gap" between what program providers feel participants need in terms of education and what community members indicate they need from a family literacy program, a source of frustration to program staff looking for common ground. Providers documented a significant number of community members without a high school diploma or the equivalent. At the same time, they had difficulty reaching this large potential audience. As one adult education teacher said, "The statistics show that a majority of these adults don't have the education they need. . . . The survey shows they are more interested in aerobic exercise. Why?"

This discrepancy was discussed within the context of several other programs. Even those programs not actively evaluating the needs of potential participants expressed frustration about the difficulty of recruitment. Often this difficulty led back to the question, "Are we providing what people want? If so, why aren't they here?" At West site, for example, program staff expressed concern that parents were not taking advantage of the educational opportunities the program offered them. Intake records revealed a substantial number of adult parents without a high school degree or the equivalent, yet only a small proportion of that number attended GED classes. West site Level 3 evaluation activities were designed to shed light on why that difference existed. As we have shown the answers ranged from lack of interest to lack of encouragement.

In contrast, South site found that community members expressed a desire to obtain a GED. Indeed, the majority (74%) of individuals surveyed without a high school diploma wanted to complete a GED. Perhaps even more surprisingly, 58 percent wanted to pursue a college degree. When asked why they had not pursued their educational goals, most cited child-care and transportation difficulties.

It should be noted that the questions asked by the surveyors at the two different sites had two distinct orientations. The North site survey asked adults "What activities would most help you help your child?" At South site, the question was "In what areas are you interested in improving your skills?" Obviously, the first question implies a family-oriented motivation, the second, a personal one.

The needs assessments from all the sites suggest several concerns for family literacy program providers. First, it seems possible that potential participants do not perceive their own educational goals as directly relevant to improving their families' lives. When community members were asked "What would help you help your child?" they were more likely to cite parent support, vocational, or recreational activities. On the other hand, when adult community members were asked what educational goals they had, they frequently answered high school equivalency and college, indicating that their personal and family-oriented goals may be at odds.

The indications for program providers is that family literacy programs must be relevant to the lives of potential adult participants because their participation is critical. Relevance, obviously, is individually determined and contextually based. Some individuals are interested in learning to help their children with homework, others in using literacy to get a job, still others in obtaining their GED in order to go on to college. Individual goals should be supported and encouraged. Indeed, without respect for them, it is unlikely that participants will be easily recruited or retained.

In addition, the findings from the South and North sites suggest that adult participants may have personal interests and goals that differ from their family-oriented interests and goals. Program activities should be designed to incorporate the various goals and interests of the family members and integrated across components such that they support and sustain each other. For example, the activities of adults in the adult component should bear some relation to their personal goals and their family goals. Similarly, the adult–child activities should also support and incorporate these goals and build on activities occurring within the adult component. Relating individual and family goals strengthens the relationship among the components, affirming both individual and family aspirations, and moving the family literacy program toward a holistic model.

The needs assessment of the North site school also pointed up a divergence between how teachers feel parents should be involved in their children's education and how parents perceive they should be involved. At a meeting of staff and participants, one parent voiced her anger at a teacher who, in her words, "treated me like I didn't know anything about how my child learns. I tried to help out in the class-room, but she made me feel unwelcome." One of the teachers rejoined, "Not all teachers are like that. We want parents to help, to be involved but there have been some bad situations where teachers have been physically and verbally threatened by parents." The discussion continued for some time. It was clear throughout the exchange that both the parent and teacher had the interests of the children in mind. Several people observed that resentment had been building between parents and teachers in general and that this quarrel was a manifestation of a larger trend.

Other program providers expressed frustration that teachers and principals sometimes "stood in the way" of an effective family literacy program. In the words of one

> This school was a tough nut to crack. Some of the teachers still don't want us to encourage parent participation. These teachers want to be the "experts" with "their" children. What they don't seem to realize is that the parents are with their children much longer than they [the teachers] are. At the very least, if the parents don't know what the children are learning, they can't enforce it and the kids don't retain it.

Obviously, this teacher–parent or parent–school conflict is a significant issue for providers of family literacy services. For those programs that operate in or work with the schools, building mutually respectful relationships among program staff, teachers, and parents is of primary importance.

Family literacy programs have the opportunity to assist parents in negotiating the sometimes confusing and difficult role of being their child's education advocate. Program staff can facilitate it in a number of ways, not the least of which is improving communication between teachers and parents. Family literacy programs can and should encourage teachers to see the value of parents who are well informed about their children's education and who promote learning both inside and outside of the classroom. Similarly, family literacy programs can and should aid parents to see their own as well as the teacher's role as educator of the child.[4]

The needs assessment of the North site also indicated that engaging men in family literacy programs is still a major challenge. The community questionnaire asked "Why do you think more women than men attend school programs?" and "What things do you think would encourage more men to come to school programs?" Although a formal analysis of the data was not completed, a preliminary inspection revealed that respondents (32/33 of whom were women) felt that women were "more involved" with their children. Respondents also suggested implementing programs of "interest to men," such as sports and carpentry projects, to bring them into the school. The coordinator of North site, Paul, hopes to survey men in the community in the near future. It will be interesting to inspect the results.

The needs assessment process was deemed a success by the coordinators at both sites. The providers found the community surveys to be particularly enlightening. At North site, at least part of the survey's success stemmed from using a community member as part of the survey team. According to the consultant in charge of the survey, "I don't think we could have done it without her. She took me into neighborhoods where, alone, I might have gotten a much different reception. With her asking the questions, people were willing to talk."

It was interesting to observe that at both sites, the needs assessment process also served as a recruitment and public awareness tool. Each home visited received information about adult education/literacy and family literacy classes and sessions. This increased use of home visits for recruitment may point to another logical link between program development and evaluation. A first contact that asks potential participants what they want from a family literacy program may increase their stake in it and thus their level of involvement.

Level 2

The Level 2 investigations conducted by Metro, West, and South strengthen the notion that participant and program knowledge is the foundation of effective family literacy programs. It is critical that program staff have a thorough understanding not only of the services being provided, but also of the services that could be provided. Most important, staff must have a well-developed picture of their students as individuals and as family members.

The Level 2 data analysis revealed that programmatic isolation was perceived as a major problem for networking programs. A reoccurring theme heard throughout the study period, from the model sites and others, was "How do we integrate the many services which we offer?" Even when all components of a family literacy program were housed under one roof, they were not always coordinated. In some situations, such as at West site, staff members working in different components were unsure what other services were offered. At another site, one of the GED teachers had never met one of the preschool teachers. Although the GED teacher knew he was part of the family literacy program, he had no contact with and very little knowledge of the preschool program. This circumstance underscores the need to integrate program components rather than treating them as distinct and unrelated. A shared vision of what family literacy is and how the educational goals of all family members relate to one another can alleviate isolation among the network of providers, which in turn is likely to improve service delivery to participants.

West site staff suggested that one way to improve service delivery is to provide each family with an ombudsman – someone knowledgeable in the services offered, familiar with the family, and willing to give encouragement and support. As in a case-management approach, this person would be responsible for helping the families, together and individually, to tailor the services to their needs. Metro staff made a parallel conclusion. They found that getting to know students in depth – their interests, hobbies, and dreams for the future – improved the program's ability to provide individualized, relevant services.

It is clear that such intake is an important step in the service delivery process. Providers expressed an interest in finding instruments and procedures that "told them something useful about the families in the program." Some providers found standard intake procedures to be demeaning and to reflect a deficit model of family education. Not only that, but standard demographic data was not generally found to be useful in curriculum development or individualized instruction. Rather, providers expressed an interest in determining "individual family needs, learning strengths, and immediate goals in order to assist family progress and facilitate productive interaction in the process." Metro staff found that the information they gathered was useful in educating staff members about the students. According to Dale

> The next question asked the adults how their children helped them. While most of the parents said that their children helped them with small tasks around the house, one mother responded that if it weren't for her kids, she would be on the street. Although this powerful response does not directly affect program development, it does help Metro's staff and volunteers appreciate the strength and determination of the adult students enrolled in the program.

Level 3

The informal collection of anecdotal records for Level 3 evaluation demonstrated that the satisfaction of family literacy program participants was generally high. Providers at all six sites described families who reported that the program had changed their lives.

Metro staff were able to determine themes and patterns of interest among program participants in a unique way. Metro's Level 3 evaluation centered on the question, "How can we better serve our participants?", and an important answer emerged from their data gathering. Through a content analysis of participant discussions, Metro staff determined that participants are more likely to engage in learning activities when they are relevant to their individual family lives. As Dale, the Executive Director, said,

> The most significant finding to emerge for the Parent Discussion Group minutes from January through July 1991 is the importance of spoken and written stories in the lives of adult students. An analysis of the Parent Discussion Group minutes indicated that the students' stories were most frequently related to their important childhood relationships and experiences, their positive and negative school experiences, their plans for the future when they are competent readers and writers, and their hopes and dreams for their children.
>
> The minutes indicate that the students frequently repeated their stories, especially when a visitor was observing the program. For example, one member of the group repeatedly told how he couldn't even write "it" when he came to the program. He credits his wife and his tutor with his success. Another student spoke several times about the help she received from her sixth grade teacher. According to this student, her teacher understood how difficult it was for her to read and write and was helpful, supportive, and encouraging. This positive experience contrasted to the rest of her schooling and marked the high point of her education.
>
> The students also talked about what they would do when they could "really" read and write. One student talked about his plans to write his whole life story. He told the group that he was waiting until he could write just like he spoke. This comment indicates the importance of helping the students develop their own voice in writing.

Program staff built on this foundation by transcribing spoken stories and preparing them as family books. In this way, Metro staff supported and facilitated the learners' understanding of the importance of reading and writing to their families and to themselves. Staff at West found that adults wanted some impetus, some push to begin an educational program. It seems logical that this impetus should relate to personal or family goals.

Level 4

Data collected about participant progress suggests that small increments of change can be demonstrated for participants in family literacy programs. The goal-setting activity conducted at East indicates that progress is tied to individual goals and can be measured by completion of their sub-tasks. The success of the "Where Do I Go from Here?" assessment indicates that participants enter the program with a variety of different individual goals, which they can break down and reach in a series of small steps.

Staff at South found a small increase in the number of adults reading more with their children after the program but a much higher percentage increasing their use of the library. This data also supports the notion that change takes place incrementally, though it should not be discounted.

The process of ongoing steps in the goal-setting is noteworthy. East site staff found the goal-setting activity rewarding in itself. By helping clients set and see progress toward their larger goals, East site staff noticed improvements in their self-esteem and motivation, indicating to family literacy program providers that participants benefit from monitoring their own progress. Providers in turn should demonstrate appreciation of this progress.

Data collected at Level 4 also reveals that program impact may be moderated and influenced by administrative factors such as staffing and funding. The mixed results of South's reading evaluation raised concern among the staff about their ability to effect change with their limited amount of intervention (six hours of parent training) and at East the biggest problem continued to be not having a coordinator on site on a daily basis. While the point of these evaluation activities was not to compare different durations of intervention, this data analysis suggests that further research should be done on program intensity.[5]

The Level 4 processes were moderately successful in demonstrating participant and program progress, though clearly much work needs to be done at this level. While it was beyond the capacity of the project, documenting learner progress fully is critical. Although the ILRDC supported a portfolio approach to documenting learner progress, most programs were only able to begin this process. When information was collected, there was not sufficient opportunity to examine and reflect on it, either by students, teachers, or program coordinators. This predicament is part and parcel of the short investigation period as well as the newness of this methodology. Means of assessing student progress other than by way of standardized tests was also of great interest to providers at all sites. The East site "Where Do I Go from Here?" assessment and the South's pre- and post-questionnaire are two examples of alternative assessment methods. Additional evaluation activities with promise include skills inventories, anecdotal records, case studies, and surveys, among others.

According to all of the program providers involved in this project, these evaluation systems are, and will remain, an integral part of each program. That all providers have incorporated these techniques into their service delivery reflects well on the technical-assistance process and the framework. Part of the project success must be linked to the dialogical nature of the process. Sites were able to develop instruments unique to their particular goals and interests that ILRDC staff, the evaluation consultant, and the providers were able to examine and discuss. The project's success must also be due to the usefulness of a framework that provides an effective, integrated system to contextualize evaluation in program development. This evaluation project demonstrates that all types of programs, even small community-based ones, can implement useful evaluation activities – which is not to say that all programs can or should engage in evaluation at all levels and in all components. Rather, programs should implement evaluation strategies that are or will be useful to program development and that assist students in their educational quests.

The evaluation findings support the notion that becoming literate is a process, not a discrete event. It is not just gaining a set of skills, but making meaningful, personal change. Providers should concentrate on supporting families as they choose their individual paths toward their ultimate goals, perhaps on providing them a variety of opportunities to demonstrate change, and broadening the notion of what counts as a legitimate effort to meet the goal of literacy.[6] The emphasis on individual, personal, and family growth and change supports the idea that participants should be encouraged to examine what they already bring to a family literacy program. This approach is not just a reorientation away from a deficit model, but literally, a new standard which recognizes the importance of success as a motivating force to continue forward.

Notes

1 For the purposes of the investigation, *family* is defined as the significant others identified by the person or persons participating in the program. Clearly, this definition places the locus of control on participating individuals. Thus, family may include related or unrelated individuals significant to the project participants. Obviously, this concept of family incorporates intergenerational relationships. However, intergenerational programs which pair individuals not defined as family (such as a program in which older adult volunteers read with children) would not be included in this definition of family literacy.

2 Information on how to obtain copies of the site reports is available from ILRDC.

3 Every sixth family on the roster.

4 An interesting ancillary observation was that parents and teachers often had positive relationships when the children were in preschool. When the children went on to elementary and secondary education, however, parents had less aaccess to the classroom and greater difficulty advocating on their child's behalf. Parent participation dropped off significantly, and distrust of or indifference toward their child's education was more frequently noted.

   This situation may be at least partially accounted for by the Illinois Pre-School Initiative. This well-funded state initiative had a primary goal of boosting parental involvement at the preschool level. No such funding or support exists at the elementary or secondary levels.

5 Various adult education researchers such as D'Amica-Samuels (1991) have demonstrated a correlation between contact hours and student progress.

6 A parallel can be drawn between this notion of incremental steps toward becoming literate and recent thinking about how welfare recipients move toward economic self-sufficiency. Herr, Halpern & Conrad (1991) argue that

> If leaving welfare is understood as a process, welfare-to-work programs should begin to focus more on the intermediate steps along the way, recognizing small gains, shaping them into gradual progression, providing ongoing support for the transitions from step to step (p. 3).

Not only that, they also argue that the path to self-sufficiency is not always linear. Participants will follow individual paths. Some of these paths may take a participant backward as often as forward, and some may have periods of no movement at all.

References

D'Amico-Samuels, D. (1991). *Perspectives on assessment from the New York City adult literacy initiative.* New York: Literacy Assistance Center, Inc.

Denzin, N.K. (1989a). *Interpretive biography.* Newbury Park, CA: Sage.

Denzin, N.K. (1989b). *The research act, 3rd edition.* Englewood Cliffs, NJ: Prentice Hall.

Heath, S.B. (1983). *Ways with words.* New York: Cambridge University Press.

Herr, T., Halpern, R. & Conrad, A. (1991). *Changing What Counts: Re-Thinking the Journey Out of Welfare.* Evanston, IL: Center for Urban Affairs and Public Policy, Northwestern University.

ILRDC (1990). *The mechanics of success for families. Report No. 1, Family Literacy Programs.* Rantoul, IL: Illinois Literacy Resource Development Center.

ILRDC (1990). *The mechanics of success for families. Report No. 2, Evaluation.* Rantoul, IL: Illinois Literacy Resource Development Center.

ILRDC (1992). *Fine Tuning the Mechanics of Success for Families. Report No. 3, Evaluation and Program Development.* Rantoul, IL: Illinois Literacy Resource Development Center.

ILRDC (1992). *Fine tuning the mechanics of success for families. Report No. 4, Policy.* Rantoul, IL: Illinois Literacy Resource Development Center.

Jacobs, F.H. (1988). The five-tiered approach to evaluation: Context and implementation. IN H.B. Weiss & F.H. Jacobs (Eds.), *Evaluating family programs.* Hawthrone, NY: Aldine De Gruyter.

Lytle, S.L. (1990). Living literacy: Rethinking development in adulthood. Paper presented at AERA Symposium, *Adult literacy/child literacy: One world or worlds apart,* Boston, MA.

Street, B.V. (1984). *Literacy in theory and practice.* London: Cambridge University Press.

Taylor, D. & Dorsey-Gaines, C. (1988). *Growing up literate.* Portsmouth, NH: Heinemann.

Weiss, H.B. (1988). Family support and educational programs: Working through ecological theories of human development. In H.B. Weiss & F.H. Jacobs (Eds.), *Evaluating family programs.* Hawthorne, NY: Aldine De Gruyter.

Part 5

Commentary

11 Enhancing Literacy Development: Programs and Research Perspectives

Catherine E. Snow

I spent many afternoons in 1981 interviewing mothers in low-income families about their lives, their children, and the literacy practices of their homes as part of a research project that was reported in *Unfulfilled Expectations: Home and School Influences on Literacy* (Snow, Barnes, Chandler, Hemphill & Goodman, 1991). Most of the children in these families had already encountered or soon would encounter academic problems in school, problems related to poor reading skills, low vocabulary, and undeveloped writing skills. The living rooms where the interviews took place were typically dominated by a television, and only in a few households were books visible. Yet all the women I interviewed said they hoped their children would graduate from high school and go on to college. All said they had bought books for their children and helped them with homework. Some had gone to extraordinary lengths to support literacy development, enrolling their children in book clubs, subscribing to children's magazines, and encouraging them to watch "Sesame Street." Almost all thought of their children as bright and competent, and those whose children were encountering academic problems were puzzled and dismayed. Those women, and their daughters who are now raising children of their own, understood the importance of books and of reading books with children. But they did not have the benefit of the sorts of programs described in this book, programs to ensure that the full benefits of book reading are made accessible to young children, especially those most at risk for school failure.

The chapters in *Bridges to Literacy* can be read both as a set of guidelines for improving literacy among America's youth, and as a basis for understanding what literacy is by analyzing the contexts in which it develops successfully. From the first perspective, the practical perspective of the program developer, the book provides an array of recommendations that is so rich and varied that they could only with difficulty be distilled into a short set of prescriptions. Almost a dozen different programs are described, all of which have their own structure, organization, characteristics, and philosophies, and all of which are described as working to improve literacy among at-risk children. From the more theoretical perspective, though, the perspective of the researcher interested in literacy development, the varied nature of the successful programs constitutes an analytic challenge. Do all these programs introduce some common experiences and opportunities for learning, despite their differences in clientele, mode of delivery, and intentionally targeted behaviors?

The programs described here have certain structural similarities. All are planned interventions, except for the work reported by Beals, De Temple, and Dickinson, in which naturally occurring variation in teacher behavior is used as the basis for identifying the characteristics of excellent preschool programs. All are focused ultimately on improving the literacy achievement of children, though most operate through parents or teachers rather than intervening directly with children. All include a component of book reading as a crucial literacy-enhancing experience for children, though in some programs promoting interactive book reading constitutes only part of the intervention. All focus on children who are at risk for educational failure because they are growing up in families with little money and low levels of parental education.

Beyond these common features, we can also summarize the ways in which the various programs differ from one another:

1. *Target of intervention.* Some programs (those described by Edwards; Toomey & Sloane; Segel; and Handel & Goldsmith) consist primarily of efforts to train parents to interact in new ways with their children; others (Karweit; Shimron's summary of Feitelson's work) involve providing training and/or materials to teachers for use in large group settings. Still others (Arnold & Whitehurst) have been used with both parents and teachers. And two (Nickse & Quezada; and Ryan, Geissler & Knell) emphasize the need to integrate the provision of services so that parents, teachers, and important figures in other institutions that serve families are all involved.

2. *Age of child.* Whitehurst's intervention is designed for one- to three-year-olds; Beals, De Temple, and Dickinson describe conditions of literacy enhancement for three- and four-year-olds. Most of the other programs reported seem most useful for children aged five to eight, though many of the parent training programs do not target child age so specifically. The Feitelson intervention described by Shimron is

unique in being of particular value to older school-aged children, for whom continued development of literacy skills is prerequisite to success in the full array of academic pursuits.

3. *Participation structure.* Whitehurst is clear that the intervention he describes works best in dyadic interaction, or with at most three or four children. The training programs for parents in general provide techniques and strategies of interaction meant to be applied in dyads with their children, but the work of Feitelson (reported by Shimron), Beals, De Temple, and Dickinson, and of Karweit is relevant to large-group or whole-class settings.

4. *Nature of evaluation.* The chapters differ, too, in the degree to which they report formal evaluations, and in what is taken as evidence for effectiveness. The work of Beals, De Temple, and Dickinson, that of Whitehurst, and that of Karweit use posttests of child outcomes to demonstrate consequences on language or (pre)literacy skills. Segel reports effects on teacher judgments of children from one of the intervention models she reports. The other interventions are evaluated primarily through the enthusiasm and continued participation of the adults being trained, and their reports concerning the effects on their own and on their children's literacy activities.

5. *Conduit for training.* In some of the interventions, the major activity is workshop-based – getting parents or teachers into relatively formal training sessions. In Segel's, Toomey and Sloane's, and Feitelson's studies, on the other hand, a major component of the intervention involves simply providing books, letting the children become the active agents in soliciting parental participation. Karweit reports that producing effective change in teachers' behavior required providing them with materials and ideas for supplementing their normal models for reading to children.

These dimensions of difference, though, mask some important underlying similarities among the programs presented in these various chapters. First, all focus on helping teachers or parents do what they want to do, namely, contribute to their children's learning. Edwards presents a sophisticated discussion of the ways in which interventions like these can be misinterpreted as intrusive; but her work with parents and teachers, like Karweit's with teachers, shows clearly that many well-intentioned adults who believe in the value of book reading with children still benefit from training in how to do it. In Edwards's study, teachers who read to children regularly still had difficulty articulating the principles that guided their reading. Like the mothers reported on in *Unfulfilled Expectations,* the parents in the various studies described in *Bridges to Literacy* valued information about how to read with their children.

Second, all these studies emphasize the value of high-quality, attractive books. This value is particularly highlighted in Segel's and Toomey and Sloane's chapters, where the attractiveness of the books is seen as a key characteristic in getting children interested and thus active in motivating their parents to read (and, eventually, borrow or buy more) books. But the power of good children's literature to capture imagination and inspire devotion is a factor in all the interventions described. Feitelson emphasizes that "quality" in children's books must be defined by children; the Hardy Boys and Nancy Drew might not constitute great literature, but they hook kids' interest sufficiently to provide lots of practice in reading and lots of enjoyment. Educators who disdain such series as frivolous lose the sympathy of all of us who have improved an airplane ride or a sleepless night with Agatha Christie or Stephen King.

Third, the affective component of successful literacy is acknowledged in all these chapters. Literacy accomplishment is a serious business, a prerequisite to grave matters like school success, employability, and good citizenship. But it is also, if successful, lots of fun. Children fall in love with reading; they start to demand bedtime stories, insist on revisiting favorite books, and introduce elements from their books into everyday life. When my son was six, he moved from careful decoding to fluent reading because of one book – *Little House in the Big Woods*. He fell so under the spell of Laura and the Ingalls family that he spent all his free time plodding through the book, coming to ask for help with a word several times a page. When, after a couple of weeks, he finally finished the book, he started again immediately at the beginning and read it through in an evening. Then he went on without pause to *Little House on the Prairie*, *Little House at Plum Creek*, and all the rest, finishing the series within a few months. His tested reading level had, in the process, moved from grade one to grade eight, because those books would not let him loose. This kind of emotional power is a crucial component in all the interventions treated in this book.

Fourth, all the interventions treat reading (especially in its earliest stages) as a social activity, not an independent, autonomous, personal confrontation with a book. While it is commonplace to assume that young children need the mediation of adults to enjoy books, it is less common to remember how normal in adult literacy practices social support is. The social support for adult literacy might be less ubiquitous, or less obvious, but it is certainly there. If adults did not need personal–social mediation for literacy, we could close the universities and send students home with textbooks and reading lists; we could cancel all scientific meetings and substitute address lists for the exchange of papers. Social mediation of adult literacy accounts for the rise in sales of books once they become films or popular television presentations; seeing the story and talking about it with friends does not substitute for reading it, but rather encourages and supports the reading. As a somewhat inconstant sports fan, I find the sports pages of any newspaper largely incomprehensible, except for the reports of games I have actually seen and talked about with other viewers. Highly literate adults participate in book circles, in reading groups, and in journal clubs in order to enhance their autonomous literacy activities with social support and mediation. Few of us are truly autonomously literate in all domains; like the preschool child sitting on her mother's lap, we benefit enormously from hearing others' views of the text in addition to formulating our own.

Fifth, and perhaps most important, all the successful routes to literacy development discussed in this book promote talk as much as reading. What preschool and primary school children learn from reading books with adults may have as much to do with how to think and how to talk as with how to read. The chapter by Beals, De Temple, and Dickinson and that by Whitehurst argue that learning to talk in a certain way is a route to learning to read. Sorsby and Martlew (1991) showed that maternal speech during book reading is more complex than during an instructional, clay-modeling task, echoing findings by Snow, Arlman-Rupp, Hassing, Jobse, Joosten, and Vorster (1976) from almost twenty years ago that book-reading talk was more complex than talk during caretaking or play, for working-class as well as for middle-class mothers. Book reading is often thought of as an activity, but it can perhaps better be viewed as a microenvironment within which certain kinds of events are likely to occur, events like: learning new words, asking *why* questions, learning scientific facts, or seeing connections between one's own life and others' lives. Though not all the chapters in *Bridges to Literacy* focus on the nature of the talk that occurs around books, all do recognize the importance of the interaction. Just giving books to families, or just telling parents to read, clearly does not work to enhance children's literacy development; interaction around the books, with the carefully modeled questions and reactions of Arnold and Whitehurst's "dialogic reading," or with the somewhat less well-prescribed reading strategies of Edwards or of Handel and Goldsmith, or even with the relatively simple instructions to respond to children's interest, is prerequisite to the positive consequences of parent–child book reading. The talk is the site of the learning; the book reading is important because it is the site of the talk.

If talk is the real mechanism for the learning that goes on during book reading, then of course we should also consider the alternatives (or supplements) to book reading – the other places in children's lives where interesting, engaging, and mind-expanding talk occurs. Dinnertable conversations, oral story-telling, and visits to museums probably constitute contexts potentially as rich in opportunities for learning as book reading. But these other contexts do not recur so predictably; the learning that occurs in book reading can build from repeated exposures to the books. A central component of the intervention described by Karweit was that a class spent a week on a single book – going back to it daily and reencountering the story in novel ways. Programs that send books home with children provide the chance for those books to be read and reread. A second or third reading of a story gives a chance for deeper processing, more probing and reflecting. It provides for the active engagement that is crucial to mature uses of literacy.

The program developer has available from the chapters in this book a wealth of ideas about how to enhance literacy development for at-risk children. The problem is not to design programs, but to institutionalize them, to make them so much a part of the fabric of children's lives that literacy moves beyond personal accomplishment to social achievement, and beyond being the responsibility of the school or the family to being the responsibility of the entire society. The chapters by Nickse and Quezada and by Ryan, Geissler, and Knell sketch out the possibilities of programs that make promoting literacy development as much a shared responsibility as ensuring access for all to food, housing, and health care.

References

Snow, C.E., Arlman-Rupp, A., Hassing, Y., Jobse, J., Joosten, J. & Vorster, J. (1976). Mothers' speech in three social classes. *Journal of Psycholinguistic Research, 31,* 424–44.

Snow, C.E., Barnes, W.S., Chandler, J., Hemphill, L. & Goodman, I.F. (1991). *Unfulfilled expectations: Home and school influences on literacy.* Cambridge: Harvard University Press.

Sorsby, A. & Martlew, M. (1991). Representational demand in mothers' talk to preschool children in two contexts: picture book reading and a modelling task. *Journal of Child Language, 18,* 373–96.

12 Implications for Family Literacy Programs

Sharon Darling and Susan Paull

The bridges to literacy described on the preceding pages are encouraging reminders of something parents and educators have long believed to be true and research has consistently supported: Children who are read to tend to become better readers, to read for pleasure more often, and to have better success in school. They also provide examples of other strategies being employed with parents and/or children to enhance the literacy learning of children and families. These reports are especially encouraging because the number, variety, and duration of the programs indicate that many people all over the world are acting on what they know and believe and that many parents and children are profiting from their efforts. It is heartening to be reminded that parents can be taught effective techniques for reading to their children, that they can become enthusiastic readers and supporters of their children's emerging literacy, that both school and home environments can be enriched with the tools of literacy, and finally, that these relatively basic interventions can make a real difference in parents' and children's literate behaviors.

Research Findings of the National Center for Family Literacy

The findings reported by these programs are similar to the outcomes of more intensive family literacy programs affiliated with the National Center for Family Literacy (NCFL). The NCFL promotes policy in support of the broad field of family literacy and provides training and technical assistance to programs affiliated with a wide range of organizations and utilizing a variety of program designs. However, early in the history of the NCFL, we were instrumental in the development of the Kenan Family Literacy Project, and since the field of family literacy is still fairly new, much of our research comes out of our experience with these "Kenan model" programs – those adopting the design developed for programs originally funded by the William R. Kenan, Jr., Charitable Trust.

The original Kenan model programs were located in Louisville, Kentucky (three sites), and in Fayetteville, Henderson, Walnut, and Wilmington, North Carolina. The programs served undereducated adults (parents and primary caregivers) and their three- and four-year-old children, and employed a program design that was a refinement of the earlier Parent and Child Education (PACE) programs in Kentucky.

The original Kenan model and the adaptations of that model that have come to be known as "family literacy" programs have broader goals than most of the programs described in this book, but they share the commitment to encouraging and supporting young children's emergent literacy. Because their goals are broader, the programs are designed to provide intensive, long-term educational services for at-risk parents *and* their preschool children. The primary aim of this family-focused approach is to break the intergenerational cycle of undereducation and poverty by improving parents' skills and attitudes toward education, developing children's skills, and uniting parents and children in a positive educational experience.

In Kenan model programs, four components comprise the basic core of program services: adult basic skills/literacy education for parents, a quality preschool experience for children adapted from the High/Scope curriculum, a parent education and support group (Parent Time), and regular parent and child interaction (Parent and Child Together – PACT). Parents and children in the original projects participated in all four components each day, three or four days a week, and the programs operated the entire school year. All the projects were located in elementary schools, and as an additional part of the program day, parents volunteered in various capacities in the schools, gaining work experience, getting acquainted with school personnel, and becoming comfortable in the school setting. The volunteer activities not only provided the parents with valuable experiences to further their own goals, but also encouraged their continuing involvement with the schools and support of their children's learning.

In the years since the establishment of these programs, through training and technical assistance from the NCFL, many programs across the country have adopted and adapted the model to their communities and organizations. Outcomes at many of these sites offer encouraging evidence of the effectiveness of these intensive, comprehensive programs.

Studies conducted in 1989 and 1991 at selected Kenan model sites show, among other things, that parents developed parenting skills, improved attitudes toward education, and family practices that directly supported their children's learning. Parents reported that their home environments had changed since they enrolled in the program. They felt that they were better able to "promote" the value of education after having returned to school themselves. Many stated that their relationships with their children were improved and that attitudes of even older (nonparticipating) children were affected. These changes were also reported by the children's teachers. Changes reported by parents in a 1991 follow-up study included helping children with homework, reading to children, having more books in the home, having more patience and more "quality time" with children, feeling comfortable talking to school personnel, attending school functions, and volunteering at the school. Recent follow-up studies with programs all over the nation are even more encouraging. Whether measured by parents' self-evaluations, scores on parent–child interaction scales, school attendance records of elder siblings, or level of parental involvement in the schools, parenting is improved for participants of the family literacy programs. And that shows up in the later school success of the participating children.

The children, who would likely be placed in the "at risk" category without intervention, benefited from the varied program services in many ways. At least 75 percent of the children in the follow-up study were ranked by their current teachers in the upper half of their classes, and were rated as average or better in motivation to learn, attendance, behavior, self-confidence, and probable success in school. In addition, none of the children in this follow-up had been retained in grade, and only 25 percent had been placed in remedial or special education classes – a much lower incidence than would be expected for this population.

Parents also reported observable changes in behavior. They said their children had become eager to learn, were on the honor roll regularly, and were determined to go to school everyday. Parents noticed improved social skills and maturity as well. More recent data from programs funded through the NCFL by the Toyota Motor Corporation show that the children in family literacy programs also make significant gains on standardized measures. From these results it is clear that most of these otherwise "at risk" children are achieving as well as or better than their peers, both in the short term, at the end of their family literacy experience, and in the years following.

Parents and Children Reading Together

The "bridges to literacy" highlighted in this book address a variety of issues related to support for early literacy. The program findings have implications for parents, teachers, administrators, and all who are concerned with enhancing the literacy skills and behaviors of America's children. Of special interest for family literacy programs are the numerous examples of parent–child interaction, primarily parents reading to children and using techniques to expand their children's story comprehension, language use, imagination, and thinking skills.

Several programs developed designs for training parents in techniques for reading to their children. The "dialogic reading technique" described by Arnold and Whitehurst is especially interesting. It involves asking questions and expanding on children's responses to gradually increase children's use of oral language and level of interaction with the story. Parents in the original study came from middle- and upper-income families and were trained to use this approach in two half-hour sessions. The fact that results (significant increases in oral language of two-year-olds) were positive after such a brief training period and that an adaptation of the training also achieved positive results with low-income families suggests that this technique might be integrated into other parenting and family literacy programs. It appears that a particularly potent strategy is to combine use of dialogic reading by teachers in preschool and parents in the home. This finding supports the approach taken by family literacy programs that combine instruction for children and parents with an emphasis on transfer of literacy skills and practices to the home setting.

Toomey and Sloane also focused on encouraging parents to read to their preschool children. In this case low-income families participated, and instruction took place in the early stages of the project during weekly visits in the home and later in preschool classrooms. Books were also sent home and training provided for parents. The researchers learned a great deal about what works with children and families both in the home and in school-based settings. The study supports the notion that low-income and working-class parents are interested in supporting their children's development, and suggests ways that preschools can encourage home reading and parental involvement. Lessons learned during the home visits will have special significance for home-based service providers.

Segel, Edwards, and Handel and Goldsmith have also worked with parents at a variety of skill and income levels to foster home reading. All of these programs have demonstrated the effectiveness of two basic ingredients: direct teaching of specific reading and interaction techniques to parents, and providing the tools of literacy – books for parents and children to enjoy. It is good to know, that in a world characterized by complexity and ambiguity, this simple, direct approach can be effective in encouraging and enabling parents to share the gifts of literacy with their children.

Meeting Parents' Needs

Many of the programs discussed in this volume recognize another important variable in children's developing literacy – the skills, needs, and concerns of their parents. If parents are their children's most important teachers, then efforts to enhance children's learning must include parents as partners in the learning process. But when working with children from impoverished, low-literate homes, partnering with parents may require special efforts to accommodate their needs, interests, and abilities.

These parents are no less concerned about their children's success in school than are middle-class parents. In fact, they often express a determination to ensure that their children will succeed – a commitment that is grounded in their own frustrations about school failure. These parents want to make sure their children learn, but they may not know what it takes. They may not have the skills to help with homework. They may not understand how children learn and how they can build oral language skills and thinking abilities through simple communication and play activities, using household items and taking advantage of daily routines and family events.

Even when the skills and awareness are there, however, the stressful realities of life on the margins of society often take their toll. Hard physical labor, inconvenient work hours, unreliable transportation, inadequate housing, unsafe neighborhoods, poor health, uncertain income, broken families, abuse and addiction, low self-esteem, underdeveloped skills in problem solving and stress management, weak or nonexistent role models for parenting, low literacy, and dying dreams – these are realities in many American homes. But, those very same homes also have strengths, real assets that keep hope alive. Parents, even in the poorest of environments, have learned survival skills – emotional, social, financial, and literacy skills. Many have developed friendships and support networks, found time to talk, play, and read with their children, learned to draw strength from loving and caring for their families, and developed a fierce protectiveness of their children.

Some of these parents have even managed to cultivate, in the face of terrible odds, a sense of hope and possibilities.

Programs that seek to develop the literacy skills of disadvantaged children must understand these families. In order for these parents to support their children's learning, they may need assistance with their own needs. They may need help to recognize their own strengths and to plan and set learning goals for themselves. They may need the chance to develop social, academic, or employability skills in a supportive, yet empowering atmosphere in which they can begin to approach their own potential as healthy, confident, capable adults, and good role models for their children.

Several of the *Bridges to Literacy* programs address the needs of parents as they work with their children. Toomey and Sloane suggest a fascinating classification of parent "types" that provides insight into the characteristics of the low-income families in their program. The classification lends credence to the contention that low-income parents are in general supportive of their children's learning but vary in the attitudes and abilities that they bring to the teaching task. Their description of the families should be valuable to family literacy program providers as they recruit participants, train staff, and plan activities.

In this connection Handel and Goldsmith raise an important question. They suggest that family literacy programs may choose to focus on the most hard-to-reach or the ready-to-learn parents. Segel also notes that the Read Aloud Parent Clubs reached parents who were "already committed to furthering their children's learning and who have sufficient energy and self-esteem to come out to meetings." This distinction has implications for program design. Those who choose to serve the hard-to-reach will find it necessary to offer more intensive educational services and provide for noneducational needs as well. Many family literacy programs have learned this lesson well.

But, as Handel and Goldsmith point out, even if the choice is to work with those who are more ready to learn, it is still important to provide meaningful experiences for the adults as well the children. Their findings indicate that adults come to understand that they themselves are learning as they read to their children. Over time, they become aware that the experience is beneficial in many ways. They build vocabulary, improve their own reading skill, develop awareness of their need for further education (in some cases), and acquire specific teaching techniques. But the program recognizes that from the start, parents should see "what's in it for them." To ensure that parents understand that this training is relevant to their needs, trainers spend time demonstrating how the techniques they are learning to help their children apply to their own reading comprehension.

Segel's Read Together program offers tutorial instruction for low-literate parents and provides free books and volunteers to read to their children during the tutoring sessions. Programs like this one aim to improve the literacy skills of adults, while meeting the parents' needs for child care and offering their children positive experiences with books. This approach is one way to get around the fact that some parents are unable to share the gift of literacy with their children.

Patricia Edwards agrees that "poor, minority and immigrant parents want to give their children linguistic, social, and cultural capital to deal in the 'marketplace' of schools," and further asserts that they can and should be taught how to read to their children to promote their literacy learning. In the "Parents as Partners in Reading" program, she developed a course for the primary teachers who trained the parents. Her sensitivity to the needs of African-American parents led her to include in the course syllabus readings that would help teachers understand the special characteristics of the literacy environments and learning styles in African-American homes.

These programs recognize a basic tenet of family literacy programs serving at-risk families: You must reach the parent to serve the child. If programs are not able to work with parents to develop both skills and awareness, if they are not prepared to accommodate their needs for basic skills instruction and noneducational support services, teachers will be less successful in helping children learn. If we really want to help disadvantaged children over the long term, we must work with their parents to enable them to create home environments that support children's learning.

Collaborations

Collaboration is another vital element in effective family literacy programs. These programs take a holistic approach to assisting at-risk families, bringing together the various elements of the fragmented human-service delivery system that exist in most communities. In order to provide educational services for both parents and children as well as necessary support services for families, staff must cross departmental, disciplinary, and agency lines in program planning and implementation. As Nickse and Quezada report, this collaboration, to be most effective, must involve organizations and agencies at "three dif-ferent levels of action" – program, community, and state / corporate levels. As they point out, collaboration in family literacy begins at the program level with the joining of adult educators and early childhood teachers into an integrated team and the participation of parents in program planning. Teamwork at this level is what makes programs work for families on a daily basis. At the community and state level, agency collaborations provide for the family support and funding needs of programs.

Collaborations may be vital, but many programs have learned that teamwork is much easier to advocate than it is to practice. Nickse and Quezada note that barriers are most common at the local community agency level. Barriers include a lack of sufficient authority on the part of agency team members, time constraints of members, and turf issues. These findings will come as no surprise to program staff, who will likely applaud the emphasis on the need for developing the skills of collaboration. It is true that though we mandate collaborative efforts (as in the Even Start legislation), "too little attention is paid to the process of being a part of collaborations . . . the collaborative process can be taught and learned." The Community Collaborations for Family Literacy project provides a good example for program planners and especially for policy makers at the state level.

In this connection Nickse and Quezada recommend that those preparing to enter the field of family literacy and related human services should have broad, multidisciplinary educational preparation, including human development, life-span education, and "the process of working in teams" as a mechanism in human service delivery. They also recommend the development of regional training and technical assistance networks to meet the expansion and staff development needs of a growing field. We heartily concur in these recommendations. If it is to prosper and expand, the family literacy movement will require a national infrastructure.

Program Evaluation

The Bridges to Literacy programs are notable for having conducted evaluations to determine how they have succeeded in or fallen short of their goals. Many have also attempted evaluation designs involving control groups. This commitment to assessing effectiveness has been a hallmark of family literacy programs since their inception. The Even Start legislation built in an extensive national evaluation, and each local project has funds to support evaluation as well.

This commitment to evaluation is exemplified by the statewide efforts in Illinois described by Ryan, Knell, and Geissler. Family literacy programs should find the framework adapted by the Illinois Literacy Resource Development Center to be helpful in planning an evaluation design. Specific examples of the use of this framework make the process concrete and demonstrate that even small programs can develop a workable plan.

The Illinois report concludes with a recommendation that family literacy programs "should implement evaluation strategies which are or will be useful to program development and that assist students in their educational quests," an important reminder of how often we forget the true purpose of evaluation. In adult education, for instance, it is the emphasis on satisfying mandates of state or local education agencies that has given evaluation a bad name. Because so many have viewed the process as involving only pre- and posttesting with standardized instruments, and have made no effort to integrate assessment and instruction, assessment is often seen as virtually meaningless to both teachers and learners. Instead, we need to develop assessment strategies that inform program development and curriculum and also help learners to identify their needs and progress. If we aim to create life-long learners, we need a process for measuring learning and growth that allows adult students to understand the true nature of learning and to monitor their own progress. If literacy is a process, as this study rightly suggests, then we must construct personally meaningful measures of progress along a continuum. We will always be concerned with evaluation that communicates with external stakeholders, of course, but we should also attend to strategies that help us develop and improve programs to serve the needs of learners.

This last point is especially important for family literacy programs that have broad goals related to meeting the distinctly personal and individual needs of families. Progress in these programs is shown in affective as well as cognitive areas and is expressed in improved attitudes and interactions as well as behaviors that are more easily measured. Family literacy programs must develop meaningful evaluation that tells the whole story of families learning and growing together. The Illinois report shows how valuable a good evaluation can be, not only for local staff, but also, when efforts are coordinated at the state level and results disseminated, for many others as well. The report includes a wealth of specific information covering a broad range of program concerns.

What Is Family Literacy?

Since a variety of approaches are described here, along with a possible classification scheme (Nickse and Quezada) for the program types, readers of this book are in a good position to consider the thorny problem of defining family literacy. Definitions are important to family literacy program development so that the field can sort out the program outcomes and draw conclusions regarding effective practice. As Nickse and Quezada note, "the proliferation of many approaches has led to a difficulty in documenting effectiveness," without a framework that "helps identify characteristics of programs." Without definitions and distinctions, we are not only comparing apples and oranges, we are unable to say with any degree of confidence what works and how well and under what circumstances.

So, to complement Nickse's typology we would like to suggest a way to view definitions that includes these variables:

1   Target population for direct services
2   Program goals
3   Duration and intensity of services

When considering the approaches detailed in this volume, it is helpful to remember that while many would characterize themselves as family literacy programs, and each is able to point to success stories, each is defining success somewhat differently. All the programs provide "bridges to literacy," but they often have different goals. These goals are related to their target populations. Some target only disadvantaged families; others aim more broadly. Some work primarily with children in a school or preschool setting; others aim instruction at parents. Those programs that work with parents may focus broadly on basic-skills instruction or, at the other extreme, specifically on techniques for reading to children. Still others, including the Even Start programs, work with both parents and children. It seems clear that programs with more limited goals may have a significant, but relatively narrower impact than those with more comprehensive aims.

We at the NCFL prefer to define *family literacy* as a holistic, family-focused approach, targeting at-risk parents and children with intensive, frequent, and long-term educational and other services. These programs include four components, integrated to form a unique, comprehensive approach to serving families. The components are (a) basic skills instruction for parents or caregivers, (b) pre-school or literacy education for young children, (c) parent education/support activities, and (d) regular parent and child interaction. Typically, program goals call for improving (a) the skills and educational level of undereducated parents, (b) the developmental skills of young children, (c) the parenting skills of parents in support of their children's learning, and (d) the quality of parent – child relationships and interactions. Using Nickse and Quezada's typology, these programs are a subset of the larger set of Type 1 programs.

The details of service delivery are less important in characterizing family literacy programs than are the goals, target population, duration and intensity of instruction. Whether home- or center-based, school- or workplace-sponsored, day or evening programs, these ambitious undertakings aim for a number of significant effects on families. Their broadest aim is, quite literally, to change the messages communicated in the home – messages related to the value of learning and literacy, the connection between education and quality of life, and the expectation of school accomplishments and life successes. As a result, parents become more confident and skilled, children are better prepared to succeed in school, and parents and children are united in lifelong learning. If both short- and long-term program goals are accomplished, the stubborn cycle of undereducation and poverty can be ended, one family and one community at a time. Surely this is what family literacy is about.

Most of the studies and programs described in this book have this aim in mind, but their specific goals and approaches often differ greatly. In conceptualizing the interrelatedness of programs, we recognize that all of these efforts help build bridges to literacy, but it may be helpful to distinguish within this larger group those four-component intensive programs that may be more appropriately called family literacy. Family literacy programs recognize that we cannot hope to make lasting changes without broad goals and a multifaceted, long-term intervention. Families have had many years (in fact generations) to become what they are. We cannot expect change to happen quickly or easily.

Common sense tells us that literacy is a complex phenomenon, that there is more to raising literate children than reading bedtime stories. If that were the only key variable, we would be without an explanation for the fact that the children of illiterate parents are quite often good readers. As Beals et al., point out, if "literacy is not a single activity, but a conglomeration of interconnected skills and abilities, it follows that the skills and abilities a child needs to learn can be (and may need to be) learned in a wide variety of interactive settings".

Arnold and Whitehurst recognize the limitations in the research showing a correlation between success in learning to read and the experience of having been read to as a child. As they point out, there may be another, unidentified variable: Perhaps, "reading at home is simply a marker of parental values," which lead to a constellation of stimulating, interactive, and literate behaviors. If this is so, then aiming broadly to affect these values makes good sense. If we cannot yet pick out the significant factors in the home, then working to improve skills, awareness, self-esteem, attitudes, relationships, and interactions through broadly focused intervention may hold the best hope for making real changes.

All of this is not to say that programs that choose to concentrate on more specific behavioral goals are not making valuable contributions to the cause. There are many factors in program planning. Funding limitations and service orientations of sponsoring organizations will determine focus. Planners may prefer a clearly defined approach with limited, easily measured objectives. And of course, some may see a simpler approach as the first step in the evolution toward a more ambitious effort. In any case we must value all efforts that further the cause of intergenerational literacy.

But we want to emphasize that complex, deeply rooted problems will not likely yield to simple, short-term solutions. We must look at the research and the experiences of programs, and we must support each other and work together to fill in the missing pieces and link the existing pieces of our fragmented system of service delivery for at-risk families. In order to provide optimal support and resources for our families, to avoid oversimplification and unmet expectations, we must think clearly about defining our varied efforts to build bridges to literacy. This book is a valuable tool in furthering the process. Family literacy programs and other service providers will find it illuminating and thought provoking.

Epilogue: What Next?

David K. Dickinson

Key lessons to be learned from the programs described in this book have been outlined clearly by each author and additional insights provided by Snow and Darling and Paul. In this epilogue I wish to look toward the future, sketching some promising directions worthy of consideration by program developers and researchers.

Understanding Interactions Between Program Types and Needs

We know far too little about which kinds of programs work for which families and children. In this book we see a broad range of program types, each of which seems to have had some beneficial effects. Unfortunately, we are in a very weak position to determine how intensive a program is needed for particular families because we often have minimal information about the particular families involved in the program. Dealing with this issue will require the development of dimensions along which we can sort families, children, and programs – a formidable task in its own right! Experimentally controlled intervention work would be ideal, but systematic collection of data on program effects by ongoing projects as well as careful longitudinal study of families also can help advance our understanding of the impact of particular literacy-related experiences on particular family constellations.

The Place of Oral Language in Literacy Programs

Programs that involve book reading have repeatedly been shown to have effects on oral-language skills, but no recent efforts examine whether interventions that do not use books improve them. One way to use such approaches in homes would be to learn if parents have routine settings in which they have time to talk with their children (e.g., meal time, during dinner preparation, in the car, before bed).

Strategies for encouraging the type of rich talk described in chapter 1 during such times could have effects comparable with those for book-reading programs. Programs based in preschools or schools have even greater latitude for generating such episodes of "rich talk." Once again, routines would have to be established and mechanisms developed to help teachers engage in cognitively challenging discussions. In home or school programs, the ultimate goal would be to see if the situation-specific strategies begin to spread to a broader range of adult–child contexts. Should this occur such oral language projects might prove to be quite powerful.

The Place of Writing in Literacy Programs

Writing is nearly absent in the programs described, even though emergent literacy research has emphasized the close connections between reading and writing. This situation is especially unfortunate for groups who are marked by a sense of powerlessness, because writing is a powerful tool that would seem to hold special promise for family literacy programs. One natural way to incorporate writing would be to have parents write materials to read to their children. One example of such an approach comes from Chicago, where Hal Adams from the University of Illinois has published parents' writing in *The Journal of Ordinary Thought* and distributed it to the schools.

In preschools and kindergartens writing could be incorporated into dialogic reading routines. For example, an intervention that I have been developing over the past two years involves having Clark University students read to small groups of primary grade children. One variant is to have the group dictate their ideas about their favorite parts of books and to list any "hard" words from them. In groups where this intervention has worked teachers report that their children enjoy the routine and seem to expect that they will eventually write about recent experiences.

Where Programs Are Provided

Most of the programs described are based in preschools or schools, though libraries and other community agencies are included. Programs could well be implemented in a broader range of settings. For example, Segel reports use of doctor's offices, a setting that Needlman, a pediatrician, has exploited by giving away books and literacy advice to children at every visit until the child is six years old (Fitzgerald & Needlman, 1991; Needlman, Zuckerman, 1992). Components of some programs might also be delivered in a variety of social service agencies that serve low-income people.

Collaborations also could develop among more diverse groups, with, for example, groups of preschool children walking to neighborhood businesses, nursing homes, libraries, etc. to engage in literacy-related activities. Collaborative ventures between universities and either preschools or schools also are relatively rare, with Handel and Goldsmith's Family Reading program being the exception (see also Juel, 1992). Such programs can work to the advantage of both the university students and children. At Clark University the volunteer reader program that I am developing has given many college students their first exposure to urban schools and children. This highly structured setting provides an ideal initial opportunity for students in developmental psychology or teacher certification programs to have satisfying and edifying experiences with children.

Examining Affective Factors

Running through many of the programs are discussions of how affective factors support literacy development – reading growth as a result of a new-found enjoyment of books, deepening of interpersonal relationships through book reading, building of a sense of self-confidence. Generally discussion of affective factors occurs in asides, with no systematic examination. We need to understand better the interactions between affective factors and literacy. We need examination of the kinds of program features that have special impact on such issues as motivation, self-concept, and mother–child relationships. We also would benefit from better understanding of the impact of such affective factors on program outcomes. For example, it would be of practical and theoretical interest to know how the quality of mother–child relationships might affect the use of book-reading strategies and to know whether the use of effective strategies when reading books influences interactional patterns in other settings.

Institutionalizing Programs

If we are to have significant, enduring effects on large numbers of low-income families, we must set up programs that endure over the long haul. To do so we need to understand what factors lead to long-term implementation of programs. Factors likely to be important include: (a) feasibility given available resources, (b) adequacy of training procedures, (c) stability of funding, (d) the extent to which a collaborative program serves the interests of all agencies involved. A number of these issues are explored in earlier chapters (especially 5, 6, 8, 9, and 10). It should be noted that the importance of these variables is likely to be quite different for single-agency programs as opposed to collaboratives.

Continuity of Services

If we are to improve substantially the literacy of the children most in need of help, we must develop programs that serve them for several years, because, as both Karweit and Toomey and Sloane point out, successful outcomes are most likely when support can be provided over time. There is a special need to find ways to serve families as children move from the preschool into the elementary school years, because this is the point when responsibility for providing services to families tends to shift from community-based agencies to the schools. Finding ways to provide continuous services may require collaboration among different agencies, though the community library is one institution that may be able to provide such continuity (see chapters 3, 4, 9).

Improvement in the continuity of support for literacy growth will need to do more than overcome organizational hurdles; it will require recognition that it is still possible to have a major impact on children's literacy skills in middle to later childhood. During these years both schools and homes can have a major effect on children's literacy growth, with each setting being able to compensate for weaknesses in the other (Snow et al., 1991). Similar compensatory effects would be possible with intervention programs devised for middle-grade children that extend the efforts of projects that serve families during the preschool years.

Bridge Building

Programs that strive to support literacy growth are emerging from many diverse disciplines and orientations. The profusion of initiatives is exciting, but coordination of efforts is minimal. In site after site lists of books to use are developed anew, and ideas for parent workshops created from scratch. Questions of evaluation pose daunting challenges in one site even though solutions exist elsewhere, and program developers devise initiatives without being aware of the experience of similar projects.

Equally important, communication between theoretically oriented researchers and service providers is limited. As Nickse and Quezada suggest, this gap might shrink somewhat if university programs would provide a more multidisciplinary education. However, central forums for communication such as the newly established Family Literacy Conference run by the National Center for Family Literacy in the United States might be helpful. In addition, new publications might help develop a community of researchers and practitioners interested in literacy programs.

References

Fitzgerald, K. & Needlman, R. (1991, September). Read out and read: A pediatric program to support emergent literacy. *Zero to three*, 17–20.

Juel, C. (1992, April). *At-risk university students tutoring at-risk elementary school children: What factors make it effective?* Paper presented at the annual convention of the American Educational Research Association.

Needlman, R. & Zuckerman, B. (1992, February). Fight illiteracy: Prescribe a book! *Contemporary Pediatrics*, 41–60.

Snow, C.E., Barnes, W.S., Chandler, J., Goodman, I.F. & Hemphill, L. (1991). *Unfulfilled expectations: Home and school influences on literacy.* Cambridge: Harvard University.

Index